Testimonials

"*Charting A Wiser Course* is an important dialogue that needs to happen through all layers of the aviation industry.

As an experienced practitioner of the old traditional, and often-confrontational, methods and behaviors of negotiation, I could be used as an example to show that you can teach an old dog new tricks.

I've had the valuable opportunity to utilize the tools and experience the benefits of this common-sense approach to decision-making and agreement-shaping in labor/management negotiations when an interest-based concept was new to the industry. Unequivocally, with true commitment from both sides, more elegant solutions can be crafted when both sides cooperatively work to solve each other's problems.

I've also learned valuable lessons from mistakes along the way of trying to pioneer sea changes in behaviors and attitudes in an industry entrenched in the old ways of doing business. But the good news is that those mistakes need not be repeated.

Imagine where aviation can take us if we all work to design a new set of wings for the Phoenix.

Charting A Wiser Course can help us do just that.

Denise Hedges
Former President
Association of Professional
Flight Attendants (1992-2000)

"In the new global economy, it is clear that we need new tools to conduct business. The concept of winners and losers in negotiations must be modified to achieve a win for all parties, or we ultimately suffer losses in common. The principles and examples cited by the authors show that this can be achieved utilizing alternate currencies and genuine concern for each other's goals. It is clear that integrity and cooperation can help us reach the ultimate solution. We may not find all the answers in this book, but it will help us move in the right direction."

> Steve Tosi
> President
> Magellan USA

"Kaye gets it exactly right. Today's business leader is confronted daily by opportunities disguised as threats. The leader typically chooses 'perfectly rational but equally wrong' actions, resulting in alienating customers, suppliers, employees, and, eventually, shareholders. Since 1994, when I first participated in the Negotiating Solutions workshop, Kaye has challenged us to consider that business leaders can and must change their assumptions and behaviors to uncover the abounding opportunities. She makes it clear that creating trust through integrity, and developing a profound understanding of needs, can expose opportunities and build durable, mutually profitable, relationships. By focusing their energies on changing not the masses but their own assumptions, leaders can enable new behaviors and results. It is an extremely rewarding, and surprisingly easy, journey, once you know the way. Kaye is an able and experienced guide."

> Jon H. Stevens
> Vice President, Logistics Services
> SKF

"Making the change from positional-bargaining to interest-based negotiation has had a dramatic impact on the way we deal with our customers, partners, suppliers, and, of course, co-workers. With the state of the industry as it stands today, there is no way our company would have been able to remain in a leadership position without such a behavioral change. The aviation industry as a whole would benefit from a similar paradigm shift."

Larry Alexandre
Vice President, Sales & Marketing
Sermatech Manufacturing Group

Additional comments on the value of Charting A Wiser Course

"As a company that is trying to change the way we work – IPTs, teams, international alliances – the approach should be complementary. I just had a long conversation with a senior manager about why bright ideas and good change initiatives don't "take." Applying the interest-based approach to organizations, not just to one-off negotiations, is a way to improve the odds."

VP & Managing Director

"I agree with what you have to say and how this change can address today's needs. It's sort of like saying, "If you always do what you always did, you will always get what you always got. And that ain't good enough anymore.""

Director, HR, IT, EH&S, & Legal

"Sometimes when you're living in the chaos, it's hard to rise above it to see the patterns of what's going on. Not a day passes that I don't talk to associates outside the industry who are asking me, 'What's going on?'"

Counsel, Employee Relations

"The paradigm shifts that are taking place as we speak are monumental, and we must move even faster than we have."

Aircraft Maintenance Manager

"We are...in a watershed period for the industry and possibly, due to geopolitical events and the interconnectivity of economies, a global one. For many if not most folks in the USA and many other countries, if there is a winner, it therefore follows that there's a loser. A very big and compelling case for why it's better to be interest-based, which implies each side is satisfied, rather than just a "winner" needs [to be] made."

Director, Aircraft Maintenance

"The GE world has continued to shift towards assuming people are assets, commodities, costs – unfortunately. It is an unsustainable model. The European guys take a longer view. Now that we have them as a partner, we have to operate reasonably interdependently. When someone has equity in your company, you can't do to them what you've done to others."

President & CEO

"We now reach our goals by letting people go and claiming we are doing more with less. When do the laws of diminishing returns come into play?"

General Manager

"First of all, I totally agree with your premises. Hell, I'd like to co-author the book."

Vice President, Customer Support

"The diagnosis rings very true of a dreadful state of affairs. It is prevalent in our industry, and in the world at large. You are absolutely correct that our response has been inadequate...so far. We attack the symptoms, not the cause; the behaviour, not the value paradigm underneath. In some cases we only succeed in making matters worse! The challenge before us is enormous! The very business model in our industry is broke."

President & GM

"For the last twelve years I have been working in an environment that...was permitted to independently pursue our vision of a 'socio-tech culture' in which everyone was expected to contribute. Traditional management was an unacceptable paradigm. Unfortunately, acquisition by a new owner is resulting in an ever-increasing reversal to historical paradigms. Can you imagine the frustration?"

Technical Director

"I have to commend you for tackling the subject since you have captured the feelings of many of us that struggle to find the blend between 'Jack Welsh'-type dogma and good responsible management in the society in which we live."

President

CHARTING A
WISER COURSE

How Aviation Can Address
The *Human* Side of Change

THE MATTFORD GROUP PRESS

A DIVISION OF THE MATTFORD GROUP, INC.
INCLINE VILLAGE, NEVADA

Cover design by Keri Lanier Smith (sticksandstones@sbcglobal.net). Formatting by Mindy Tindle (thetindles@charter.net).

"High Flight" by John Gillespie Magee, Jr., 1941, reprinted by permission of the author's family.

Excerpt from "Anything You Can Do" by Irving Berlin. © Copyright 1946 by Irving Berlin. © Copyright renewed. International Copyright Secured. All Rights Reserved. Reprinted by Permission.

Excerpt from "Big Yellow Taxi," by Joni Mitchell, © Copyright 1970 (Renewed) Crazy Crow Music. All Rights Reserved. Used by Permission, Warner Bros. Publications U.S. Inc.

Excerpt from "Rhinestone Cowboy" by Larry Weiss, © Copyright 1974 (Renewed) WB Music Corp. All Rights Reserved. Used by Permission, Warner Bros. Publications U.S. Inc.

Content/Process model © Copyright 1986-2003, The MAPping Alliance. Used by permission.

Excerpts from The Structure of Scientific Revolutions, 3rd edition, by Thomas S. Kuhn. The University of Chicago Press. © Copyright 1962, 1970, 1996 by The University of Chicago. Reprinted by permission of the University of Chicago Press. All rights reserved.

Hard Positional and Soft Positional Negotiation chart and principled negotiation concepts from Getting to Yes, 2nd edition, by Roger Fisher, William Ury and Bruce Patton. Copyright © 1981, 1991 by Roger Fisher and William Ury. Adapted and reprinted by permission of Houghton Mifflin Company. All rights reserved.

Excerpt from "The Sea is History" from Collected Poems: 1948-1984 by Derek Walcott. Copyright © 1986 by Derek Walcott. Reprinted by permission of Farrar, Straus & Giroux, LLC. UK permission from Faber & Faber, Ltd.

Library of Congress Control Number applied for.

ISBN: 0-9747328-0-X

Please address requests to print excerpts from Charting A Wiser Course to The Mattford Group Press, PO Box 5454, Incline Village, Nevada, USA 89450, or email to mattford@gbis.com.

Dedication

For Martin Bear.
For Mindy, Jason, Joanne, and Julie.
For my Mom, who didn't raise her
daughter to wash kitchen floors.
For our students and colleagues.
For Barb Williams' son Rob.
And for my Uncle Jay.

Table of Contents

Chapter		Page
Foreword		i
Introduction		1
1.	What's Going On Here?	14
2.	Lessons From Our Shared History	25
3.	The End Stages of Once Useful Models	102
4.	We Have Met the Enemy and He Is Us	116
5.	Current Change Efforts	121
6.	Paradigms, Master Models, and Paradigm Shifts	126
7.	How Managerial Models Embed and Persist	133
8.	Assessing Our Current Behaviors and Objectives	148
9.	Changing Behaviors	172
10.	Getting To Our Master Model	179
11.	Implementing This in Our Environment	193
12.	Isn't This The Same As "Win-Win" Negotiation?	232
13.	Some Lessons Learned	239
14.	Taking Our Organizations From Here To There	281
Appendix A: Some Resources		303
Appendix B: How You Can Help		307
Acknowledgements		308
About the Authors		310
Footnotes		311

Foreword

The aviation industry has always been about connections, and today that description applies more than ever before. Starting with the simplest connections - supplier to operator, operator to passenger, passenger to destination - aviation has evolved into a complex of interlocking and overlapping connections of alliances, joint ventures and partnerships.

Underlying all of these new forms of relationships is the labor/management connection, a relationship in some ways little changed from the days of its birth.

Aviation was one of the first truly global industries. In fact, it was on the back of aviation's travel and transportation capabilities that the other great industries of the world rode into the global market, achieving the scope and scale that have brought new levels of prosperity and hope to nearly every corner of the planet. And yet aviation itself has been stopped from becoming truly globalized by a network of laws and prejudices that only now are beginning to crumble as serious business thinking takes over from romantic and often provincial ideals born in the 1930s. Those falling barriers open the door to a new generation of business relationships.

Today's levels of interconnectivity find previously adversarial groups with common interests requiring a unified response while the adversarial relationship remains to some degree. Now airlines find themselves in alliance relationships with other airlines that had been fierce competitors, and, given the track record for shifting allegiances, may be direct competitors again. A manufacturer enters a joint venture with another manufacturer on one project while understanding that the partner of the moment is likely to become a competitor's partner on another project. Operators buy equipment with complex after-sale parts and maintenance agreements in which the performance of the vendor has a direct bearing on the profitability of both. And labor groups enter into talks with airlines with an eye not only on the labor groups and expansion plans of alliance partners, but those of their regional airline partners, as well.

In short, never before has there been a time in which the ability to construct a useful deal while maintaining healthy relationships between the parties in the deal has been more important. The days of slash and burn deals in which the loser is left a smoking hole in the meeting room floor is a thing of the past for those who know that there certainly will be more deals in the future, and that while the aviation industry may span the globe it is a very small community, indeed. Your adversary today may be your partner tomorrow.

A new way has to be found to enable the various business entities to come together, fashion a deal in which all parties achieve sufficient benefit to prosper and yet retain sufficient good will that future dealings will not be poisoned by excess advantage taken in the current transaction. With the complexity of the deals escalating with the increasingly complex business environment, that necessity becomes all the more urgent.

That need to find a new way to strike a strong business deal while fostering a positive relationship is the central point of this book by Kaye and Joe Shackford.

The Shackfords have many years of experience in fashioning deals and relationships that last, and training people to achieve those results. This book is a story of how their approach evolved and how it can be made to work. While a full understanding of that approach requires a deeper immersion in the process than can be had by the simple reading of a book, the book is a good start down that road.

We at *Air Transport World* believe that the Shackfords present a most beneficial approach to the art of doing business in the aviation community, a community that we like to think stands out for the excellence of the people involved. There really is nothing about the Shackfords' ideas that restrict them to aviation, but we have to agree with Kaye and Joe that aviation is a darn good place to start.

J. A. Donoghue
Editorial Director
ATW Media Group
October 20, 2003

Introduction

It was not accidental that the September 11th terrorists targeted our core institutions of aviation, finance, and defense. The aviation industry has been in a sickening flat spin ever since. The global economy needs our industry to survive, stabilize, and rebuild. Our various businesses and people have their own passionately personal reasons to wish for the same outcome.

The task before us is gargantuan.

The good news - if you can call it that - is that much of the mess we're currently in is of our own making. If we created it, we can change it.

Throughout the industry businesses are reworking strategy, markets, products, and organizational structure. They have laid off appalling numbers of people. They are simultaneously implementing major change initiatives - lean applied to the manufacturing floor and business processes, Six Sigma, value-streaming, supply-chain management, and others. They are seeking to implement massive changes in how they work in the marketplace with suppliers, customers, and partners. And they're also trying to change dramatically the working relationships between management and employee groups.

But there's one key element that no one is paying sufficient attention to. Without it, these other efforts won't succeed.

To chart a wiser course in aviation (and in our other infrastructure industries*), one that will let us achieve our objectives, we must address this element as well.

What's encouraging is that businesses can start to address this critical element now without massive expenditure of resources.

Implemented wisely, this element will immediately start to provide them with better results, and will make more attainable the rest of the work they need to do. It will also give their people some respite, improvement, and hope, even as they're working to identify and shift towards the large strategic changes more appropriate to today's environment.

It has to do not with the *content* side of change, but with the *process* side of change, with what Douglas McGregor called "the human side of enterprise."[1] It has to do with how we do what we do with one another.

So what is this key element? It is a mind-change about the nature of reality. I intend to make a case that the environments in which we must now be effective, and our own strategic objectives, have changed so much that *we literally can't achieve those objectives using our current behaviors.*

----

*Though the examples I use are from the industry I know best, our students from other industries suggest the logic is as compelling and important for their industries as it is for mine.

I then will describe why we must, and how we can, align our behaviors with our objectives so we can accomplish the monumental task of rebuilding our businesses and industry.

Aligning your behaviors with your objectives sounds like a simple thing to do. In actuality, accomplishing widespread and lasting behavior change across an organization or an industry is hard. Perhaps because it seems that this should be simple, until now management has given it short shrift. It certainly has not been included in business plans and measurements.

Those who have addressed it at all have sought to get people to change behaviors through managerial pronouncements, mission and value statements, intentions, and exhorting them to try harder.

Sometimes they invested in skills training.

Nothing really changed.

The challenge is even more daunting because the very folks who need to establish, lead, and manage this paradigm-shifting change are precisely those people *least* prepared by training, inclination, or prior experience to do the job. They are the operations managers and leaders of their businesses. They didn't earn advanced degrees in organizational behavior or human psychology. Their degrees are in aeronautical engineering or mechanical engineering or finance or marketing or business administration. Or they have Airframe & Powerplant licenses. Or they came up through the ranks.

Many of them have few skills at, and little interest in, what tends to be dismissed as the "touchy-feely" side of business. This touchy-feely stuff has just never seemed that important.

Yet if their businesses don't effect corporate-wide behavioral change at the paradigm-shift level, the Herculean change efforts they're now attempting will fail.

Union leaders traditionally focus on preserving jobs and improving the conditions of employment. Operations managers usually look to their human resources and employee relations people to take care of "that stuff." This might be all right when union leaders and managers are operating within an existing paradigm. But it's not all right when they need to change the paradigm. In the midst of the rest of the upheavals, this, too, has to be their responsibility.

I think I can transfer to you the concepts and tools so that you can take this on wisely. I invite you on a journey with me to understand why it's necessary, why it's harder than it looks, and how it can be done.

If this book does what I expect, you should have a better appreciation for where we came from, what we learned, and what we've somehow forgotten. You'll understand better how our past is sabotaging our present. You'll have more clarity about how to move forward, an understanding of some of the roadblocks and quagmires, and you'll have the mental resources to begin. The book won't get you all the way there, but it should give you the concepts you need to prepare the rest of your plan in ways appropriate to your particular responsibilities.

The path I propose to take you on is sometimes a bit convoluted and theoretical. Much of it comes from life in the trenches; I hope it resonates with your own experience and causes you to smile or groan in recognition. It may put together for you elements you've known about but may not have linked before.

4

Most people take journeys they choose to go on, with some idea of the benefit to them from staying the course; so I want to preview the logic and flow of my argument.

Chapter 1 sketches out the growing crisis in our industry prior to September 11th. It describes the unintended consequences of the business model Jack Welch brought to GE, now broadly emulated throughout our industry. His efforts to undo the assumption that the corporation owed lifelong employment to its employees, coupled with widened span of control, ever increasing requirements for double-digit growth, and an annual edict to eliminate the bottom 10% of each manager's employees, had some nasty side effects. This model destroyed personal identification with the organization. It created a situation in which hours escalated endlessly and family life suffered. We were treated as and came to treat each other as commodities. Loyalty was to myself. We began to dismantle our own infrastructure of support and to tread the slippery slope of ethic in order to get results. I propose that everything we've been doing in order to get results is not only *not* getting us good results, it's actually getting us *lousy* results and making it harder to get better results in the future. I then propose that there is a better way – one that is sustainable, effective, and human.

Chapter 2 suggests that in order to figure out how to get to where we need to be, we first need to remember how we got to where we are now. I take you back into the major themes in the industry in the 1972 to 2003 period by inviting you along to visit my history at GE Aircraft Engines. I identify what working with others to make tough things happen in a tough industry taught me about organizational and personal effectiveness. I suspect you have learned many of the same lessons. My purpose is to trigger your memories of your own history on a business and a personal basis, head and heart, in order to craft a shared launch platform.

Chapter 3 makes the point that though our current models worked surprisingly well for a long time, they aren't working now. I briefly describe the end stages of a once useful business paradigm. I raise two questions: What is the best model for our environment now, and what happens to people in organizations as we approach the useful end of problem-solving models that once served us well? I note that some of our best and brightest have been experimenting with other models – some inside our large businesses, others by opting out and setting up in smaller businesses to do it their way. So alternative experiments already exist; *we're positioned for a paradigm shift.*

Chapter 4 addresses the need for us to understand that we have within ourselves equally great capacities for good and for evil. We need to understand this if we're going to confront the change needed in *our own* models, assumptions, and behaviors. Most of the problems in our businesses today are derived from things we're doing to ourselves and to each other, not because we're pathologically calculating and callous, *à la* Enron, but because the cultures we're part of have supported these behaviors, because we've concluded we must do them to succeed, and because it's crept up on us over time. Yet the capacity to make other choices not only exists in us, in many of us there is a hunger for "there's got to be a better way." This hunger is now a key basis for the hope for change.

Chapter 5 reviews how our managements have been seeking to get significantly better results. In most of our organizations, we've dramatically revised our strategic objectives and written cascading sets of mission and value statements. We're implementing major change initiatives. Yet management has been frustrated at the apparent lack of willingness of employees to step up to the opportunity in spite of the massive resources that are being poured into the efforts. Employees have been equally frustrated by what they see as a disconnect between management's strategic vision, mission and value statements, and management's own *behaviors*.

I propose the reason: Change initiatives this massive can't be accomplished within our current paradigm for how we work together – our *behavioral* paradigm. To succeed, we have to change how we actually work with one another, day-in, day-out, inside the organization and out in the marketplace.

Chapter 6 makes the point that if we're going to consider whether to effect a paradigm shift, we need to reclaim what it means. I review Thomas Kuhn's 1962 book, *The Structure of Scientific Revolutions,*[2] drawing parallels between what he calls "the practice of normal science" and what we can call "the practice of normal business." He notes that the rigorous training scientists receive teaches them to think *inside* existing models. He takes paradigms "to be universally recognized scientific achievements that *for a time* provide model problems and solutions to a community of practitioners." For long periods the existing models work. There then come periods in which problems you should be able to solve elude solution. Though you have to overcome tremendous inertia and investment in the old paradigm, investigations begin that "lead the profession at last to...a new basis for the practice of science."

As we look for parallels between his world and ours, it becomes clear that the formal and informal educational indoctrination we received exerts a deep hold on *our* minds as well. We, too, derive insight from the success stories of our industry's hero-leaders. The model problems they've solved, and the business models they've built, become the basis for our models. And sometimes we, too, reach points when models that once served us well can no longer solve the problems we need to solve.

The chapter concludes by suggesting that our paradigms are models or maps. Sometimes they're useful; they help us navigate the terrain. Sometimes they aren't. *And sometimes the terrain changes.* When that happens, it's important to change the map.

Chapter 7 describes how managerial paradigms embed and why they tend to persist beyond their useful lives. This chapter explores how each of us figured out how to make the world work. It relates our early models to how we moved into our organizations as problem-solvers, managers, leaders, and creators of organizational culture. Those of us who rose did so because our personal paradigm for problem-solving worked wonderfully well in the environments in which we found ourselves. These models are deeply embedded in our instincts and deeply related to our self-identities. As we rose, we embedded our personal paradigms into our organizations' paraphernalia of culture. Southwest is as different from American as Herb Kelleher is from Bob Crandall.

This is why, if our managements, managers, and leaders decide to take this path, they will need mechanisms to remind themselves and their staffs that many of their instincts won't work - mechanisms for holding these embedded reflexes in check.

Chapter 8 introduces two basic premises: 1) the purpose of our behaviors is to achieve our objectives in a particular environment, and 2) negotiation, which *Newsweek* magazine calls "the game of life," underlies most of the behaviors we use to achieve our objectives.

Linking these ideas lets us use the research findings from the Harvard Negotiation Project[3] to identify our current model for dealing with each other. They describe it as two sides of the same game: hard positional negotiation and soft positional negotiation. Most of us in aviation tend to play the hard side of this positional game. We can then look at the relationship between our current behaviors and our objectives. To do so, I review a sampling of objectives culled from actual corporate strategic objective and mission statements. I hold hard positional negotiation behaviors against these objectives and ask two questions: Does this compute? *It doesn't.* Can we get from here to there using these behaviors? *We can't.* Soft positional negotiation won't get us there either. *If we intend to achieve the objectives, we have to change the game.*

Chapter 9 notes that historically, when we've decided we needed to change our behavior, we have *intended* to change and *tried* to change. And then we've sent people to skills training. Nothing changed.

Einstein says that *you can't solve the problem at the level of the problem.* In this case, you can't change behaviors by seeking to change behaviors. That's not where our behaviors come from.

I introduce an A→B→C→D model for behavior change. Our *Assumptions* derive from our master model – our paradigm – and drive our *Behaviors.* Our *Behaviors* tend to elicit *Reciprocal Behaviors.* In combination, these *Behaviors* have certain *Consequences.* The model says that if we don't like the *Consequences,* we can make a *Decision* to change. Usually, when we decide to change, we seek to change the *Behaviors.* It doesn't work. To change, we have to revisit the master model and change it. The good news is that when we change our model, we can do with relative ease things that felt like pulling teeth before.

Chapter 10 reviews how it takes three things to change our behavior:

1) a cathartic event,
2) our personal identification with the event, and
3) a readily available alternative model - ideally, one already pre-tested in our system.

In terms of the alternative model, the research of the Harvard Negotiation Project in the late 1970s set out to identify the best way to come to agreement *without giving in.* This led to the identification of the elements of interest-based negotiation. I hold these behaviors against our industry objectives, asking the question, "How about this instead?" It is, I believe, a far better fit.

Chapter 11 addresses how we can apply these concepts in our environment. I take us back to Chester Karrass's doctoral dissertation at USC in the late 1960s.

There was a time when you could take your time to play the negotiating game. You could erode relationships and accept sub-optimal results. Then the world got very, very interconnected and needed to flow smoothly together. We need our suppliers as much as we need our shops. We need repeat customers. We need to be in functional worldwide alliances. We need an educated, involved, committed workforce. We need to do more and more with less and less.

Neither hard nor soft positional negotiation can get us there. Interest-based negotiation and interest-based management can. But how do we apply interest-based concepts in our interdependent world of business, profits, and bottom-line results?

The chapter introduces several elements that apply, build on and extend the Harvard research to the industrial setting. And it reviews a simple statement: What goes around comes around. We're all interconnected, far more than we thought.

Chapter 12 addresses the misperception that interest-based negotiation is the same as "win-win" negotiation. Win-win negotiation has gotten a bad reputation throughout our industry, especially with some key union groups.

Most organizations that decided to shift to interest-based negotiation or bargaining had notified everyone that they would now behave with each other in win-win ways. So we dutifully set out to "try" to function in this new way. Operating inside our old mind-sets, *seeking to change our behaviors rather than our paradigms,* all we did was switch from the hard side of the positional game to the soft side of the same game, calling it "win-win." We experienced "win-win" as "win-lose," and we were right.

Perhaps more than anything else the failure of hard positional negotiation and of "win-win" soft positional negotiation points to why it will take widespread training at the paradigm-shift level to get the results we so badly need.

Chapter 13 reviews some of the evidence that this alternative model works in our industry. It describes some of the folks in aviation that Joel Barker,[4] author of *Paradigms: The Business of Discovering the Future*, would identify as "paradigm pioneers." These are the people who took a step in faith to apply the new paradigm before there was overwhelming evidence supporting it, and before their organizations embraced it. They did so because it seemed to work better. Paradigm pioneers have been at work throughout our industry. They have stories to tell. Many are good news stories. The chapter also addresses some of the things we learned the hard way - among them that short-term gains can sabotage long-term objectives, and that when management doesn't understand the change taking place on its watch, it can mismanage the change process disastrously.

Chapter 14 describes how you can take yourself and your organization from here to there. Scope out your total business change process and objectives, considering all eight of the stages that John Kotter describes in his book *Leading Change.*[5] *Then add the ninth factor.* Change your managerial and behavioral paradigms as a key and necessary element of the entire change process. Once the mind change occurs, if your business culture allows even some of it, you won't go back.

Clearly, some folks are going through this change on their own. Evidence exists that a "global mind change" is underway. But if we wait for it to happen naturally, it won't happen in our current organizations. Too many corporate culture mechanisms are in place to hold us where we are.

The chapter proposes ways to drive and guide this change inside our organizations. Though it will take time, persistence and resources to implement fully, immediate and visible benefits will occur wherever you begin.

The reason for doing so is simple: We can't accomplish our strategic objectives within our current managerial and behavioral paradigm. By changing our paradigm, we can.

* * * * * * * * * *

So these are the highlights of the journey I invite you to go on with me. Now I need to involve you in the whole picture.

Chapter One

WHAT'S GOING ON HERE?

We all knew that the aviation industry and our own businesses were fragile before September 11th.

The crash of the dot-com companies had depressed the stock market and was rippling through the economy, resulting in reductions in air travel, making airline overcapacity even worse. This led to a corresponding cutback in aircraft orders, spare parts usage, and repair work. Companies were already battening down the hatches – laying people off, slipping orders, reducing travel budgets and canceling training.

Airports and air travel were nightmares to navigate. Long slow lines at hub-and-spoke airports; questionably handled flight delays and cancellations; reduced seat pitch on planes that jammed even short people's knees against the seat backs in front of them; combined with service cutbacks and cavalier treatment by frustrated airline personnel, were creating pressures that boiled over as Air Rage. Congressional committees were threatening to investigate the industry. The vast chasm between advertised images of air travel and its reality further compounded the problem.

A cascade of unsustainable negotiated labor agreements precipitated by United's agreement with its pilots' union in 2001 threatened to sink the industry. In most airlines and many aviation companies, union/management relations approached all-time lows in terms of lack of trust between the factions. Union members, still smarting from earlier concessionary agreements, and in no way sympathetic with the fact that profitability had peaked a few years earlier and was on a downward slide, identified management as the enemy and declared it their time to "get theirs back."

Statements by management that these demands played out across the organization would bankrupt the company were seen as meaningless negotiating ploys. A similar crisis in air travel in 1990 to 1991 and a mutual end-game of industrial chicken between management and union leaders had led directly to the demise of Eastern Air Lines.

The Internet was undermining whatever command-and-control authority existed in union halls. Members of every persuasion set up their own rogue web sites, making it difficult, if not impossible, for members to sift disgruntled disinformation from the true facts - chaff from wheat.

In many of our organizations, managements had imported whole cloth the *modus operandi* of Jack Welch of GE.

Among other initiatives, starting in the early 1980s, he had set out to undo the complacent and rampant assumption that the corporation owed lifetime employment to its professional employees. "Loyalty," he declared, "is an outmoded concept." He went on to explain that the company's obligation to you was paid in full with each paycheck, and that you should always "be prepared to go and flourish elsewhere."[1]

Span of control was widened, with far more people reporting to each manager. The original purpose was to drive decision-making down into the organization to the people who had the knowledge. This purpose was frequently subverted by the continuing requirement that every manager know and instantly be able to report on everything that was going on in his or her bailiwick. Decision-making, for the most part, remained controlled at the top, and managers just worked longer and harder, with greater stress.

In the 1990s, another twist was added. Managers were required to identify the bottom 10% of performers in their organization each year and get rid of them.[2] The 20% at the top were to be identified and rewarded. Though there may have been an initial logic to this requirement, it soon reaches a point where you really can't "grade on the curve." Everyone who is left is good.

Satisfying the requirement to identify the bottom 10% becomes more and more a matter of chance, timing, or partisan perceptions. Who's on a new job or struggling with a difficult territory? Who stood his or her ground and royally annoyed a new superior or didn't cave to a customer? Who appeared to not be as gung-ho as others, even if he or she did fine work? Who had a life outside of work and wasn't eager to put in eleven-hour days?

Justifying the decision to get rid of people required creating a track record of "kiss of death" contact reports and evaluations in their personnel folders, which further eroded commitment to the organization. Managers who resisted identifying people to get rid of were informed that those who weren't able to differentiate would soon find themselves in the "bottom 10%" category.

These changes, played out over the years, had some unexpected side effects.

This purposeful breakdown of the psychological contract between company and employee, when added to an endless requirement to deliver double-digit profits, along with a continuing reduction in manpower and an erosion in the organizational infrastructure of support, in many organizations produced legions of middle managers working not in support of company interests, nor in support of the customer, nor as good stewards of the people and organizations that reported to them, but as individuals in overstress, primarily reduced to protecting their backsides and chasing their own personal incentive compensation parameters.

Loyalty was to myself; everyone else was a temporary resource toward - or an obstacle to - my short-term ends. In an environment where most of us didn't know how we were going to meet the ever-escalating demands our own organizations had placed on us, it was all too easy to slip into a siege mentality in which everyone else was the enemy.

Customers saw suppliers as the enemy. Many procurement organizations had been encouraged to take a page from Wal-Mart's playbook. Negotiations were reduced to "take it or leave it" situations involving little other than price. Many took place in rooms with bare tables. Buyers were sent in two-by-two to assure that one of them wouldn't cave. Purchasing's litany all too often was, "Five percent off your price or you're off our list."

An infamous memo from the executive office to GE purchasing managers said in part, "If your supplier likes doing business with you, you're not doing your job."

Somehow no one extracted the learnings from the end game of Boulwarism[3] in relation to union relations in the 1960s and applied it to the marketplace.

Not infrequently, supply chain people found themselves pressured to meet their *own* department's metrics, even when these measurements were in direct conflict with the needs of their internal customers. Those who resisted found their competence being questioned, which raised their anxiety about their *own* exposure. If they didn't meet the measurements in an environment where their organizations were still reducing people, or where they'd just merged, maybe they were the next ones out the door, with mortgages to pay and kids in college.

Suppliers frequently agreed with the "enemy" assessment in mirror-reverse: The customers are out to get us. Let's get them back, or get them first.

One prominent aviation company's sales organization espoused a concept known internally as MAG. It stood for *Maximum Allowable Gouge*. A major services business from a highly respected Fortune 500 company periodically sent out its employees to "screw the customer" to prove their loyalty to the organization. The same organization engaged in a process called "clawback." Get a conceptual agreement, have top management from both sides announce the deal as done and publicly claim the mutual benefits. Then wait until the customer turns the details of finalizing the agreement over to underlings, and send your killer contracts guys to "claw back" everything that was vague in the sales agreement, to ensure you got the profit level you needed, counting on the fact that wanting to avoid the political embarrassment of being the one to undo an already announced deal would drive those lower down in the organization to cave.

They were not alone in this practice.

Those folks who were part of more moderate sales organizations found themselves dreading that "five percent off your price" litany. Frequently they knew far better ways to serve the customer, to craft better solutions, but day after day they found themselves dealing with junior buyers fresh out of university who thought negotiation was a football game, and who were severely limited in their authority, and after a while they just gave up on seeking to propose those better ideas.

Our colleagues in sales found themselves making promises to get the contract they weren't sure their shops could deliver. Roger Fisher's ACBD concept (Always Consult Before Deciding)[4] was not a norm for how they dealt with their own shops. They had been reduced to making sure they met their own insular measurements: They were measured on sales volume; the shops were measured on cost, delivery, and quality.

Our shops described the relationship as one in which the sales organization periodically floated an order over the wall that separated the two organizations, rather like a paper airplane on a light breeze, with no idea whether the shop could do it, and no prior conversations about how best to integrate what sales offered with what the shops could produce in terms of volume, line of balance, or the impact on cost effectiveness. Shop managers, not surprisingly, did not feel a high degree of ownership for the delivery terms and conditions of the contract.

On a personal level, more and more of us decided, mentally if not physically, "If this is the way the game is played, I'm outta here."

John Drake, founder of Drake, Beam, Morin, wrote a best-selling book called *Downshifting*. In the preface, he states:

"This book is for you if you are
- Fed up with the 12-hour work day and want to cut back.
- Scared about the risks that come with working less.
- Looking for more satisfaction in life.

- Making a good income, but wondering if the price is worth it.
- Questioning 'Is this all there is?'
- Wanting more time for your family or yourself, but uncertain about the best ways to achieve it."[6]

He describes how, as the founder of a very successful human resources company, he found himself alone night after night in interchangeable hotel rooms all over the country, when all he really wanted was to be home with his wife and kids. He sold his share of the business and downshifted. His little volume is a recipe book for how to live your life more in consonance with your values and priorities.

There have always been people who weren't tough enough for this "bet the company" game called aviation/aerospace. But now it was many of our best and brightest who were choosing to drop out – some because of the endless and escalating hours, some for the lack of support from their own management, more because the business practices they were subjected to or required to practice conflicted directly with their own integrity.

Does This Make Sense?

When we commiserated with one another - over a drink on a business trip together, or late in the day in our cubbyholes or offices - about management, or the hours we were expected to work, or the results we were expected to achieve, or the deteriorated relationships between customer and supplier, union and management, we all knew this was nuts. Yet we were all caught up in it.

21

Some of us were old enough to remember different times, when we worked long hours, and the challenges were tough, but it was fun and satisfying. We felt we were part of a team and we were basically proud of what we were doing, of the recognition we were receiving, and of the organization and industry we were part of.

Most of us have started to question our own memories. Were we recalling those times through rose-colored filters of memory? Was it more fun because we were younger and less battered? Or was it truly qualitatively different?

We Seem to Have Forgotten

We seem to have walked away from or forgotten everything we thought we'd learned in the past forty years about how to manage employees for maximum effectiveness. We've forgotten Frederick Herzberg's conclusions in his classic *Harvard Business Review* article "One More Time: How Do You Motivate Employees?" that neither negative nor positive KITA (Kick In The Ass) employee motivation works.[7] We've forgotten Douglas McGregor's work in the 1960s on Theory X and Theory Y and his conclusions that most people actually want to work and like to work, and our job as managers is to clear roadblocks so they can.[8] We've forgotten Abraham Maslow's Hierarchy of Needs.[9] We've forgotten the insights of Peters and Waterman reported in their 1982 book *In Search of Excellence*.[10] We've even forgotten one of Deming's key rules on continuous improvement: Drive Out Fear.[11]

Why?

Over and over again, the answer is, "Well, that's all well and good, but I need results."

Here's the conundrum.

What if we discover that what we've been doing, the personal and business sacrifices we've been making, with work devouring more and more of our lives, time away from family escalating, our own ethic and integrity being nibbled away, turning people who work for us and with us from human beings into expendable commodities to manipulate, turning ourselves into commodities to be manipulated – in order to get results - is actually getting us *lousy* results and making it harder to get better results next time?

What if the managerial and behavioral models we've been using, as useful as they may have been in the past, are neither sustainable nor suited for what we need to do now? What if there is a far better way, one that is sustainable, effective, and human? What if we can get far better results, with far less effort, in ways that *are* consistent with our own ethic and integrity and that let us discover a better balance between work and the rest of our lives?

What if we can get those far better results for our company and our shareholders in ways that are also better for our employees (union and non-union), suppliers, customers, and alliance partners, in ways that extend out into our various environments?

What if we can get those far better results not just now but over time, so that we create organizations that endure and enrich our communities as well as ourselves?

What if?

I'm convinced we can. A lifetime in aviation has led me to this conclusion. More than fifteen years of running what our students refer to as a "boot camp for culture change" has confirmed for me that though it takes commitment, work, persistence, and some major retooling of our paraphernalia of culture, it's infinitely possible.

And it's perhaps never been so necessary.

* * * * * * * * * *

If we're going to explore how to get to where we need to be, it's important to recall the path we took to get to this place where the excesses of the very things that made us good are now causing us to implode.

I invite you to surface your memories of your own personal journey. To do that, I want to take you on a tour of my thirty years in aviation.

Whenever and wherever you entered our industry, I very much hope that my experiences will trigger memories of your own – the events themselves, your reactions to them, and what you learned from them.

If my experiences illuminate spaces carved out by your own life and times, and ring true, please record them in some way.

Perhaps our shared history can become a base that can help us reshape what we're doing and how we're doing it to better fit the challenges and opportunities we now face.

Let's see.

Chapter Two

LESSONS FROM OUR SHARED HISTORY

Aviation has been my home since 1972. Not only have I worked in it since then, I fell in love with, married, and adore an aeronautical engineer. (Some aeronautical engineers truly are adorable.) My husband Joe and I fly small planes and read *Av Week* and *Air Transport World*. Models of a Cessna Citation, a Bell 206B Jet Ranger painted in the colors of the helicopter that Joe soloed, DC-10s, 727s, and a beautiful DC-3 painted in Delta's colors serve as major motifs of our interior decorating.

High Flight, the hauntingly beautiful poem John Gillespie Magee, Jr.,[1] wrote at age 19, just a few months before he died when his Spitfire collided with another plane over England on December 11, 1941, hangs on the wall in our home.

Sharing his passion, I still thrill to my core at the smell of avgas in the predawn air as I walk out onto the tarmac before the rest of the world is awake.

> Oh, I have slipped the surly bonds of Earth
> And danced the skies on laughter-silvered wings;
> Sunward I've climbed, and joined the tumbling mirth
> Of sun-split clouds – and done a hundred things
> You have not dreamed of – wheeled and soared and swung
> High in the sunlit silence. Hov'ring there,
> I've chased the shouting wind along, and flung
> My eager craft through footless halls of air.
> Up, up, the long delirious, burning blue
> I've topped the wind-swept heights with easy grace
> Where never lark, or even eagle flew --
> And, while with silent, lifting mind I've trod
> The high untrespassed sanctity of space,
> Put out my hand, and touched the face of God.

Thrilling from the very first time I climbed into the left hand seat of a little airplane was the feeling that comes when you push the throttle to the firewall, then pull back on the yoke as your little plane reaches V_r speed and the ground starts to slip away beneath you and you're up in the sky alone.

Every time I file aboard a commercial airliner with the rest of the passengers, I take quick sideways glances into the cockpit. The pilgrim soul in me wants to just turn ninety degrees left and slip into the pilot's seat, into that environment of altimeters, airspeed indicators and LCD screens, altitude encoding transponders, noise-attenuating headphones, detailed checklists and the entire world to traverse.

Long before I came to work in this strange, over the edge, exuberant industry, I was in love with aviation and aerospace.

Back in the Fifties, as a young kid in California, I would lie awake at night and plot what I needed to learn and do to have a chance to be the first female astronaut. It may have been woefully insufficient, but it was tremendously heartfelt.

I decided I had to be good at math, learn to fly, and, of course, learn Morse Code. My little brother and I spent endless evenings tapping out secret messages to each other, or sending queries out into the ether over our uncle's magical ham radio set – dah-di-dah-di, dah-dah-di-dah. CQ, CQ. "Can anybody out there hear me? Please respond. Let's talk."

I devoured science fiction and science fantasy – Isaac Asimov, Robert Heinlein, and Theodore Sturgeon. Red planets and space cadets and light curving back on itself, and is there life beyond us out there in the universe?

I had the great fortune to have an uncle who was a physicist and an adventurer. Jay shared his love of science with me. He had a natural teacher's ability to bring all of science alive with wonder. For many years, he served as the head of the Office of Naval Research in San Francisco. He'd pick me up at school and take me with him to meetings at Varian Associates and Stanford Research Institute, where I learned about klystron tubes and nuclear accelerators. When I was in ninth grade, my birthday present from Jay was a subscription to *Scientific American*, renewed annually for years afterward.

* * * * * * * * * *

GE's Aircraft Engine Group asked me to come in to interview late in 1971. By then, the Equal Employment Opportunity Commission had been authorized to bring class action suits on behalf of client populations. They were targeting major corporations for sex and race discrimination. The suits, once filed, gave them the rights to nose around everywhere, into *all* of a company's policies, practices, and results. Those sued companies became painful and costly examples to others.

It was therefore good business policy to make sure your numbers made you less of a sitting duck than other companies. I strongly suspect my being a woman was the reason I was asked to interview. I'm not sure I was hired because I was a woman, but it certainly opened the door. At the time, hiring a white woman was a less bitter pill for many mid-level managers to swallow than hiring an African-American man.

They brought me in for what became a series of interviews with folks who would be my peers in human resources, with my potential client manager, and finally with the top HR manager. It isn't over until the fat lady sings. In this case, the fat lady's name was Don Lester.

The interview with Don Lester sticks in my mind to this day. He asked about my early childhood. He wanted to know, in disagreements between my father and mother, who prevailed? Of the four children, who did my mother like best? In disagreements between my three brothers and me, who won? I told him I wasn't sure the questions made sense in the context of our family. As the interview progressed, I told him I was divorced. He asked, "In the financial settlement, who came out ahead, you or your husband?" I told him that wasn't how we approached it.

After a series of questions along the lines of "Who won? Who came out ahead, you or him?" I swallowed hard and said, "I'm curious about your line of questioning. You seem to see the world in terms of win/lose, of hierarchies." He allowed as how that probably was an accurate observation. I said, "I see it in terms of 'How do we work things out together?' Given that you see it in win/lose terms, and given that you're the head of Human Resources, why are you even taking the time to interview me? And why have you staffed your organization with human potential movement change specialists?" "Well," he said, "I could be wrong. Let's say I'm hedging my bet."

It took a long time for me to realize he was walking a balancing act, enabling needed culture change while maintaining his power base. He *was* hedging his bet.

He worked for and very closely with a highly authoritarian, hierarchical, and brilliant group executive named Gerhard Neumann, who thrived in the hardball world of military aviation. Gerhard Neumann was seeking to lead GE to success in commercial aviation after a disastrous early entry with the engine on the Convair 880 program. Top-down, the company was managed in a command-and-control way, one step removed from a military structure. Yet Don Lester hired and supported a group of highly creative, Theory Y human resource and organization development managers, and he turned them loose to work wonders at the mid-levels of the organization.

At some point, you ask, "Why?" Why not just stay straight command-and-control? Why hire and turn loose change agents to develop an interactive, self-directed, empowered work force?

Two words come to mind: realism and need. Realistically, Gerhard Neumann and his top managers weren't going to change. Realistically, Don Lester needed to maintain his credibility with them by remaining one of them. Yet he knew the organization needed to unleash the creative energy of thousands of employees. As employment skewed more and more towards knowledge workers who required autonomy and participation, command-and-control authoritarianism wasn't going to get us there. And though I never was privy to his thought process, he may just have concluded that culture change is generational. If he could immerse lower-level and middle management in these different models, assumptions, behaviors, and results, when top management retired, the next generation stood ready to inherit the mantle.

If that was what he was trying to do, it worked fantastically well - for awhile.

So a disconnect was built into the organization – hierarchical and authoritarian at the top, human potential-driven in the middle.

* * * * * * * * * *

Two-thirds of the way through the day's interviews, when I learned that work at the GE Lynn plant started at 7:30 a.m., I stopped the interview process, said, "Thank you," and left. I was a single mother with two young children. I lived thirty to forty minutes away, depending on traffic, and my kids couldn't even get into their school until 8:20. My purpose in working was to provide a life-style and a future for my kids and me; this wouldn't do it.

I also had a problem with the product – jet engines that went on fighter aircraft and military helicopters.

My potential client manager called me up a few days later and said, "If you can come to terms with the product, we can deal with your hours. You can come to work once you drop your kids at school and add the time on to the end of the day."

I talked at length with my Uncle Jay. In the best of all possible worlds, he said, war and the machines of war are insane. In this less than perfect world, you can do more to contain the escalation of conflict if you control the machines of war than if you let others control them. And if you don't, he said, others will. I concluded that being a grownup in a complex, imperfect world means doing a balancing act of my own. Could I keep my ethical compass in this less than ideal real world?

Don Lester signed off on hiring me. He and Bill Lindsay, my client manager-to-be, then went out of their way to help me say yes. I would continue to struggle with the product, but I said yes to GE. Flextime as a policy was still years in the future. Don't assume we're setting precedent here, Don Lester said.

* * * * * * * * * *

I started work in February of 1972, immediately upon completing a Master's in Adult Education at Boston University, the closest to a change management consulting degree I could find and afford. I was to be an Organization and Development Representative in Lynn, Massachusetts. I was the first woman in the role in that locale for some thirty years, when Marion

Kellogg had entered GE and then rose with her mentor to become a vice president of the corporation and a member of the Board of Directors.

I remember driving up the Marsh Road in Saugus, Massachusetts, toward GE's sprawling Riverworks facility on my first day, with the early morning mists rising into the chill winter air out of the swamp lands that fringed the road. I watched with awe as the plant's smokestacks and depression-era brick buildings loomed up through the mist. I'm a change agent, I thought to myself. My job is to change this place.

Joining GE straight out of graduate school was like jumping from the top of a railway car going twenty miles an hour to one going a hundred and twenty miles an hour. For weeks afterwards, until I adjusted to the rhythms, speed and assumptions of the place, I would drive home with my windows rolled up, banging on the steering wheel and yelling, "The world is not like that!"

By the time I joined GE, I was almost thirty. I had been working since I was sixteen. I was the mother of two school-age kids. I had worked for a company that made hi-fi equipment, at a large teaching hospital, in civil rights in the South in the 1960s, as a teacher, in program development for a National Education Laboratory, and as associate director of an experimental urban ministry. I knew what the world was like, and the world was not like *that!*

Not like what?

Nothing moved at a moderate pace. Everything was time schedules and Gantt charts and signing up for targets and goals you had no idea how to reach. There were all these meetings, recounting what had

32

been recounted at other meetings about other meetings. Every day everybody wrote up Items of Interest ("IOIs" to the in-crowd) about what they'd done that day. They'd then affix routing slips to them and send them around to everyone else, who would check off their names, add items to their lists and send them around to another routing slip full of people. You could spend your entire day reading and writing IOIs.

I got in trouble with my human resources boss when I started saving up the writing of my IOIs. Every couple of weeks, I would write a small book's worth and deposit them in his in-basket. It seemed to me better to be busy making things happen than documenting them.

He had a different perspective. "How do I know what you're doing if you don't keep me informed?" he asked. "Why should I bother you with what I'm doing if it's on track and ahead of schedule?" I asked. "What if my boss asks me what you're doing?" he parried. "Well, you could check with me and get back to him," I offered. He let me know that all managers at GE needed to know at all times exactly what all their people were doing.

There were continual meetings about where we stood against target and schedule and who had screwed it up and how were they going to fix it? How did you ever get work done, with all those meetings, and all that blaming?

Communication was in acronyms and terminology I'd never heard of – AEG, IOI, MTO, MSO, EDM, AOG (*that* was an important one), FOD, and a couple of thousand more. We once published a booklet called FUI (pronounced "Foo-ey") when we realized that many of us much of the time didn't understand each other's acronyms. FUI stood for Frequently Used Initials.

I sat in on the weekly staff meeting of the Manufacturing Technology Organization, well aware that my job was to change this place. I didn't understand one word in four of what was being said about laser drilling and EDM'ing, investment castings and fine fiber introjects causing catastrophic failure in René 95 powdered metallurgy disks and blisks.

How can you change a place when you don't even understand what they're saying? Change would have to wait for a while.

Then one day, in staff meeting, our Advanced Materials Quality Manager was leading a discussion on problems one of our suppliers was having with inertia welding. I understood the conversation; it sounded like English. It made sense. It was a Twilight Zone moment.

I flashed back to a class in college twelve years earlier. My anthropology teacher, Mr. Katz, had described an event that occurred during a recent field study on a Polynesian island. He had been sitting in the living room of a home with the male members of the village when the sister-in-law of the homeowner entered the room. This was a forbidden act. Every man there, himself included, was shocked and outraged. He then had a visceral reaction to his reaction – shock that he was seeing the world through the taboo and value mindset of *their* culture, not through his own.

* * * * * * * * * *

It was not long before GE's horizons became my horizons. I could sit in my desk chair and spin around and all around me were people who saw the world the same way and who used the same terms to describe it. The organization's goals became my goals. I was being rewarded, respected, and included for making impersonal, goal-oriented things happen fast and well. My self-perception was changing. My assumptions, conclusions, vocabulary, and behaviors were changing as well. I could now be effective *inside* this brave new world I'd entered, but I was losing that perspective that might have helped me to help it operate *outside* of its boundaries and reframe itself.

I no longer drove home yelling that the world was not like that.

I went through a period when I swore like a trooper. It was the language of the shop and I was one of them, right? Only I wasn't. I saw me from the inside - one of the guys, as I'd been one of the kids growing up with my brothers. They saw me from the outside. They had their own expectations about appropriate behavior for women. Their expectations had to do with school teachers, wives, secretaries, nurses, and - it being Boston - nuns.

I cleaned up my mouth. It wasn't about women's liberation; it was about getting things done in what was still a man's world. I learned to soften my approach instead of confronting directly. And I got things done that were useful to them. Because their expectations of women were so low, they gave me greater credit for accomplishments than would have been the case had I been a white guy. They didn't change their minds about women; they just exempted me from the class. "Oh, well, Kaye," they started to say to each other, "she's different." It was a compliment.

We struggled with how to improve productivity in the organization.

One of my colleagues drew an input-throughput-output model[2] of organizational effectiveness for me.

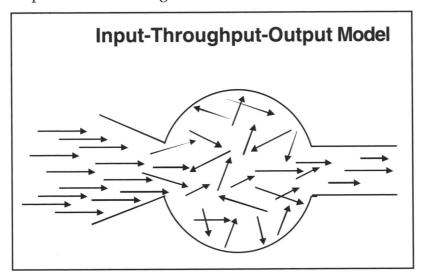

Input-Throughput-Output Model

Adapted from a colleague's hand drawing, ca. 1975.

We joked about it, but it was true. All we had to work with was the sum of our available energy. We could use that energy to bounce off walls and bounce off each other. To the extent we did, it was gone, and not available for productive work. The continual question was, how can we align our energy so it *is* available for productive work?

I initially assumed that the sum total of energy was a constant, but it's not. When we worked in opposition to each other, the battles themselves drained energy out of us, so the total shrank. When we unleashed our creativity and commitment and played together toward results, we fed off of each other's energy, playfulness, and ideas. Energy grew. I started to understand that managerial responsibilities included growing and aligning available energy.

The metaphors of the place abounded with terms drawn from sport, warfare, and aviation. "Win the engine competition" or "Win the fly-off." "Beat the forecast." "What's the thrust of their position?" "How do we triangulate on it?" and "Let's not auger in on this one."

We prepared to negotiate *against* our adversaries. We didn't ask our negotiators if they'd gotten a good agreement; we asked, "Who won the negotiation?" We didn't talk about power utilization; we talked about power *exploitation*. Whatever our job, we were to meet our measurements and get it done, whether with, around, over, or through other people, functions, or companies.

We read a book by Michael Macoby called *The Gamesman,*[3] and it struck us as true. We read a book about the aviation industry called *The Sporty Game*[4] where major decisions were "bet the company" decisions that could affect your business for the next twenty years, and it struck us as even more true. All of business was a game, we were playing in the Big Leagues, and our job was to win.

And *win*, in this context, meant *beat*. Not just in the marketplace, but cross-functionally in your own organization. Manufacturing saw Engineering as an obstacle to its success; both saw Projects as suspect. Walking into Building 40, where Projects were headquartered, was a bit like stepping gingerly into enemy territory. Later, when I'd moved to Evendale, the headquarters of our large commercial engine business, Engine Sales occupied the first floor of Building 100; Projects and Customer Support occupied the second floor. Occupants engaged in what they accurately referred to as "Stair Wars."

We worked in a matrix organization. I reported solid line to a human resources manager and dotted line to Bill Lindsay, my client manager. Shortly after I joined GE, Bill asked whether my first allegiance was going to be to Human Resources or to his organization and staff. "You have to decide," he said, "whether you're here to 'fix' us according to HR's view about what's right and wrong, or to help us in ways that are helpful to us as seen by us." I chose to seek to help them first, satisfy HR second; I found myself engaged in another balancing act.

My colleagues also taught me something else very fast. I had been one of those bright kids beloved by teachers, the kind who raises her hand to be called on and who answers in complex paragraphs rather than short phrases. It had served me well in school; my mother delighted in my grades.

Now, working in groups, when my mind leapt to obvious connections and I leapt to propose the self-evident solution, it didn't serve me or anyone else well. My colleagues rolled their eyes: "There she goes again."

I learned fast. The best answer isn't necessarily the right answer. There are lots of right answers. The issue is coming up with an answer the group can and will support and implement. The shortest distance from point A to point B is not a straight line; it's rather serpentine. Everyone who will be affected by the decision has to have a chance to be heard and to shape the outcome.

This, by the way, is very different from manipulating folks into thinking it was their answer. I learned that even if our colleagues and counterparts are not as bright as we are (and that assumption is usually highly questionable), they're not a lot dumber, and they certainly are smart enough to know when they're being manipulated.

Was I willing to work *with* people, to lead by helping create an environment in which we could solve problems together? Was I willing to take the time to let a good decision evolve, even if it meant biting my lip or sitting on my hands? As I learned to shut up for all of five minutes, then finally all of ten minutes, I was amazed to discover that other people came up with awesome ideas and built on each other's input.

This helped when I worked with client managers, especially engineering managers. Many had been promoted into the managerial role because they were the best design engineers. Now suddenly their job was to create an environment in which other folks got to do the fun stuff, the design stuff. Too many couldn't keep their hands off the design and problem-solving process.

After awhile, the better engineers who reported to them would find jobs elsewhere. Their logic was, "Why knock myself out when my boss is going to second-guess everything I do?" Those who remained were content to push more and more of the problem-solving work onto the manager, thereby confirming the manager's perception that, "These guys are useless. Can't trust them with anything. If it's going to be done right, I've got to do it myself."

People's energies at work focused more on putting out fires than on strategic and tactical planning and implementation. Fire fighting got your juices flowing. Fire fighting was also rewarded.

Colleagues and I once ran a session with young managers about how to get ahead. What was the advice the young managers gave each other? "Get a job. Screw it up. Pull it out. Be a hero." You got far more credit for saving something that had deteriorated into a disaster than you got for running your part of the business smoothly and well. If it ran smoothly, your management would conclude that it must not have been difficult. You would stay below the radar and not be identified as having The Right Stuff.

* * * * * * * * * *

GE Aircraft Engines in Lynn, Massachusetts, was filled with 6,000 folks like my Uncle Jay. I loved it. I loved those no-nonsense, make-it-happen people who would sign on for challenges they didn't know how to accomplish, and then somehow set a path, figure it out and make it happen.

I wanted to learn, and I was fascinated with what these people did. They opened up their specialties and their challenges to me.

My job was to help them align their knowledge, energies, structures, systems, and behaviors with their objectives. Sometimes it required organizational redesign, sometimes a training program. Sometimes it required new ways to work together across organizational silos.

I worked first with Manufacturing Technology and with Advanced Engine Programs back when the

CF6-80 was just a baby and the T700 was a sweet little Swiss Watch of an advanced engine design.

The 1970s were a remarkable time in that facility – the era of the human potential movement. Key HR folks – strategic and tactical thinkers - had been exposed to Douglas McGregor's concepts on Theory X and Theory Y; steeped themselves in the Eupsychian Management[5] concepts of Abraham Maslow and his wonderful Hierarchy of Needs; read Peter Drucker and Warren Bennis and Chris Argyris; incorporated concepts from Sid Simon's Values Clarification workshops[6] into the personal development training sessions we ran for our clients; attended workshops sponsored by the National Training Labs[7] in Bethel, Maine; and worked with Eric Berne's Parent-Adult-Child ego state concepts.[8]

They worked to put these concepts into action to help individuals and groups function better.

Change was in the air as we struggled with how to manage knowledge workers who knew more about the content matter than their managers did. How did you manage engineers for creativity while maintaining at least the appearance of control? How could you build effective involvement in the precursors of continuous improvement and Kaizan – programs with titles like Zero Defects and Bring Quality to Life (BQ2L)?

We implemented leading edge processes in career development. In the early 1970s, a person's career and job growth were in the hands of management teams who made job-change decisions behind closed doors. If a position came open, the hiring manager needed first to know of someone who might be able to do the job. That person's current manager had to give permission before they could be approached. If the current manager said no, the individual never heard there was interest. If a manager or the HR representatives didn't know of a qualified candidate working in anonymity in some outlying building, that person never had a chance to be on the candidate slate.

Don Lester approved my colleagues' suggestion that we move the locus of responsibility for job and career growth to the individuals themselves. The project process involved hundreds of managers and individual contributors designing *for themselves* an open job posting system. Such a system had to reflect their interests in their own job moves and career growth tempered and balanced by their interests as managers in the system.

I witnessed first-hand the power of involving people in those things that affect them. As soon as the job posting process was developed, it was implemented. Normal resistance never surfaced. Maybe, I thought, normal resistance isn't "normal," if normal means "unavoidable." Maybe it's natural resistance that arises when people don't have a say in things that affect them.

My own client manager was open to learning everything I knew. I taught him what I knew about Transactional Analysis; we then worked with his staff to make the policies inside Manufacturing Technology more adult/adult, less parent/child.

We also played with ideas: "If we really wanted to help minorities and women succeed and grow in this place, what would we do? How would we do it?" And then we did those things inside his organization, with remarkable success.

Shortly thereafter, his boss raised the need to open up career paths for minorities and women throughout the department. The economy was in the doldrums, so career growth was stagnant. No jobs were being vacated, therefore no jobs were being posted.

Drawing on the success of the Manufacturing Technology experience, we suggested that mentored workshops be run to help people make wiser decisions – not just to bid on individual jobs, but to do so with a career plan in mind.

I proposed the concept at a department staff meeting. The department manager said, "Do it; include white males." It was a brilliant amendment. At that point, the members of his staff, each of whom had his own favorite son or sons, chose to support the program.

We created a coaching system, making it legitimate for those being coached to petition a top manager to be their mentor. We published role précis on the current members of the manufacturing staff so everyone could see the paths each of these people had taken to get to their current roles. Participants could visit managers of their choosing to find out what they did and what roles existed in their organizations. They then sat in private with their mentors to identify strengths and gaps in their own backgrounds thus far, and to agree on a logical sequence of growth steps through various roles. And then the mentors met to swap individuals and jobs according to agreements they'd made with those they represented.

If natural growth was non-existent, we could still give people the chance to move *laterally* and learn another job. Most of these people went on to substantial careers in the company. Many point to this lateral job-swapping program as the event that shifted them from neutral into high gear.

The same department manager called me in one day and said, "We need a materials and processes curriculum." I had only the slightest idea what materials and processes *were*. His logic was sound. GE had long assumed that if you could manage, you could manage anything. We were growing folks from one process area to another, as they progressed from foreman to production control analyst to process control supervisor to manager of shop operations. After a few such moves, they frequently didn't understand the manufacturing processes they were managing, didn't know when to ask for help from a process expert, and didn't know what to do with the advice when they got it. And the folks they managed knew they didn't know. Respect was hard to maintain. And bad managerial decisions were being made.

I had heard about an education-by-objectives instructional design being used to create an entire medical school curriculum in Illinois and a nurse midwifery program in North Carolina. We pulled together a team of our top technologists – world experts in metallurgy, sheet metal, metal forming, conventional and non-conventional metal removal, all the way through to current assembly, inspection, and test procedures - and we brought in instructional designers from Chapel Hill, North Carolina.

The first time the instructional designers came in, they taught those fifty technologists how to construct a curriculum and sent them off to do it. The second time they reviewed their draft curricula and taught them how to develop instructional objectives. The third time they reviewed the homework from the second step and taught the next step in instructional design. I learned that our technical experts, who were truly among the best in the world, loved the chance to share their knowledge with others, to leave a legacy. Curriculum development was done as an add-on to their regular jobs.

We used me as the benchmark for materials development. If Kaye could understand the booklet or the script for a self-instructional video and could pass the post-test, the logic went, anyone would be able to.

By the time we were done, we had a seventeen-week long modularized materials and processes curriculum complete with slide shows and self-instructional videotapes. Students could familiarize themselves with the material at the Learning Resources Center before they ever went to class. Class could be used for problem-solving and taking learning further.

We designed a program-wide pre-test with an 85th percentile pass level and administered it to the department staff at one of their regular staff meetings. Several didn't pass. They laughed and signed themselves up for the program.

It was the first time manufacturing professionals and managers had a chance to understand the entire process of engine design, operation, and manufacture from basic metallurgy through to assembly, inspection, and test. A high potential mid-level manufacturing manager told me that for the first time he understood where a part he'd been making actually went on the engine, what it did, and why it was designed the way it was.

If students chose, they could take pre-tests to competency out of certain modules. The top metallurgist in the plant took the course even though he'd competencied out of the metallurgy module he had co-authored. The manufacturing manager in charge of making rotating parts competencied out of the module on lathes. But he took the rest of the program.

The program was taught after hours by the technologists who had developed it. An unexpected side benefit resulted. A buyer in Materials was able to ask our top coatings specialist how he could tell whether a part at a supplier's plant had been coated, as the drawing called for. Throughout the plant, contacts were made that lasted far beyond the course. The technologists' expertise could be honored and shared; everyone grew in their sense of being part of a larger whole and working toward overlapping self-interests.

When I moved from Lynn, Massachusetts, to Evendale, Ohio, to be the HR manager for Materials, we were already well into course design for Materials and Processes, Level II, aimed at helping professionals actually work with the technologies.

I was in Evendale when Materials first started to reduce input cost by sending value/process engineers to the suppliers' plants to work with them on manufacturing process changes. The supplier got to keep the benefit of the change in that year's contract; we split the benefit in the years that followed.

I worked with folks in Materials Quality when they first shifted away from inspecting for quality on the receiving dock toward the then-radical idea of building quality into the manufacturing plans at the suppliers' plant, and then monitoring whether or not the plans were followed.

During the early 1980s, when we were ramping up at an incredible rate, I worked in private with unit and subsection Materials managers who had concluded our current organizational structure was getting in the way of results. We met for weeks, carving out time in the early evenings and on weekends, putting together a speculative proposal to reorganize.

The department manager agreed to let us present it to his staff; no promises. After the presentation, the presenters were excused from the room; I stayed on in my role as HR manager for the department. The section managers dismissed the entire concept as absurd. They then reworked it themselves, coming up with a design about 95% in common with the proposal they had dismissed out of hand. When the department manager announced this radical organizational change to the entire department, he went out of his way to use the same viewgraphs that had been used by the lower level folks. He never mentioned it, never owned it, but each and every one of them knew.

Yet there was a meaner side to the business that I never understood, especially at the higher levels. It seemed to take over more and more of the life of the business as we entered the 1980s. We had been able to effect changes at the mid-levels, but the mindset from the top still held sway.

Our group executive, Gerhard Neumann, had a sign on the wall behind his desk that read, "Be insecure." Those granted an audience with him found the focus of their eyes shifting back and forth from his face to that sign located just behind his head.

It's possible to put a positive interpretation to the sign, to remind yourself to continually think about what you haven't considered, to remember never to become complacent about what you've done or what you may still need to do.

But, in truth, Mr. Neumann chose to pit his key people against one another. He regularly sent out memos – dutifully reported at cascading staff meetings at division, then department, then section, then subsection and below. The memos had a common theme: "I've assigned the responsibility for this challenge to Jim Worsham, but if Jim isn't up to it, Brian Rowe (or Jim Krebs or Neil Burgess or Bob Hastings or Ray Letts) is waiting in the wings."

He was comfortable that internal competition produced the best results. Have folks compete against each other! Have organizations compete against each other! Winning, beating, and pitting folks against each other is how you stay in fighting trim, bring out the best in people and programs and ensure survival of the fittest. He was not alone in this belief and practice.

He defined business strategy in short, clear, memorable prose that everyone could grasp. Everyone in GE Aircraft Engines understood our strategic purpose: "Beat Pratt." Not "serve the customer." Not "grow our market value." Not "enrich our community."

Beat Pratt.

Yet somehow you felt you were part of the winning sports team, and "Beat Pratt" seemed worth going after year after year. We aligned our energies to make it happen. We joked about having the GE Monogram stamped on our souls and delicate parts of our anatomy. We struggled in disbelief when, from time to time, a trusted colleague quit GE and (how could they?!) went to Pratt. Even as we competed with each other for the next job, we joined together to win in the marketplace.

In fairness to "Beat Pratt," there was a deeper logic to this business strategy. GE entered the aircraft engine business in support of the war effort for World War II. The U.S. Government needed to ensure the survival of two strong engine manufacturers. For each engine decision, the Department of Defense competed GE against Pratt & Whitney in an engine competition and fly-off. Engine development costs were awarded to both companies, but when it came to the production run, they chose one or the other. They didn't split the order. And the winner didn't subcontract part of the work to the loser, which did happen with airframes. It was all or nothing.

The driver for the engine competition was to beat Pratt technically so the DOD would choose us.

GE's employment population rose and fell in the 1970s with these DOD decisions. So, in mirror reverse, did Pratt & Whitney's. If you took Pratt's military employment totals over the years and laid them out on a chart with GE's totals, one charted upside down, they would dovetail into an almost perfect whole. Seeking to stabilize this employment roller coaster was a driving reason for steering GE into the commercial aviation engine business.

It wasn't just us.

Some years later, in the mid-1980s, the *Wall Street Journal* reported on the Great Engine Wars, which GE withdrew from when the price of staying in the game became too steep. The opportunity:

to be the airlines' engine of choice on the new 757 aircraft. All three engines were qualified on the airframe. Pratt & Whitney and Rolls-Royce each committed contractually to outperform the other over the life of the aircraft, with annual penalty payments to be paid to the customer if their engine choice performed less well than the other.

> "Anything you can do, I can do better.
> I can do anything better than you.
> No you can't.
> Yes I can.
> No you can't.
> Yes I can.
> No you can't.
> Yes I can,
> Yes I can." [9]

I have a twenty-two pound, fourteen-year-old American Eskimo dog. His name is Turbo. He's small but supercharged. Dog hierarchy is determined in part by who pees highest on the post. When Turbo was younger, he would bend his little body over backward to ensure an upward arc to his stream that far exceeded his height.

Beat Pratt.

I later learned that Bob Crandall at American Airlines clarified the underlying energy behind American's marketplace stance with similar clarity.

Two words: "Competitive anger."

* * * * * * * * * *

50

Another more insidious meanness permeated our worldview, one I absorbed by osmosis without it ever rising to the level of consciousness necessary to question. I had been told upon entry to GE that I was "exempt."[10] I was special. I got to drive into the plant to park in spaces reserved for exempt employees.

I carefully glued a decal containing my badge number to the inside left-hand corner of my car's windshield. I learned to flash my badge casually to the guard as I drove in through the gate.

There were three classes of employees in our little universe: exempt, non-exempt, and hourly. Non-exempt and hourly workers parked outside, often blocks away, and walked in.

Hourly workers, I assumed, were "different." For years, our paths crossed only when I had to traverse the first floor of Building 40 – a major manufacturing building – to get to the cafeteria. The corridor that ran through the center of this cavernous building was flanked on either side by multiple rows of lathes, grinders, and milling machines, and by the hourly workers who operated them. Whenever possible, I walked through the parking lot to get to the cafeteria. Winter storms drove me inside. At these times, I would scoot down the central walkway, clutching a protective notebook to my chest. The guys in the shop would whistle and catcall. I'd hunch my shoulders defensively and scurry faster, eyes averted, face reddening.

In the midst of one such episode, I decided this truly was ridiculous. I stopped, turned, took a few steps towards my tormenter, looked him up and down, made eye contact, grinned, and said, "You look pretty good to me, too. I'm Kaye. Who are you?" He smiled, came forward, wiped his hand on his coveralls and, shaking my hand, told me his name. His co-workers hooted and clapped. Something changed.

It's easier to lay people off when you conclude they're not like you. It's easier to justify preferential work conditions or benefits advantageous to you. It works the other way, too. It's easier to continue class warfare when you're "union" and they're "management" or "suits."

* * * * * * * * * *

Work for exempt and non-exempt workers started at the GE plant in Lynn, Massachusetts, at 7:30 a.m. Thousands of sleep-deprived engineers, technicians, secretaries, managers, and lab assistants stumbled out of bed each morning of their working lives at 5:00 or 5:30, in order to be at work prior to 7:30, largely because Gerhard Neumann was a morning person who thrived on four or five hours of sleep a night and couldn't wait to get to work in the morning. Cars full of sleepy people would queue and stream into the plant in the predawn hour, their headlights forming a sparkling golden stream that sliced through the surrounding darkness.

Not infrequently, Gerhard Neumann would take his binoculars and climb to the rooftop of Building 45, which looked out over the arriving line of traffic. Starting at 7:31 a.m., he'd dictate to the subordinate at his side the license plate numbers of the cars entering late, to be correlated that morning in the Security Office with the name of the owner of the car. An official dunning note would be delivered promptly to the in-basket of the offending driver. To the best of my knowledge, Mr. Neumann never climbed to the rooftop after 4:15 p.m. to determine the license plate numbers of the cars leaving late, or to check to see if the late arrivals correlated in any way with the late departures, or to require the Security Office to send notes of appreciation for the long hours of casual overtime.

I learned later that Sikorsky did much the same thing. Their lower level people parked in an external parking lot and walked in through a gate in a high chain-link fence. At Sikorsky, the gate itself was closed precisely at starting time. Those arriving one minute late entered through the guardhouse to sign in as tardy. Their managers would later clarify for them the working hours at the plant.

I imagined this early Best Practice spreading around the industry, shared perhaps among chief executives at annual Conquistadors del Cielo meetings.

One of my close colleagues, a man identified by his peers as one of the top stewards of the business over the course of his career, quoted the theme song from *Rhinestone Cowboy* as uneasy justification for decisions he found himself increasingly required to make as he advanced in the organization hierarchy. He needed me to understand that I, too, would have to make them if I was going to climb the ladder:

> "There's been a load of compromisin'
> On the road to my horizon.
> But I'm gonna be
> Where the lights are shinin' on me."[11]

It may not have been the message he intended to send, but the message I received was that the closer I got to the top, the harder it would be to remain true to my own ethic.

* * * * * * * * *

My tenure in Evendale bridged the time when Materials changed its name to Sourcing.

Years before, as an English teacher in a junior/ senior high school in a rural North Carolina county, I had learned that if kids didn't have the word, they couldn't think the thought. If they didn't have the concept, they couldn't receive the thought. Now I learned again how the very words you use shape your assumptions, behaviors, and results.

Think of the difference between the word "vendor" and the phrase "external source." We had internal sources - our shops - and external sources. Both sets of sources mattered to the success of our business, not just now, but over time.

Most of us worked differently with a source than we did with a supplier or, God forbid, with a "vendor." You knew you needed your external sources to remain healthy, as much as you needed your internal shops, so you worked with them not just on the specific situation but out of respect for the long-term relationship.

This was a far cry from the '60s and early '70s, when we would cherry-pick specific items from this vendor, and others from that one, competing them annually against each other, even though in some cases we participated in pushing the very folks we needed toward bankruptcy.

Others of us mouthed the new words while our arms and legs kept moving in the same old ways. Suppliers talked among themselves about the gap between our talk and our walk. "When GE says 'Let's partner,'" some of them advised, "slap your hand over your wallet."

And I learned about trust and trustworthiness. When Bill Lindsay addressed the need to make major changes in a highly critical part of the business, he brought in Armand Lauzon from our satellite plant in Rutland, Vermont, to head up the operation. "I don't know if Armand's any better than some other guys I could have chosen," he said, "but I just *feel* better knowing he's on the job."

I later watched my Materials client manager make similar decisions involving Skip Kundahl of Mal Tool. Whenever our manufacturing shops couldn't do something, or couldn't do it on time, Jim Walz knew that Skip Kundahl and Mal Tool could get it done. For a premium. But done, done well, done on time. A reputation for reliability, I would later learn from Roger Fisher, is powerful.

* * * * * * * * * *

And my clients taught me about the relationship of measurements to objectives, or, more frequently, the failure of measurements to support objectives or encourage desired behaviors. They also taught me about the time-honored game known as "Beat the Measurements."

A raw materials buyer at GE Evendale in the early '80s first taught me about the disconnect and the game. His name was Art Thom.

Each year, the Division Manager of Manufacturing issued cost reduction edicts to the departments that reported to him, Materials among them. These edicts were divided up and cascaded down so that each individual buyer had annual bogeys he or she was measured against. Notice that no one participated in deciding what realistic cost reductions *should be*. We were told what they were and what our individual contributions would be.

It was framed as a competition. Whoever won the Cost Reduction Competition received a substantial cash bonus plus dinner for two at a local Five Star restaurant. The winner was invited to the appropriate upper manager's staff meeting and introduced to the staff with applause all around. Hands were shaken, photographs taken. The event was reported in the plant newspaper. It was a big deal. Positive KITA.

Year after year, Art Thom won the Cost Reduction Competition.

One Saturday morning, as I wandered around the Materials area, I noticed that Art was also at work. I dropped by his cubicle to talk. "Art," I said, "how come you always win the Cost Reduction Competition?" He laughed and said, "It's easy."

Then he described the ground rules. A cost reduction, he said, is determined as a percentage basis of the difference between what you pay for your "first buy" and what you pay for the follow-on buy.

He said, "I buy forgings. I always place the first buy in less than lead-time, so I have to pay a premium to get the material delivered on time. Because it's in less than lead-time, they can't deliver it in near-net shape; they have to send me a huge forging. Our shops have to hog the part out of the forging, so there's lots of waste material. I pay by the pound, so the price goes up. When it's time for the follow-on buy, it's a snap to get a huge cost reduction. Works every time."

This started me on a path to understand the managerial danger of defining success by whether your people meet their measurements. The lesson came across again when I learned to fly small planes. Set the course, make corrections as necessary for wind, weather, and other environmental effects. Don't chase the compass needle; you'll zigzag all over the sky, wasting resources, and wasting time. If you set your course right and allow for corrections, the needle will come in by itself.

But we have to measure people, my client managers would say. Otherwise, how do we know how they're doing? I'm convinced that we can indeed measure most things, but we need to make sure that our metrics encourage positive action in the direction of our organizational goals, in ways consistent with our values. Most don't. And perhaps people need to be consulted on what the objectives and measurements should be.

* * * * * * * * * *

In late 1977, I hadn't ducked fast enough when Jim Worsham, our vice president for military engine programs, decided that our marketplace people didn't know how to close. In fact, he concluded, they didn't know how to negotiate. He had brought in a one-day crash course in negotiation for himself and his staff run by Chester Karrass' organization. Now he asked for an internal workshop in negotiation capable of being run for thousands.

I was identified to design such a program. Before I agreed to the assignment, I went to the top managers of functions that negotiated in the marketplace. "If we designed and ran such a program, would it be useful to you and your people?" I asked each one. The head of

Materials summarized their input: "If you really can help our marketplace people be better negotiators, it's as valuable as anything you will ever do for this organization."

"Keep me honest, then," I said to each one. "Give me your best person to be on the design team – someone respected in the organization, someone who knows the marketplace, knows your people, knows where you are now and where you need to be."

That's how the team was formed – representatives from materials, military and commercial product support, military and commercial contracts, human resources, large commercial and small commercial engine sales – people who would make sure the end product was useful to their folks. With their input and involvement, I wrapped a week-long residential workshop around Chester Karrass' conceptual material.[12]

We went off to the New Hampshire woods with sixteen high potential mid-level managers to pilot test it early in 1978. The first session was so bad we stopped in the middle and, with our sixteen participants, redesigned it on the spot. A few months later, the second session got a "thumbs up." We brought the participants back a few weeks later to review every part of the design and tune it further. For years afterward, Thursday morning of the workshop was dedicated to an evaluation of the program – what was helpful, what wasn't, what would be more helpful?

I learned again the importance of designing for your customers, with their input. They can tell you what is useful and what isn't.

Soon we were running it fourteen times a year. Starting in 1983, we took it to Europe and ran joint sessions with Snecma, our partner in the CFM-56 family of engines.

My job quickly became training teams of people to run the program. With their involvement, I spent nine years teaching thousands of GE people and people from their partner organizations to be very good hard positional negotiators. (I now stand in front of every group and tell them I'm spending the rest of my life doing penance.)

Initially the program was only offered to marketplace people.

Then one day a program manager entered my office, got on his knees, clasped his hands together and begged to attend the program. "You don't understand," he said, "all I do all day long is negotiate."

Sales managers pleaded with us to invite engineering. "You don't understand," *they* said, "one design engineer can do more damage in one meeting with the customer than I can undo in months."

And I started to understand why *Newsweek* magazine, in an article written around that time, had described negotiation as "the game of life."

I designed the workshop around Malcolm Knowles' concepts of learner/teacher teams.[13] The driving reason was pragmatic: I didn't know anything about negotiation. How could I presume to stand in front of a group of highly experienced marketplace people and say, "Hi, I'm this well-meaning woman from HR who has the gall to think she can teach you to negotiate better." We always ran the program with two trainers – a process co-trainer who understood group process, psychological process, and learning process, and a content co-trainer who was an experienced and respected manager of negotiators.

So we provided a framework for learning, and we provided the best conceptual material available at the time. Our students formed themselves into cross-functional subject matter teams. Each team reviewed a chunk of the content material in the context of our business and ran the workshop for an hour teaching everyone else the material in the light of their experience. I was amazed again at the power of turning people in the organization loose to teach one another, drawing on and sharing their own hard-earned experience. Again, I learned that people like to share what they've learned and what they know. When you've made it safe to risk, they also share what they don't know and what they're still struggling with. That's when real growth and change can start.

In the process, I learned a lot about tactical, positional negotiation – time tactics, authority tactics, bottom line tactics. *Kick It Up to Higher Authority* and *You've Got to Do Better than That*, legitimate and illegitimate escalation, *Good Guy/Bad Guy*.[14] All the fun stuff.

And it *was* fun stuff; it was an intricate game, an intricate dance. We thought of ourselves as grownups in a tough business. We assumed we were dealing with grownups on the other side. Our job was to exercise the marketplace until there was no more movement; their responsibility was not to do anything that wasn't wise for their own organization.

The pie was fixed; negotiation was about claiming value; we looked out for our interests; they looked out for theirs. Our mutually exclusive objectives were to get as much as we could.

But I also learned that our best negotiators always understood that they'd be working with these folks again and again and that aviation was a very small community.

My husband Joe and I once had a long conversation with Granny Frazier, the long-time head of Boeing's Propulsion Systems Division. Granny described his relationship with the engine manufacturers as a marriage. He said that he'd never take inappropriate advantage of the folks he dealt with. He'd negotiate hard, and so would they, but he'd never push the engine guy beyond decency, even when he could. It would reach the point that they go out together, sit down with a good bottle of Scotch, drink together, and flip a coin or split the difference. Even employing the assumptions and tactics of hard positional negotiation, he made sure he kept the relationship intact and the other guy's self-esteem inviolate.

The waiting line to attend the workshop quickly became so long (people were queuing for up to two years) that we rationed slots in each session for different organizations. This had an unintended side effect, that of profound and lasting team-building across organizational lines.

When purchasing, engineering, supplier quality, manufacturing, contracts, finance, legal, sales, customer support, tech reps, field sales, HR and ER folks all attended together, working long and hard on teams together, they became resources to each other for business effectiveness and personal growth. Mutual respect and understanding grew and extended beyond the workshop back into the workplace. Networks flourished. People in manufacturing now had someone they knew and trusted in sales, or engineering, or materials to call and ask what was going on. Before, they had just assumed it was "those morons in engineering, those idiots in sales."

People better understood the entire organization and how their roles fit in it. It was easier for them to align their priorities and actions in support of the business, not just in support of their function. We were producing graduates more able to be turned loose in the environment to work for the good of the organization, people empowered to make the deal.

Several years into the workshop, I happened to sit next to Don Lester at a Management Association dinner. His unique form of expressing pride in you was to rib you mercilessly in front of your peers. He complained loudly to everyone around us about this skunkworks project I was running that he was pouring endless resources into. After the spotlight had shifted to another victim, I told him quietly that if he took a list of program graduates, nailed it to his wall, threw a dart at the list, and called that person, whoever he called would tell him the workshop was the most meaningful and useful training in their career. The next morning, I brought in one of my son's darts, packaged it with a list of program graduates, and sent it to Don.

Don called his predecessor, Bob Miles, and asked him to conduct an exhaustive evaluation of the program. Among Bob's findings were these comments:

> "To categorize NSW training as anything less than outstanding would be an injustice to the value of this training as seen by participants and their managers."

> "Relatively few people above subsection level take the course. In

LESSONS FROM OUR SHARED HISTORY

time this will lead to an inverse skill and knowledge situation in the management hierarchy. A frequent comment was that superiors are giving away the shop because they are not skilled negotiators."[15]

At the time, Harry Stonecipher (later of Sundstrand, McDonnell Douglas, and Boeing) ran our Commercial Engine Business. He agreed with Bob Miles' report. He commissioned three executive sessions of the program. High potential subsection, section, and some department managers attended. They, too, taught each other about the marketplace and built cross-functional understanding and respect. But though additional managerial support for the program grew, we never got our top management team or a critical mass of our upper level managers to the program. The split in the organization between those at the top and those below remained, now more clearly visible from below.

Running the workshop had put me in contact with our sales and product support folks. They introduced me to the worldwide nature of our business, and the impact of ego. Did we really understand the continuing support costs of successfully selling engines for one 747 that would be located in a small country in Africa? In Asia? Was it worth the sale to get one more tail logo for our display wall?

They also helped me see other gaps in the organization.

At the time, our sales people weren't privy to the financial implications of their actions. Management didn't trust them with the financials, assuming that if they knew they'd give too much away. Their job was to get the sale; top management's job was to tell them when they'd gone far enough.

We never reduced the engine's list price; we just gave away items from concession packages until we'd reached the bottom line set by management. When the subsection or section level sales managers reached their bottom-line and started saying, "I've gone as far as I can go," the customer would escalate, calling our top management to complain about the non-responsiveness of the sales guys. One of our top managers would then leap on an airplane, fly halfway around the world, dump millions of dollars on the table, and "save" the sale.

It didn't take the customers long to figure out they should always escalate to higher authority. It didn't take our sales folks long to realize their credibility at the customer organization approached zero. Those who stayed in the roles shrugged and did their best. If management wanted to be heroes, regardless of the business impact, it was beyond their pay grade.

This particular little manager-subordinate game, played out over and over again, had been part of the pattern that had caused Jim Worsham to conclude years earlier that our sales people didn't know how to close.

And I learned the impact of partisan perceptions. Management truly wanted sales people to be more able to close and to negotiate better; it was with resignation that they kept leaping on those airplanes to save the sale (though it was enormously gratifying). Sales people truly wanted to work with their customers. Each was frustrated; each felt justified. The behaviors were visible, but no one examined the assumptions that drove the behaviors. The expensively non-optimal game went on.

Again, words drive your self-concept and your actions. We had customer support representatives and customer support managers, but the organizations themselves had different names: military *product* support, commercial *product* support. There's a world of difference between supporting the product and supporting the customer.

And what do you mean - give the engines away and make your profit in spare parts usage? Why did we always have fourth quarter fire sales in order to meet yearend profit commitments to Corporate? Didn't we know the customer would just wait until fourth quarter to buy spare parts, and our shop guys would stand around the first few months of the following year without enough to do? How much true profit were we walking away from year after year by conducting business this way?

What did it mean to partner with Snecma on the CFM family of engines when our strategic objectives and drivers and theirs differed so widely? Who had been smart enough to come up with the idea of *revenue* sharing rather than *profit* sharing, so that they could staff their organization far deeper than we staffed ours - to satisfy the need of the French government (Snecma's owner) to provide employment - while we could structure ours to let us turn in more profit?

And how did we learn to function in trustworthy ways with one another, when we were collaborators on the CFM and competitors in the military, and when they were from France and we were from Cincinnati? And how did they learn to work with us, when until now they had been content to conclude that Americans were merely defective Frenchmen, devoid of Descartian logic and incapable of understanding the importance of truly superior bread and potatoes?

* * * * * * * * * *

Something else happened that caused me to rethink my world view.

We worked in a matrix organizational structure. Each engine project had to get its work done through engineering, materials, manufacturing, and assembly. Each project manager vied with the others to ensure that his materials got procured, his production and assembly schedules met. In a scarcity situation, the power games were reaching destructive proportions.

A temporary organization was set up to coordinate these decisions among and between the Projects and the functional organizations. Everyone in the new organization was a high potential manager who'd succeeded thus far by getting his job done through direct control. Now no one reported to these guys. They had to get their jobs done through influence, coordination, and persuasion, and they were struggling. They asked for help.

I, too, had been rewarded for my ability to get my job done no matter what, or who, the obstacle. Like them, I was convinced my success had been based on overcoming obstacles, most of them of the human kind.

Sometimes the bases of your success turn out to be other than what you think. The research that underlay a training program developed by the Forum Corporation called *Influence*[16] helped me to help them. It also started to retool my own thinking.

In the late 1970s, the Forum Corporation had concluded that the next major obstacle to operational success was going to reside not in what you did within your *own* function, but in your ability to get work done *across* functions, and in the success of temporary work teams.

Members of these teams came from different areas in the organization. Each brought their own interests and needs; each represented the interests and needs of their own functions.

The people at Forum wondered if there was a pattern to what it was people did who were especially successful in these influence environments, environments where you needed to get work done with others over whom you didn't have direct control and where there were no already-established organizational structures for problem-solving and decision-making. They set their sights high. They were looking for people who were seen by their peers as highly effective, and seen by their managements as promotable. And they were looking for behaviors that differentiated the high performers from the average performers.

As their research progressed, they found the behaviors that differentiated high performers clustered in three areas – those things people did to set up an effective structure for working together, those things they did with others to gather the data and solve the problems, and those things they did to set up mechanisms to ensure the solutions actually got implemented.

They called the three areas *Building Influence, Using Influence,* and *Sustaining Influence.* They discovered that one core element differentiated people in each of these areas. Each core element was surrounded by a constellation of other behaviors that helped them achieve their objectives.

They kept your attention anchored by directly tying the program concepts to work that mattered to you. Prior to the program, you were asked to identify a major project you were working on. You then mapped your influence network, identifying the functions and individuals you had to work with in order to get that project done. For each functional area, who did you have to work with at your organizational level, who below you, who above you? They asked you to map the *frequency* of your interactions with each of those people, and the *quality* of your interactions. And from that set of people in your actual influence network, they asked you to identify six people most critical to the success of your project. These became the people you asked to provide anonymous data about you in relation to specific influence behaviors.

The people you identified each answered a set of questions about the extent to which you behaved in those ways. They answered a corollary set of questions about the extent to which those behaviors were critical to your getting your job done. Their answers went into a central computer at Forum headquarters and were compared to a database of people in roles like yours.

Your capabilities, and the importance of those capabilities to your success, were reported to you as percentile scores against folks in roles similar to yours. Those behaviors you were lousy at but that weren't critical to your success didn't matter much; nor did those you were good at, but that didn't matter. What did matter were those behaviors you excelled at that *were* critical to your success, because these constituted your true power base. Even more important, perhaps, were those you weren't so good at that were seen as critical to the success of what you were trying to do.

Now, here's the kicker: In relation to *Building Influence*, the core behavior was being willing to help others in the pursuit of their interests and needs. In relation to *Using Influence*, the core behavior was being willing to share your power in the interest of the overall organizational goal. In relation to *Sustaining Influence,* so that projects actually embedded and lasted, the core behavior was behaving in ways that caused others to trust you.

If the program hadn't been anchored in feedback from our own colleagues that directly linked these concepts to our success, my clients and I would have blown them off. What do you mean, being helpful to others in relation to their objectives? What do you mean, share power? Our job was to gain and exploit our own power, wasn't it? What do you mean, behave in such a way as to cause others to trust us?

Forum was kind enough to format the data so that my clients not only got individual feedback, they also got group feedback from the organizations they had to work with – projects, engineering, manufacturing, and assembly. My clients used the data to change how they worked with the individuals and the organizations. They also went back to each organization to report on what they'd concluded and what they intended to do differently. Effectiveness increased with communication and feedback.

Little tumblers started turning differently in my mind. Coming from the battlefront mentality I'd been surrounded by, where everyone else was a potential obstacle to your success, these thoughts blew me away. At that point, I had two choices. I could deny them. Or I could play with them. I chose the latter.

* * * * * * * * * *

In 1981, Jack Welch inherited the top job at GE Corporate. Shortly thereafter, Brian Rowe, our new Group Executive at Aircraft Engines, found himself required to provide ever more profit quarter after quarter to Corporate. Gerhard Neumann had managed to keep us a development business; now it was time to be a cash cow.

The raucously innocent, in-your-face enthusiastic, absurdly non-optimal, confrontational but can-do nature of the business started to change. Engineers ran it less, finance managers more. (Risk management wasn't yet a factor, but it was coming.) Meeting your measurements became paramount, and it was "your" measurements, not "our." Instead of humanistic management spreading, analytical, numbers-driven, bottom line measurements gained sway. If top management didn't produce their numbers, they were gone. They passed this obligation down the managerial chain.

At the same time that Jack Welch was encouraging people to "take a swing," internal dynamics made it far riskier to try something and fail. People already working very hard were being asked to do more and more with less and less.

As the pressure to produce intensified into the 1980s and the sense of unique community lessened, several highly visible, successful, admired, and relatively young managers self-destructed from overwork and overstress. It shook us to the core. Ned Hope died of a heart attack in his hotel room on a business trip. He disregarded the warning signs (indigestion, pain radiating down his arm) and the long-distance pleas of his wife to go to the emergency room because he had a dinner he had to go to and meetings to prepare for. Another fell over at his desk, dropped by a burst aneurysm in his brain. These gentlemen and others had clear advance warning signs, but the discipline of doing whatever it took and subordinating their own personal needs to the needs of the business kept them from heeding those signs.

And it was becoming less fun to come to work in the morning. Life was getting more administrative and less personal. Our internal organizational development efforts diminished as outside experts - the McKinsey's and such - were commissioned to conduct multi-million dollar audits producing cookie cutter reports and recommendations that no one identified with or owned. Internal ownership of a job posting design team or internally developed job swapping opportunities diminished and died as we hired external training companies to develop programs run by consultants and trainers who didn't know us, our product, or our industry. More and more, improvement initiatives imported from Corporate pushed aside local efforts.

The proud sense of community was evaporating in the exhortations to push product, push employees, squeeze out profit, and become more consistent with

Corporate. We were laying off successive waves of people, not because the work was going away, but in order to meet higher and higher profit commitments to Corporate. Layoffs always coincided with the Thanksgiving and Christmas holidays; you needed people off payroll before year end so you didn't owe them vacation time for the following year.

At roughly the same time that we were seeking to implement Deming's continuous improvement concepts, a falsified time card scandal at GE Aerospace in Philadelphia (surfaced by the company to the government and resulting in huge fines) led top corporate management to conclude they needed to appear more proactive in monitoring integrity. A few years later, collusion between a GE Aircraft Engines' field sales manager and an Israeli general for their individual and illegal gain, involving activities that dated back to the mid-80s, was surfaced by a whistle blower who never attempted to let upper management know what he was discovering. The ensuing debacle resulted in the destruction of the careers of nearly twenty of our best and brightest. They were fired or demoted not because they had been part of the conspiracy, but primarily because they had put their signatures on documents on the basis of trust. (You will recall those documents placed in front of you complete with tiny colored tabs that direct you to the signature lines and perhaps a hand written Post-It ™ note that reads, "This looks good to me. Please sign.")

To prove to the government that we were responding vigorously, the corporation set up "integrity hotlines." Anyone could accuse someone else of operating without integrity by making an anonymous accusation through the hotline. All tips had to be investigated, no matter how ludicrous, false, or self-serving. The people accused had no rights to know or confront their accusers.

The truth is, business runs on trustworthiness and trust. Trustworthiness in that the pattern of your actions over time causes people to conclude that you are worthy of their trust; trust in that once you have established your basic trustworthiness, people make themselves vulnerable to you by trusting the information you give them, the timeliness of that information, your interpretation of its factual and political significance, and the basic soundness of your judgment.[17]

No one appreciated the irony in the lack of integrity and basic democratic principles in the assumptions that underlay the integrity hotline. Integrity isn't about setting up Gestapo mechanisms to look responsive to your government; it's about operating in such a way that your outer actions are congruent with your inner values. If we were operating with integrity by setting up and managing integrity hotlines, I shudder to think what our inner values were.

So I learned another valuable truth, this one sadly. Culture change isn't linear and cumulative. It can move in one direction, picking up steam. Then new management can enter, the environment can change, and it can take a hard right turn.

I had also assumed that businesses get wiser over time. What I came to realize is that individuals open to self-critique and environmental feedback tend to get wiser. They also get older and fall off the edge of the organization into retirement or death with great regularity. And eager thirty-year-olds with more ambition and testosterone than sense too often take their place, and here we go again.

* * * * * * * * * *

Something else happened that profoundly affected my worldview. I was now in a new role as manager of marketplace education. I had headed up the design team for the negotiation workshop, now an organizational best seller, while still the HR manager for Materials. Don Lester created this new role for me. His very unsentimental instructions: Institutionalize the workshop so it can continue even if you get run over by a truck. And, by the way, design or find other marketplace programs with similar impact.

I tripped over a brilliant sales account strategy program developed by a man who lived in the Indian Hill suburb of Cincinnati. His name was Rich Hodapp; his company was called The MAPping Alliance. His Decision MAPping® process[18] contained a concept radical to us: Don't compete against the competition; satisfy the customer's needs better than any alternative reasonably available to them.

It was not so much a training program as a way of running the business. It held the promise of reconciling the partisan perception gap between our sales guys and their managers. Account teams worked together to identify the decision the customer was seeking to make that we were seeking to influence. Rich taught us to ask ourselves: How does the customer make decisions such as this? Who in the customer account is or will be involved as the decision evolves? What factors will drive their decision this time? Where do we stand in relation to those factors? Where do we need to be in order to get a favorable decision? Can we get from here to there within the available timeframe? What's enough to realize a favorable decision? What's unnecessary or unattainable?

Decision MAPping® contained even more radical thoughts. It required us to collaborate across organizational silos. The issue wasn't sales or contracts or customer support. The overarching concern was the management of an account over time in ways good for the customer that maximized your product mix, sales volume, and profitability consistent with your business plan and strategic objectives. Realizing the account opportunity over time wasn't the role of an individual; it was the joint and manageable role of an account *team*.

It was possible to MAP both the entire account and a specific account opportunity in a way that intuitive thinkers and analytical thinkers could communicate with each other. Management could review different accounts in relation to common patterns. MAP provided management a consistent framework for identifying opportunities, solving problems, and applying resources across multiple opportunities.

However, to MAP an opportunity honestly so that joint decisions about how to proceed could be made, you had to identify what you knew and what you didn't know, what you'd done and what you hadn't done. You had to make yourself vulnerable to a management that had long assumed you were genetically deficient if you didn't know everything about your job at every moment.

To admit that you didn't know the status of a decision or that you hadn't met all the participants in an account's decision process was grounds for public flaying. One such public flaying was sufficient to produce sales people wildly unenthusiastic about supporting such a process. A few key top managers, sworn to function as mentors and resources, displayed finely honed skills at public flaying. It just kind of slipped out of them.

And, in truth, many of our seasoned sales folks were individual contributors who circled the globe at will and liked operating independently. So long as management could see their elbows and knees moving, they had been free to do things pretty much their own way. Some would fail to notify our on-site tech reps when they would be in the area meeting with airline management. They had little interest in becoming part of an operation managed for the organizational good, or in people back at the factory or in other roles second-guessing their activities.

So Decision MAPping® flourished in the Asia Pacific sales department, whose director didn't care how strange something was if it helped them do their work better. He was able to create an atmosphere in which it was all right not to know something. It flourished in our aviation service department. Those guys were operations managers. They knew they didn't know much about sales and therefore didn't have ego issues to overcome. And it languished elsewhere, receiving polite lip service and little else.

But these ideas had taken hold in my mind. Don't beat the competition; satisfy the customer in ways that are good for you and them. Don't work just for today's sale; work the short-term and long-term simultaneously. Work together on account teams across functional lines in the interests of overarching strategic objectives. Make sure that what you do doesn't screw up your colleagues in what they need to do now or down the line. Tell the truth about what you know and what you don't know, then together identify how to find out and come up with a plan you all can buy into. Analyze and find the weaknesses in your *successes* as well as in your failures. Make fixes.

What strange, wonderful, and subversive ideas.

* * * * * * * * *

There come times at work when no matter how hard or smart you work, you can't do your job right. It happened to me when I was asked to be the acting manager for all of professional development in addition to my regular marketplace education job.

After a few months, my new manager informed me he wouldn't be refilling the professional development role. "You mean you want me to do two jobs?" I asked. "No," he said, "I mean that your one job now has two parts."

A few months later, when my life had narrowed down to working at work and working at home, and to that horrible continual pressure in the back of your head that comes from knowing you're not doing justice to either part, I went to him to ask for relief. He listened, and then, lacing the fingers of his hands behind his head, he leaned back in his big black swivel chair and said, "So you're telling me you're not up to the job."

There is no answer to that statement.

He went on, "You're telling me you don't know how to prioritize and delegate." There was no one to delegate to.

I reviewed my work scope with him and said, "Tell me the projects you consider less important and I'll stop them or slip them." He allowed as to how they all needed to proceed to completion to the timeframes we'd agreed on.

This phenomenon was taking place across the organization.

It reached crisis proportion in my own mind when we started to break our word and go back on clear commitments made in the marketplace.

Whatever else we had done at GE during my tenure - and we were tough-minded folks in a tough industry - we had prided ourselves on keeping our word, doing what we said we were going to do. Not just our contractual word, our handshake word. This is a more true definition of integrity, the kind of integrity that builds trust. And now we were walking away from it.

In the early 1980s, we had created a program called Supplier Excellence. We identified criteria that let us evaluate suppliers more impartially. Criteria included evaluation of the excellence and stability of their managerial team, the quality system they had in place, technical excellence, on-time deliveries, and reliability. To qualify as a top supplier under the Supplier Excellence program, even small companies had to invest hundreds of thousands of dollars a year to establish and maintain quality systems and to staff with monitoring personnel who would integrate with us.

We committed to them that if they made these investments, we'd understand if their prices were 1% or 2% higher than those of competitors who weren't Supplier Excellence qualified.

Just a few years later, with a different Sourcing manager eager for advancement, increased profit pressures, and new directives from the Corporate Procurement Czar, we returned to placing orders with the lowest bidder, whether or not they participated fully in the Supplier Excellence program. When suppliers complained, we shrugged our shoulders. Most didn't complain to us, since it was also a time when we were reducing our supplier base.

To their credit, more than one key Sourcing manager said, "If you make me go back on my word with my suppliers, I'm outta here." And they left. Those who remained went back on their word, or on the word of their predecessors. This is a very slippery slope. There is no such thing as situational integrity.

When you see clearly the potential for improvement that a business needs but isn't yet ready for; when you see what non-optimal things are being done in the pursuit of results that are making it infinitely harder to achieve those results; when the business is mortgaging its future and doesn't seem to care; when it is moving further and further away from your clear understanding of what needs to be, could be and nearly was; and when you can't get the attention of the people who can effect those kinds of changes, it gets harder and harder to go to work in the morning.

* * * * * * * * * *

Joe and I saw no end in sight to the trend direction of the management of the business. Our youngest child had just entered college. We opted for an adventure.

Joe had been traveling to India for years, selling jet engines to Indian Air Lines and Air India in his role as Director of Asia-Pacific Sales for the Commercial Engine business. He had spent several years seeking to convince GE Corporate and GE International of the business potential in India, which was being handled by a country manager located in Singapore.

As with many such efforts, the eventual response was the equivalent of "OK, mister, you're so smart...Go do it."

From 1986 to 1989, Joe served as GE's first National Executive to India, forging links from the Indian government and Indian private sector industries to all parts of GE on joint ventures, technology transfers, and direct and indirect sales. I lived with him in New Delhi.

I, too, worked for GE-International. I think they hired me to get him to say yes. I designed and ran training programs for GE people and people from their partner organizations in India, South Asia, and Europe – negotiation, communication, account strategy, people management. And I was Joe's eyes and ears, seeking to understand India and Indians so we could work with them in ways helpful to them and good for us.

I learned one simple lesson: All over the world, people get up in the morning, get their kids off to school, go to work, seek to make a living, need to feel special, need to be cared for and about, and thrive when they feel part of something larger than themselves that matters.

They also operate according to where they are on Maslow's Hierarchy of Needs.

I found myself managing a household of servants in a 4500 square-foot house set in a walled compound in the diplomatic enclave of New Delhi. We had a cook, a houseboy, an inside sweeper, an outside sweeper, a gardener, a part time laundryman (who washed our clothes and ironed them with a flat iron heated over coals in a brazier he set up in our backyard), a Sikh driver, and three round-the-clock chokidars from Nepal who sat and frequently slept soundly on folding metal chairs in their crisp khaki uniforms beside our wrought-iron gate, let cars in and out - saluting beautifully as they did so - and attempted to look like they were guarding the place.

Managing a household of servants was our social responsibility. Joe's monthly income was more than one hundred fold that of the average Indian. We had an obligation to provide jobs for servants, each of whom supported not just his immediate family but also his extended family back in his village.

Daily life was also such that it would have been impossible for us as foreign country nationals to manage without them. The cook spent all day seeking fresh produce, cleaning vegetables to protect us from massive bouts of dysentery or worse, and cooking for us and our guests.

So I needed to manage them. I knew how to manage. I held weekly staff meetings. Joe laughed. At staff meetings, I asked each servant to share what he was doing, what his opportunities and problems were, and what he needed the other staff members and me to know. Each time, for each person, the answer was the same: "Madam, I need more money."

Every day, the house filled with fine sifting dust. The winds found all the cracks in the foundation, around the windows, and under the doors. The marble floors needed to be washed twice a day; everything needed to be dusted daily. Our internal sweeper left things a mess. His definition of dirt and mine didn't overlap. He earned thirty-five rupees a week when the exchange rate was eight rupees to the dollar.

I struggled with the pay scale. It felt obscene. I learned to pay servants according to market-based pricing studies conducted by the American Embassy. It was dangerous to pay your servants above the average wage, in that when you left - as you would - and they needed to find another job, they'd refuse a job that paid less than what you had paid them. They would endanger their family's ability to survive before they would take a lower paying job.

I sought to use pride-in-work as motivation. The inside sweeper continued not to see dirt.

I talked to a friend who had a Ph.D. in Economics, had been a member of Indira Gandhi's kitchen cabinet, and had taught economics at the University of Southern California. He helped me see that the majority of Indians, including my sweeper, operated at Maslow's physiological, security and safety need levels. Most Americans in business, he said, operated at social, self-esteem, and self-actualization levels. Gestalt theory says that a need satisfied is not a motivator; a need unsatisfied is.

Most of the time it makes little sense to try to manage American business people at physiological, security and safety levels; they need the chance to do things that matter, to grow, to feel respected, to feel they have some control over their own destiny, to feel part of projects and missions larger than themselves.

It made no sense at all to seek to manage my servants at self-esteem and self-actualization levels.

I set a new course with my inside sweeper. I raised his pay by ten rupees a week. But I told him that every day I would review his work cleaning the house. For each spot left dirty, I would and did subtract half a rupee from his pay. It bothered me terribly.

He suddenly saw dirt. He broke even or made a little more money; my house was cleaner. But I had to inspect the house every day with him. I felt like a martinet, pouncing on dirt here, deducting half a rupee there. I didn't like being an authoritarian manager. But I learned that you also need to manage people according to their expectations of you.

And I learned that other cultures weren't sitting there eagerly waiting to be enlightened by Americans. India's culture traces back 2,500 years. Its worldview integrates philosophy, spirituality, religion, music, medicine, nutrition, and more. I discovered, in my arrogance, that they might actually have perspectives of value for us, life lessons for us.

India taught Joe and me much about the importance of family. We learned a great deal from their sense of respect, continuity, and commitment.

Elders weren't tucked away in nursing homes; they were cared for in the home. They were centers of attention and respect at family and business gatherings. They had meaning and honor in their later years. They were surrounded by the swirl of family life in a kaleidoscopic network of relationships.

Indian children (boy children, anyway) were expected to remain part of the household and the family after they were grown - none of our "Turn eighteen and you're out" mentality. You rear your children differently when you expect to be in a continuing relationship with them for the rest of your life.

India was not Cincinnati, Ohio, in funny clothes and accents, though for eighteen months I tried to pretend it was. There is in the world – as I'm sure you already know and I found out - tremendous diversity in culture and social system, and in the operant worldviews and values that underlie both. Some work better than others to make things happen in the world we now find ourselves in. Some keep their people from being able to function, or put incredible roadblocks in their way.

My friend from Indira Gandhi's Kitchen Cabinet gave me a piece of advice that grew in value over the years as I came to understand it. "You must understand," he said, "that many of us live simultaneously in the twentieth century and the fifteenth."

To be effective in India, we had to accept India on its own terms, and we had to understand how the world looked to the folks we were working with. I was not effective so long as I thought they were exotic versions of us, or so long as I was trying to "fix" them. We didn't have to agree with their worldview, but we had to see it, almost as if through their eyes.

I first bumped into this while still in Cincinnati. Joe had been brought into GEIOC (GE International Operations Company) as the new National Executive for India, a role that hadn't existed before. Reporting to him were two businesses that had existed for decades - very well thank you - without a National Executive. GE had been providing power generation equipment to India since the early 1900's. Photos exist from the early years of the 20th century of teams of elephants pulling power generators on skids over the Himalayas. Everyone in the local GE businesses was Indian, including some very capable presidents and vice presidents. One of them, Mr. A. K. Gupta, was vice president in charge of the Delhi office. He had worked for GE for over forty years.

The GE office in New Delhi occupied the sixth and seventh floors of the Archana business complex, a block office tower that rose above a shopping complex that housed an air-conditioned movie theater running "Bollywood" melodramas day and night. Joe was given an office on the seventh floor.

Temperatures in the summer hung for weeks around 120° F/49° C, with 80 to 90% humidity. When the electricity went out in the area, which it did with great frequency, the generator for Archana was reserved for the movie theater. Power was sometimes out for several days.

Joe arrived in India in his new role in early June 1986. I remained in Cincinnati until August. In mid-July, he returned to the States on business. While in Cincinnati, he received a telex from Mr. Gupta. At the time, telexes from India were transmitted via our New York office and took two days to arrive. The telex said, "Electricity out. Internal temperature in office surpasses 110° F/43° C. Request your permission to spend 1,600 rupees for metallic paint for windows to lower temperature in office."

It was another Twilight Zone moment. Joe wondered what kind of vice president had he inherited that the man couldn't make a decision to spend two hundred dollars? What were the next three years going to be like if this was the decision-making capability?

There had to be more to it than that. I started scrambling. I contacted the Indians we knew who worked in the Evendale plant. You need to understand, they said, that the business culture in India derives from the family culture and structure. In the family, the father takes all the decisions. Everyone else presents the issues to him, he decides, and it is their job to execute the decision. Should the father die, the eldest brother takes all the decisions. He may not be the wisest or the best for the role, but the role devolves to him. In this case, Joe had become the new eldest brother. Mr. Gupta had to pass the decision on to Joe, even if it took two days outbound, and another two or three days inbound.

Joe sent a return telex to Mr. Gupta that read "A.K., I entrust you to take this decision." Mr. Gupta happily took back responsibility for that decision and others.

And we had to care about being of help to them, as seen by them. If we did, they picked up on it and forgave us for lots of things we didn't even know we were messing up. When we didn't care about being of help to them, or when the people we brought in from the States presumed to dictate to the Indians what Americans had decided they needed, business had a funny way of never happening.

Those of you who have had an international living experience surely must share this insight. The more your host culture differs from yours, the easier the lesson is to learn because you can't function competently until you learn it.

India also taught me how very American I am. You don't have a clear sense of your own culture, values, or paradigms while you're immersed in them, surrounded by folks who have come to the same conclusions about what the world is and how it works. The models and assumptions that drive your behaviors are invisible to you.

When you have followed the White Rabbit into Wonderland, and all around you peons are painting the roses red, you have to find the conceptual vantage point that lets what you see make its own kind of sense. When this happens, you also come to see your own cultural assumptions as if from the outside.

* * * * * * * * * *

GE laid me off in India in 1988. It was nothing personal, my boss said. It was a head count thing. He immediately hired me back as an outside consultant at more than my prior salary. Now every program I designed and ran for them was for their use, my copyright. There were advantages.

What I learned was that of course it was personal - to me. It's always personal. I felt like my family had divorced me.

I looked around and took stock. We were eight thousand miles from home. We didn't know when we would be returning or where.

For years, back in Cincinnati, an index card had been taped to the wall over my typewriter. It read:

THE MATTFORD GROUP

Marketplace Strategies and Skills

If I had stayed with GE - more correctly, if GE had stayed with me - that would have remained just an index card on the wall. Now, eight thousand miles from home, God said, "Start your own business." So I did, with GE's concurrence.

I returned to America in 1989 in awe of and cherishing this very imperfect and far-from-complete experiment we had started over two hundred years earlier to create an evolving government of the people, by the people, and for the people. I had learned that in the world there were governments of the king and his family, by the king and his family, and for the king and his family. Governments of the dictator, by the dictator, and for the dictator.

I didn't appreciate this awesome experiment that is the United States until I left it for a while.

I also returned in despair at the cavalier way we in America seemed to be throwing it all away. We were walking away from the understanding that an informed citizenry has to be an educated citizenry, that the experiment requires each of us to be informed, to be involved and to vote. We had somehow forgotten that what makes America, or Canada, or Germany, or England (or whatever your country may be) capable of surviving and thriving is the educated, committed involvement of its citizens. It only works when citizens work not just for their individual self-interests but also for their enlightened self-interests, when they pursue those objectives that are not only good for me and mine but also good for you and yours.

I knew we needed to think of ourselves as *in this together* no matter what our differences. I knew we needed to be committed to doing our part to help the experiment work.

Lacking this sense of being a proud part of something bigger than ourselves which was worth creating and defending, and somehow having forgotten that we had carved this experiment out of something quite different *without any guarantees it would last*, we were descending in the late 1980s into a Balkanization of America and even further into a philosophy of "everyone for themselves."

This was around the time when Ivan Boesky[19] proclaimed that greed is healthy, and found few nay-sayers. The phrase remained even after he was indicted for securities fraud, to be repeated by Michael Douglas in the movie *Wall Street*. Greed is good, proclaimed his lizard-like character, Gordon Gekko. America was built on greed. What was intended to be an indictment of the character became instead a business truism. A new generation of eager managers was learning that greed is good, and it's all about money and getting mine. And if we disrupt or destroy countless others along the way, or undermine the foundations of our own businesses and industry, well, that's the way the game is played. It's nothing personal.

* * * * * * * * * *

So, in 1989, Joe and I returned not only to the United States with all its problems and potential, but also to aviation, our home. Joe rejoined GE Aircraft Engines to manage the Lynn, Massachusetts, Military Product Support organization through Desert Shield and the start of Desert Storm. He returned to an organization he had left eleven years earlier, to work with colleagues he had known for close to thirty years.

I returned, not as a GE employee, but on a short-term contract to redesign the workshop in negotiation. This was a point in time in which GE Aircraft Engines was clear that its future depended on alliances and partnerships in the marketplace, on life of the program contracts with its suppliers, and on what was being called "share to gain" with its employee groups. Hard positional negotiation – what I'd taught thousands of GE people since 1978 – was now operating in direct conflict with their own stated objectives.

I had discovered the work of the Harvard Negotiation Project[20] while in India. I had incorporated the concepts in the programs I ran for GE International. Now GE Aircraft Engines asked if I could redesign *their* program so that experienced negotiators could discover the disconnect between their behaviors and their objectives, could realize what lousy solutions they were getting and how much better solutions were available to them.

We piloted the new program early in 1990. I turned the design over to them. At the time GE was laying off huge numbers of people. They outsourced most of their training administration, turned the program over to a university to administer and chopped it up into a three-day design. But they also gave me copyrights.

I could now offer the workshop to the industry.

When we returned from India, Joe and I had agreed that he would support my early efforts to get things going with the Mattford Group. When it was up and running enough, he would join me.

You may remember the time leading up to Desert Storm. The need for military preparedness masked for a short time the extreme downturn in the military business following the fall of the Berlin Wall. As 1990 advanced, I noticed a gray pallor creep into Joe's skin that even a continuous tan didn't mask.

This was another time when no matter how hard or smart you worked, you couldn't make the world work right. The harder Joe worked, the more visible that gray pallor became to me.

After eighteen months in India, working fourteen to fifteen-hour days, seven days a week, my semi-pro baseball player, endless energy husband had come down with misdiagnosed and mistreated double pneumonia. For months, I had watched him hack and spit green mucus into a glass he kept by our bedside until we'd finally gotten him back to England and the States to an accurate diagnosis and treatment.

Now, safely back in Massachusetts, I was afraid again for his health.

In the fall of 1990, Joe came home to say they'd just completed a five-year plan for the military product support business. He was going to spend the next five years dismantling his organization and laying off people he loved. He didn't know if he had it in him. I shared his concern. I feared he'd kill himself seeking to hold together things that couldn't be held together.

I reminded him of our intentions – that he would work for GE until our little business was up and running, and then he'd join me.

The fledgling Mattford Group was caught in the same business downturn. This was not the best time to propose to strangers that they come to a weeklong, residential, relatively expensive, paradigm-shifting workshop in interest-based negotiation run by two people they'd never heard of. My marketing plan was the equivalent of selling Girl Scout cookies to relatives. I had been contacting GE Aircraft Engines alumni throughout the industry who knew us and the quality of our work, but even that was tough in this economy.

But perhaps he could join me anyway. "I need your help," I said. "I can design training programs, administer them, and run them, but I don't know beans about marketing or selling."

"That's easy," he said, "I love to sell."

GE was offering special early retirements at the time. We did the math. If he could get early retirement, and if our little business failed abysmally, one of us could go to work for McDonald's and we'd be fine. It was, as they say, a no-brainer. We said to each other, "Let's see if we can do it our way, and if we can make a difference."

* * * * * * * * * *

In January of 1991, Joe left GE and joined me. We flip a coin periodically to determine who will be president and who vice president. We have walking staff meetings two or three times a day in the meadows and woods of Lake Tahoe with our dogs. When we're not running workshops or meeting with clients, the sun wakes us up in the morning. Going to work in a snowstorm involves climbing a single flight of stairs.

We have run this business ever since, working with those in aviation who negotiate in the marketplace, cross-functionally in the organization, and between employee groups and management. We work with everyone from relatively entry-level buyers through to Senior VPs in very large organizations and Presidents of mid-sized organizations. We work with marketing, sales, customer support, finance, contracts, legal, supply chain, operations, maintenance and engineering, facilities, and distribution people. We have had the honor of working with a union president and her colleagues, and with top people in employee relations and human relations and their colleagues.

As we've run this workshop over the years, we've slowly realized the true potential and implications of what we have. I'd like to pretend I knew all this from the beginning, but I didn't. It's unfolded as we've gone along the path. As before, our clients have been the ones to point aspects out to us.

It started with a participant asking in session, "Why do you call this program *Negotiating Solutions?*" He went on to say that it was far more than that; it was about everything you do – with your colleagues, your employees, in the marketplace, with your family. You limit yourselves when you call it negotiating. People think it's going to be, "Sharpen your pencil" and "You've got to do better than that."

Fred Phillips, director of purchasing for Delta Airlines, first referred to *Negotiating Solutions* as "boot camp." When he did, I heard it as an insult. I don't think that was his intention. He proceeded to run the program for everyone in Delta Purchasing and networked out into the larger Delta organization.

When an international marketing manager for Bell Helicopter went home and told his wife that the workshop was as meaningful to him as boot camp and flight training, that didn't sound like an insult.

Later, a dear friend gave me a book called *Making the Corps.*[21] The author followed a platoon of Marine recruits through eleven weeks at Parris Island. That was how I learned about boot camp.

The purpose of boot camp, I learned, is to shock-strip away our old belief system, to discover how deeply engrained it is, to realize it's getting in the way of what we're trying to do, and to decide the benefits to each of us from changing are greater than the comfort of old behaviors that no longer serve us well. And then it's to build and practice a better model, based on values such as honor and integrity and "Don't let your wingman down." Folks are given the chance to practice the model sufficiently so that when they go out into a world that doesn't share those values or behaviors, they have a reasonable chance of staying the course.

More recently, one of our graduates, the president of a small aerospace company in Seattle (no, not *that* one), suggested a slogan for the program. She proposed: "Changing the world, 28 people at a time."

Another graduate, a very experienced arbitrator for American Airlines, described the differences he saw in himself:

> "I openly share my interests with my counterparts. Then I try to listen carefully for what they say or don't say their interests are. It has enabled me to open the lines of communication and establish trust with counterparts who are viewed as difficult and adversarial by my colleagues. It's so much more genuine, productive, trust-inducing, and

effective. Once you start practicing it,
it creeps into all of your human
interactions. This is a lifestyle change,
a better way of being in the world."

More and more people attend the program
with their real-life counterparts to solve real-life
problems.

This was leading-edge strange in 1995 when
Pratt & Whitney Turbine Airfoils sponsored several
sessions. It was revolutionary at the time to consider
inviting those you negotiate with to learn to negotiate
with you better. Mort Moriarty and his folks saw a
different potential.

Purchasing ran the sessions. To each one they
invited corporate partner suppliers. They also invited
business unit management personnel, from cell
leaders up to senior managers. And they invited
people in the greater Pratt & Whitney organization
they worked with, from functions such as
International Offset. Importantly, they invited end
user customers from Delta Technical Operations,
Southwest Maintenance and Engineering, and
Lufthansa.

The workshop has spread through word of
mouth from colleague to counterpart to constituent
for one simple reason: graduates get substantially
better results with less effort. But they also like
themselves more. They're more efficient. And they
operate with more integrity; their inner values and
outer actions are more consistent.

They come out of organizations that are another
ten years down the road of working to do more and
more with less and less. They go back into those same
organizations able to solve problems better. They see

the other guy not as their adversary, but as their counterpart. They are comfortable with the realization that they truly do need to work together not just now but over time. And they're more effective both inside their own organizations and in an industry that hasn't yet changed much.

But they also return seeing with different eyes. And their frustration is increasing. They now see what far better solutions are possible, lying there just waiting to be picked up, in cultures that still see the other guy as the opponent, cultures that believe "my role is to beat you," and that the only way to win is to be the last guy standing.

And, almost without exception, everyone I meet is still their own version of my Uncle Jay. They are decent and hard-working, creative and goal-oriented, adventuresome, enthusiastic, visionaries and realists. They are hard-headed and soft-hearted. They are doing their very best every day to be managers and leaders. To quote Warren Bennis, they are seeking both to do things right and to do the right things. And most of them, like us, love aviation and aerospace.

* * * * * * * * * *

Now, what do I hope you've concluded from all this? What experiences and conclusions from my life in aviation might intersect with or overlap with yours? And can these lessons from our recent history point toward a model for working together that does allow us to find better results in ways that let us keep our own integrity, humanity, and ethic?

First, I hope that parts of my story resonate with yours. I hope you sense that I operate from a belief in

the basic goodness of people in our organizations –
top management, middle management, those on the
line, those out on the shop floor, our folks at work
around the world - everyone.

Here is what I've confirmed thus far:

- The aviation industry evolved out of a military
  base. Much of our management style,
  marketplace orientation, and paraphernalia of
  culture still reflect an authoritarian, hierarchical,
  command-and-control worldview. This was
  especially true at the top. People at the top saw
  the world that way, responded that way, and
  succeeded. Their life lessons were that this is
  the way the world is.

- Those at the top project their personal
  worldviews onto the environment and call it
  reality. Their management style gets projected
  onto the organization. They define success; the
  organization falls into line. Those who don't
  fit go elsewhere.

- When we join an organization, no matter how
  much it differs from our prior world, its culture,
  paradigms, assumptions, and norms quickly
  become ours. Its horizons become our horizons;
  we come to accept that the world *is*, in fact, as
  our organization sees it.

- The humanistic management movement of the
  1970s explored alternative models for
  effectiveness. But it took place *within* the
  existing paradigm, and primarily within the
  organization, not out into the larger
  environment. It never reached the executive

offices. Though paradigm shifts start in the middle and at the edges, it takes true personal, visible buy-in and persistent commitment of resources by those at the top for lasting system-wide change to occur.

- Most of us want to be part of something that matters, something bigger than ourselves. Yet we also need to be unique and recognized as contributing and special. We keep our own individuality and our ability to think, reason, play, and feel. Even when we try not to, we bring our whole selves to work. It's always personal, and therein lies much of our strength in organizations.

- People respond to mentors and guides. We cherish managers who serve as good stewards of the business and responsible champions and challengers of their people. The more self-directed we are, the more we turn off at even petty vestiges of authoritarian management.

- Being brilliant and decisive doesn't make you a good leader. The issue is envisioning a direction and shaping an environment in which those involved help create solutions they all own and will support.

- Tremendous power and creativity are unleashed when people have the right to exercise control together over their own destiny. They are able, if asked, to balance their personal needs with their role needs and with the company's needs.

- "Natural resistance" may not be natural at all, but instead may be a logical result when people don't have a say in things that affect them.

- Most of us tend to make wise decisions when trusted with and given access to the information and perspective we need to make those decisions. When denied that information or perspective, our decisions are based on more narrow views.

- People in other functions or organizations are suspect until we get to know them and work with them. As we see how the world looks through their eyes, we understand more, and we can find better solutions for us all. (Occasionally, getting to know them lets us confirm they truly *are* idiots. This information is also helpful.)

- Our assumptions, which include our vocabulary and our metaphors, drive our behavior. We tend to treat "vendor" differently than "sources," and "hourly" and "non-exempt" folks different from "exempt." Bill Moyers says that when we get our vocabulary, our metaphors, right, we tend to do the right things.

- We frequently forget that real lives and families are terribly disrupted when we play child-ego-state-driven games. We are stewards of our businesses; they don't exist for our aggrandizement.

- People will kill themselves for the needs of the business. It is to the business's self-interest that they don't. Striking a balance between the needs of the business and people's personal needs is good for the business.

- The ostensible reason for measurements is to achieve results and encourage behaviors in a desired direction. Too often they don't accomplish either. Top-down demands, quarter after quarter, to meet bottom-line measurements greater than what are actually doable create miserably non-optimal and disastrous long-term side-effects.

- Beating the other guy is fun if you're the beater. We need to decide whether we want to beat the other guy or to get really good results now and over time. (Getting really good results has its own satisfactions.) We are conflicted about the honest answer.

- Don't beat the competition. Satisfy your customers, counterparts, and constituents in ways that are good for you and them.

- There is no such thing as situational integrity.

- And what we learned with Snecma: differing interests can dovetail. The more clear you are about each other's interests, the more you can construct solutions satisfactory to both.

- You deal with people differently when you expect to be in a continuing relationship with them. We live not as isolates, but in a system. Maybe they aren't the enemy...

- We respond according to where we are on Maslow's Hierarchy of Needs. In the West, manage us according to social, self-esteem and self-actualization needs. Let us stretch, but not beyond reason.

- Culture change is possible, but it isn't linear, cumulative, or inevitable. It takes a perceived need, a shared decision, persistence, and visible patterns of consistently trustworthy action at all levels.

- Businesses don't necessarily get wiser over time.

- We, for the most part, are decent, hard working, well-intended people. Sometimes our systems and cultures are aligned with our environment and objectives; sometimes they aren't. When they aren't, it's legitimate and important to search together for a better way.

- There are better ways. The question is whether we have the perceived need and courage to find them and embed them.

- If not us, who? If not now, when?

If your lessons learned in our industry overlap with mine, why are we now operating in violation of so many of them? How is it that we too often are working at cross-purposes with our own life lessons?

Chapter Three

THE END STAGES OF ONCE USEFUL MODELS

What has been going on in this industry has nothing to do with the basic decency, intelligence, or capability of its people. We are caught together in a system in crisis. This is incredibly important to understand.

But we're getting tired and burning out. And we're doing things, out of necessity or overwhelming pressure, that are at cross-purposes with our own sense of what's right to do. And we still need to solve problems, realize opportunities, shape solutions, and somehow keep work flowing. We still need to do more and more with less and less. There is no reason to think that this trend will stop. If anything, post September 11th, it has escalated.

And our old models aren't working anymore.

I want to be clear. The models worked surprisingly well for a long time.

Gerhard Neumann needed to "Beat Pratt" to maintain a military base while he guided GE Aircraft

Engines successfully away from a dependence on military contracts by carving out marketshare to position GE as a major player in the commercial business.

Bob Crandall ran an airline that had won out when the original bids were awarded for the first airmail routes. For decades, American enjoyed the protection that came from operating in a regulated environment. He inherited salary scales and cost structures shaped to that environment. He had to reform the company so it could compete domestically and internationally under deregulation, including against start-up low fare airlines that didn't share the cost structure of the majors.

Competitive anger worked. He thrived on being aviation's "bad boy." He took on employee groups with the same focus and intensity that he used on suppliers. The A and B salary scales he implemented to keep the airline competitive eventually led to employee resentment and distrust that were to fester through and beyond his tenure. As he departed the airline, he apologized for the state of employee relations, seeking to assume blame for prior sins so that those who followed could go forward without being pulled down for those transgressions. It didn't stand a chance of working. Don Carty would inherit the resultant fallout.[1]

Jack Welch needed to shake up a stodgy, complacent company that was degenerating into a conglomerate. He did. With his singular focus on financial results, he also undermined much that had made General Electric great, and set the business up for hard, hard times once he walked out the door. If his business model was judged only by stock price, it worked extraordinary well for two decades, in part driven by adulation and the "irrational enthusiasm" of the 1990s. Throughout the world, managers sought to copy his model. Warren Buffett of Berkshire Hathaway was quoted as saying, "All CEOs want to emulate him."[2] Dr. Thomas Middlehoff, Chairman of the Board of Bertelsmann AG, wrote that "Jack's vision and courage...and, of course, his success, make him the role model of entrepreneurs and managers worldwide."[3]

The issue is not whether these business models were right or wrong in some absolute sense. The issue, says Maslow, is the need to "use the objective requirements of the situation as the centering point or organizing point for leadership." What is the best model for our environment now, and "who is the best leader in this particular situation?"[4]

* * * * * * * * * *

So what happens to people in organizations as we approach the useful end of problem-solving models that once served us well?

Let's consider just those few elements I've mentioned: the imperative to produce 10+% profit, quarter after quarter, cascaded down as bogeys and measurements to each person in the system; the elimination of the psychological contract between company and employee; expanding managerial span of control while not removing the requirement for each manager to know everything that is going on; plus the need to eliminate the bottom ten percent of your employees while rewarding the top twenty percent.

Stage One: Measurements are ambitious. Given the incentive to be in the top twenty percent and the fear of being identified in the lower ten percent, folks try harder and work longer. The first years, this works fine. When you start such an effort, typically there is dead-wood in companies, or people who just aren't a fit for the environment and the challenge. Jack Welch is right: it's kinder to get them out of there sooner rather than later. So you get them out. Those identified as high performers receive major salary and incentive compensation increases. They feel recognized and rewarded. As the model continues into its fourth and fifth year and beyond, the elimination of the bottom ten percent gets more arbitrary; uncertainty builds in. Lots of people are making money, both in salaries and incentive compensation. The stock price is rising, so the promise of stock options is a major incentive. The business appears to be thriving. Home life suffers. Work becomes an obstacle course with big rewards to the winners. Some of your best and brightest are starting to wonder if this is all there is. Towards the end of this stage, measurements become meaner.

I was told of a negotiation between a sales account manager for Oracle and the senior vice president of an information systems company who was working with them on an agreement to provide computer systems technology for a major airline. It was the last day of the month. The senior vice president for the information systems company had authority from the airline to settle the negotiation within certain parameters. He came to a conceptual agreement with the sales account manager within those parameters. He made what he thought was a courtesy call to his airline customer to inform them of the terms of the agreement. The customer said, "That's not acceptable to us." The deal was off. Midnight came and went. The next morning, the sales account manager was fired because she hadn't met her target for the month. Nothing personal.[5]

Stage Two: Beyond a certain point, you can't work harder or longer. To meet our measurements, we start finding ways to beat them instead. Art Thom's creativity spreads throughout the organization; we human beings in organizations are resourceful to a fault.

Another easily available way is to squeeze benefit from someone else. We engage in "Sausage Casing School of Economics" behaviors. "Sausage Casing School of Economics" thinking assumes a finite and set amount of resource. To meet *my* needs, I squeeze the sausage casing somewhere else to plump it into my portion. To increase value for my customers, I squeeze my employee groups. To meet my measurements, I squeeze my suppliers or engage in Maximum Allowable Gouge or Clawback with my customers. Or I find ways to meet the letter of the measurement that violate the intention behind it. I'm no longer creating value; I'm just claiming more than my share.

> "If your suppliers like
> doing business with you,
> you're not doing your job."[6]

I can think of nothing that breaks down the relationship between all members of the system faster than this, with more discord and resultant wasted energy.

For some of us, this is the point at which we start struggling with depression. A clinical psychologist friend once told me that depression is anger turned inward. When you feel trapped in an abusive system, yet feel for your own success that you need to stay there, the frustration has to go somewhere. We turn it in on ourselves in backaches, headaches, weight gain, substance abuse, and depression.

A few years ago, GE's Corporate Procurement Czar instructed purchasing managers at the different GE businesses to outsource their purchases to Third World companies in order to reduce cost of input materials by 30% to 50%. This also helped with international offset on the sale of product to those countries. Pratt & Whitney at the time was playing "follow the leader" in many of its marketplace strategies. Its procurement managers were instructed to tell their suppliers that they needed to take 30% off their prices to P&W over the next several years.[7] This set up a backlash of resistance and resentment that the purchasing folks are still clearing up. At the time, PCC, a major metals company, appropriately said, "OK, you want 30%? Let's figure out how to take 60% off our cost of doing business with you – you take half and we'll keep half."

I have often wondered what would have happened if P&W had gone out to its suppliers, laid out the competitive pressures and the need to reduce cost of input materials, and said, "Let's put everything on the table, including stuff we're doing that's causing you to have to build in price or buffer. Let's figure out together how to make your input price to us more competitive in ways that are better for you, too." At a time when many of the suppliers were suffering volume losses because GE was pulling its business from them to move to those Third World sources, some very creative mutually beneficial solutions could have emerged. Working relationships could have been strengthened.

Immediately after September 11th, some major companies sent out notices to their suppliers that henceforth, invoices would be paid not in thirty days, but in ninety. Take it or leave it. I suspect they still expected their *own* customers to pay within thirty days. Reciprocity as a rule of fairness took a major hit.

These actions seem to work, but only if you're not planning to be in your current role very long. You get the quick-hit savings; the next guy deals with the disasters that follow. It's as beneficial as Art Thom's cost reductions. But it gets you through the next grading period. And for managers who are being measured quarter by quarter, their logic is, "In the long run there is no long run."

This is also the stage at which folks in the middle and on the edges are starting to shake their heads in dismay and think, "There's got to be a better way." They begin looking for and experimenting with alternative models in their own spheres of influence. It's not visible at the top.

Stage Three: Things are getting worse. You still have to meet your measurements. So you start dismantling your own infrastructure. You reduce R&D spending. You strip out legions of engineers working on advanced technologies or product improvements that won't come to fruition on your watch. I know of managers who have pulled out most of their leased copy machines in order to reduce costs. They've already dismantled their copy centers. Now professional employees have to walk half a building away and stand in long lines to use the copy machines.

Secretaries and other clerical personnel are being stripped away. I have no problem with eliminating the private secretary whose job was to sit at a desk in front of your private office, file her nails, watch the soaps on a little TV set on her console, and by her presence control access to you, thereby signaling your importance. But every strategic administrative assistant, secretary, or clerk who does a good job supporting the work of professionals makes each of those professional people twice as efficient.

And the definition of "bottom ten percent" is getting highly subjective. Instead of driving out fear we're driving *in* fear. I'm afraid to take a new job for fear of getting caught in the process of elimination because I'm not up to speed in my role. I'm afraid to have honest disagreements with my manager. I'm afraid to share information or perspective with you because it might put you above me on the list. I'm afraid to take that very swing I'm being asked to take for fear of failure. This is the point at which the answer to the rhetorical question, "An eight hour work day – what's that?" became "Sunday."

Stage Four: Everything is getting harder to make happen. You still have to meet your measurements. You start to cave on your own ethic; you cheat or you lie. The first time it bothers you a lot, but you rationalize your actions: You have to do it to protect yourself; you're being a good team player. After awhile, slippery slopes being what they are, it bothers us less. We find ourselves saying things like, "It's all about money," and, "Everybody does it," and, "We had to do it. They would have done it to us." We're chipping away at our own integrity.

One of our students, a young program administrator, summed up this stage. He had participated the day before in an exercise that looks like it's about product, sales volume, and price, but actually is about trust and trustworthiness in a mixed-motive environment. His team, in order to win, went back on a course of action he had negotiated with a representative from the other team. He had been empowered to act on his team's behalf. The two representatives had shaken hands to cement the agreement. He had returned to his own team and told them what he'd agreed to. And the other members of his team had said, "Nah, we're not gonna do that." He'd stayed with his team. They violated the agreement; the other team did what their rep had committed to do. In terms of relative numbers, his team won, though only because they'd made more than the other team. In terms of what was possible in both the short- and the long-term, both teams had lost, big time. That night, he did a lot of thinking. The next day, he told the workshop community what he'd learned: "Depending on how you define it," he concluded, "success really sucks."

Stage Five: The good news is that we're not there yet. Stage Five is despair, decay, and implosion. We're seeing it in other industries.

If we don't regroup, **Stage Six** is simple. Dinosaur time. We shutter our doors or end up much diminished as organizations, with our employees and probably ourselves having endured horrific personal pain, life disruption, and devastating economic loss. Others operating with paradigms more appropriate to current environments take over the industry.

Opting Out. Along the way and at each stage, the option remains for each of us to say, "There's got to be more than this," and to opt out.

This can be far more than the *Downshifting* that John Drake wrote about. This can be a very creative choice for the individual and for the economy as a whole. Thomas Petzinger, Jr., author of *Hard Landing*, wrote a remarkable book in 1999 that didn't get the attention it deserves. It is called *The New Pioneers: The Men and Women Who Are Transforming the Workplace and Marketplace.*[8]

He described how he "had spent nearly twenty years analyzing business for the *Wall Street Journal*." He had "covered some of the biggest takeovers, labor strikes, bankruptcies, and bust-ups in history." He had written the definitive study of the commercial aviation industry. He suddenly realized, he wrote, that "my career had been devoted almost entirely to the study of conflict. I had written about people and institutions locked in struggle not over the creation of wealth but over its control."[9] What he now set out to document were the kinds of folks he'd written about in his *Wall Street Journal* column "The Front Line." One way or another, these folks had gotten fed up with bureaucracies and had left, not to drop out, but to set up businesses to do it their way, to find out "whether capitalism can co-exist with humanism," and whether shared purposes and values can work better than "tightly drawn strategies."[10]

He documented the growing rise of an alternative paradigm for business. It is easier to start in small businesses. As they succeed, many of them will choose to grow. Some will choose to remain small because it suits their purposes better. It's not always necessary to pee highest on the post.

These experiments have been going on in large organizations, too, at least since the Sixties. They have thrived for a while, gotten sidetracked or accidentally been crushed by managements that didn't know what they had or how to manage them within our existing models and metrics.

Though he doesn't write specifically about aviation, the same phenomenon is happening throughout our industry.

David Harrelson and Chuck Esposito were in their mid-20s when they dropped out of American Airlines' Warranty Administration function in Tulsa's Purchasing organization to set up GIRO. They couldn't convince their management to finance the potential in developing Internet-based computer systems to track and process warranty administration claims. So they set out to do it themselves. Phil King, now President and CEO of GIRO, estimates that "only 30% of all warranty coverage is redeemed. Some 27% of claims are just never filed and another 12% are turned down due to lack of information...another 12% of claims are handled by unwanted material replacements."[11]

Between 1994 and 2003, GIRO redeemed over $100 million in warranty claims that would have gone unclaimed. GIRO became so effective at recovering multi-year-old warranty payments that GE rewrote its warranties so that there is now a life-limit on them, like those rebate checks that you have to cash within ninety days.

And what is their fee for their efforts leading up to processing a claim? Nothing. All they want is a percentage of the money they recover for the airline. At the core of their business, they believe in creating value. They believe in finding ways that are better for you and for them, too.

Adolfo Diaz and Virg Pizer got angry at how GE Engine Services handled the takeover of Greenwich Air Service in Miami in the mid-1990s. In keeping with the Neutron Jack tradition (vaporize the people, leave the buildings intact), a few months into the takeover more than 300 of the 600 former Greenwich people in Miami were fired. Management wanted to keep Adolfo and Virg, identified as high potentials. "Thanks, but no thanks," they said, "You've already identified the kind of culture you set up for people in your companies. We think we'd rather do it our way." They left without severance packages to set up Patriot Aviation.

In the years since, they have built their business by offering a customer-centered alternative to the aftermarket approaches of the OEMs. Virg says, "Our experience has been overwhelming. We set up to be very personal and hands-on through all phases of the business cycle. As little as we were, small and self-funded, we've built a reputation and client base that have already allowed us to set up a second facility located just off of Love Field in Dallas to be near our customers there." Their slogan: The Power of Choice.

Karen Borgnes Odegard had entered accounting after her dad suggested that wanting to be a professor or a musician was nice, but it would be helpful if she were employable. She worked for Arthur Young, then decided that she'd rather make history than audit it. She says she learned compassion the hard way, having first learned in a man's world to be a ball-buster. In 1993 she and her former boss bought Pacific AeroTech. She wanted to see if she could make a success of the business while balancing work with family. Initially working a four-days-a-week, thirty-hour, schedule, she has grown the tiny spin-off from Pacific Aviation Group from a four person, $600K/year business in 1993 to a nineteen person, $7 million/year business in 2003. There were times that meetings in her conference room meant the baby was there, too. Some staffers still avoid one end of the conference table – the end that doubled as a changing table. Because she's not always there, her managers have to take up the slack. They do. She and they take care when hiring new people to make sure their value systems mesh; it's what she thinks makes Tech unique. Flex time and "bring your daughter to work" occurs for them not as a once-yearly event, but as needed.

She e-mailed me recently to say, "You showed me that being an open-handed negotiator is a legitimate technique, rather than just a lack of guile on my part. I have participated in some amazing negotiations...just by telling the truth and asking my counterpart to work with me to craft a solution that meets both our needs." She went on to say, "When people believe you're sincere, it's amazing how easily things occur."

"We're straight," she says, "but we know what we want. I'm amazed at what we accomplish."

And Southwest long ago set a path that shows there can be a completely different business model. Maybe our job is to serve the customer.

Maybe the customer's alternatives aren't simply other airlines. Maybe their alternatives include driving the car, utilizing the Internet and increasingly sophisticated telecommunications, or doing nothing.

The good news relative to the Phil Kings and Karen Odegards and thousands of others like them in our industry is that these folks are playing with alternative models, and they're succeeding in the same marketplace the rest of us live in. The not-so-good news is that as more and more of these folks bail out of our larger organizations, they're stripping those organizations of the people and perspectives we most need to drive internal change.

So alternative experiments already exist; we're positioned for a paradigm shift. They have been tested in the very marketplace where the Americans, Uniteds, and others were once working to blow other airlines out of the sky. They're growing through hard times, both the little ones and the rather big ones. Other models – jetBlue, Ryan Air, and easyJet among them – are being tested.

Chapter Four

WE HAVE MET THE ENEMY
AND HE IS US

If we're going to have the long-term resolve to move toward system-wide change, it's important to recognize that we each have within ourselves great capacity for good and equal capacity for evil. Pogo taught us that "We have met the enemy and he is us."[1]

Some of you may remember a macabre set of psychology experiments conducted at Yale in the 1970s.[2] Students answered an ad in a college newspaper to work part-time at a laboratory. As each person reported to the laboratory to start work, he or she was met by a person in a white lab coat. This presumed scientist showed the student around the lab – very impressive, lots of dials and levers. The experiment, the student was told, had to do with the effects of electric shock on a subject. Each student was told the subject was in the adjoining room and that his or her job was to administer the electric shock under the guidance of the scientist. This was done by turning up the voltage with a dial and then pressing a button to administer the shock. The dial was marked with escalating levels of dosage - green, yellow, and red zones. The red zone was labeled "Lethal; do not exceed."

The student started out administering low levels. The scientist complimented the work and instructed the student to administer escalating levels. Soon cries of pain could be heard coming from the other room immediately following the administration of the electric shock. The scientist required the student to raise the dose. More than half of the students, even though they themselves showed considerable signs of stress and conflict, continued to administer dosage levels well into the "Lethal; do not exceed" zone.

For years after I read this, I considered it just a fascinating experiment. But I now think it's far more than that. I think it directly addresses the questions we ask ourselves with distressing regularity.

How can young Palestinian gunmen shoot up a Bat Mitzvah party in Israel? How can Serbian soldiers massacre old men, women, and infants in Bosnia? How can Protestants in Northern Ireland verbally and physically attack young Catholic schoolgirls who must walk through their neighborhoods to get to school? How can Sikh separatists crash a child's first birthday party in New Delhi, spraying machine-gun fire at the assembled guests? How can presumably idealistic young men from Saudi Arabia and other Middle Eastern countries hijack airplanes filled with normal people going about their normal business and fly them into the World Trade Center Towers and the Pentagon?

How can I kiss my husband or wife and children and go off to work to screw the customer or to administer a policy of Maximum Allowable Gouge? How can I do "a load of compromisin' on the road to my horizon" and then find the horizon doesn't materialize and all I've done is compromise myself?

Of course these choices and actions exist in degrees of kind, but I suspect their antecedents are the same. I also think that until we recognize that "we have met the enemy and he is us," the chance for success in finding a better way is very low.

We do these things because the culture we're part of supports them; those in positions of authority declare them within the rules of engagement and necessary to our success; because we have a frightening ability to segment human beings into "us" and "them"; and because we tend to let our need for inclusion in our communities or approval by our top management override our individual sense of decency and right-doing.

I also think we do it because it has crept up on us over time. Roger Fisher first introduced me to the concept of a slippery slope.[3]

You've probably heard the story about how to boil a frog. If you try to throw a live frog into a pot of boiling water, the frog isn't dumb; it leaps out. But if you put the same frog in a pot of tepid water and slowly turn up the heat, it will stay there until it cooks.

A slippery slope is similar. Bit by bit, we adjust to behaviors that, if we were hit with them all at once, we'd never abide by or participate in. I once read a book by Viktor Frankl about his experiences in a concentration camp.[4] "We become inured to horror," he said.

Now, the good news about that macabre experiment at Yale is this: Close to fifty percent of the students *didn't* stay stuck inside the rules of the game. They chose not to administer those lethal levels of shock.

> "The workshop of character is everyday life. The uneventful and commonplace hour is where the battle is lost or won."
>
> — Maltbie D. Babcock

We have within us the same capability.

When Don Lester was hedging his bets, he was authorizing the hiring into GE of people who, from the start, knew in the core of their beings that we are, in fact, all in this together. The hundreds of people who participated in designing an open job-posting system, even though they had been managed, measured, and rewarded in a basically hierarchical, command-and-control system, leapt at the chance to design and participate in a model that turned career growth responsibility back to them, one that gave them more responsibility, freedom, *and risk*. The creativity and sheer playfulness that was turned loose as fifty top technologists shared their knowledge and power with hundreds of their colleagues had always been there.

So though our behaviors have been deeply affected by the seas in which we've all been swimming, just as little boy embryos are washed in a testosterone bath, the capacity to make other choices not only exists in us, in many of us it is a hunger for "there's got to be a better way." We all know that what we're doing is nuts, and almost all of us yearn for a better way. And September 11th taught almost everyone that we have been living out of balance with our true priorities.

It is this hunger that is now a key basis for the hope for change.

Chapter Five

CURRENT CHANGE EFFORTS

O ur managements have also realized we are in trouble. They, too, have already been looking for how to get those significantly better results on a systems-wide basis. In most of our organizations, we've dramatically revised our strategic objectives. We've also set out to change organizational structure and relationship. In some cases, such as American, we have been clear that we need to change our culture. Delta has identified that it has to accomplish its strategic objectives in ways that are consistent with its values.

For some years we've been working to implement lean on our shop floors and in our business processes, supply chain management, Six Sigma, global alliances, and other major change initiatives. Delta called its early efforts High Performance Workplace. Pratt & Whitney calls it ACE – Achieving Competitive Excellence. Others are shifting to PBM - Process-Based Management.

Our managements aren't involving us in these things for the sake of novelty. They have concluded that we must make major changes in how we do business to survive and thrive in an environment that requires an ever more seamless flow of material along the value stream, and a reduction in the internecine warfare between management and labor.

These change efforts have several things in common: Our managements have crafted strategic mission and value statements consistent with the changed environment. We've developed cascading sets of mission statements and goals in support of theirs. To succeed, we need to partner effectively with others over whom we have no direct control, all of whom have values, perceptions, interests, and needs that differ from ours. These efforts require us to choose to work collaboratively together, even though our individual measurements and reward structures might be in direct conflict. They require that we operate with integrity, and that there be consistency between the strategic statements we make and the path that we walk.

And they have other things in common. Perhaps without exception, *none* of these efforts has truly been system-wide. Our walk for the most part *hasn't* matched our talk. And, if we're honest about it, we might have achieved and taken credit for admirable early results, or results in one area, but *they weren't transferring and they weren't embedding*. We don't know why. It has not been for lack of trying.

Management has been frustrated at the apparent lack of willingness of employees to step up to the opportunity, in spite of the massive resources that are being poured into the efforts. Employees have been equally frustrated at what they see as a disconnect between management's strategic vision, objectives, and value statements and management's own *behaviors*. Employees down through the ranks hear the words. They look for evidence of different actions and, though they might see random acts, they don't see consistent, persistently different *patterns* of actions. Like Charlie Brown, they are reluctant to kick the football again.

This failure of major systems change efforts to embed and spread is hard to own up to. It is made even harder by the fact that the early results have been very encouraging. Our industry magazines tend to celebrate the first waves of success. So do our internal communications and annual reports.

In 1996, John Kotter published a book called *Leading Change*.[1] I love it because it presents a pattern of the whole. It lets you hold what you're doing against that pattern so you can see not only what you *are* doing, but also what you *aren't*.

In the first sixteen pages of the book he documents the eight reasons why change efforts fail. It was like reading my life at GE – all the important and necessary efforts that started out, gained momentum and enthusiasm, got converts willing to take a step in faith and embrace the change, and then, for reasons no one quite understood, faltered, stumbled, and quietly submerged, never realizing full potential.

He then went on to identify the eight stages required for successful change and described how to implement them.[2] They included:

1. Establishing a sense of urgency
2. Creating a guiding coalition
3. Developing a vision and strategy
4. Communicating the change vision

5.   Empowering employees for broad-based action
6.   Generating short-term wins
7.   Consolidating gains and producing more change
8.   Anchoring new approaches in the culture

What struck me was how each stage rests on the other. You first have to establish and maintain a sense of urgency within the organization, and to create a guiding coalition made up of people with sufficient organizational clout and personal commitment *before* you communicate the change vision. You have to generate and advertise short-term wins to keep people's energy flowing.

Like Maslow's Hierarchy, the stages exist as a pyramid, each built on the base of the other. And, like Maslow's Hierarchy, as you advance from stage to stage, you iteratively cycle back through the lower stages, seeing them differently, making them better in the light of what has now happened.

Each of these stages, and the entire model, makes enormous sense to me *inside our existing paradigm for how we deal with one another.*

For the kinds of change efforts we must implement now, I think there is a *ninth* factor. Implementing or shifting to true lean initiatives – in operations or in services and business processes, true supply chain management, true process-based management, lasting and effective functional global alliances, can't be accomplished within our current paradigm for how we work together – our *behavioral* paradigm. I think I can demonstrate this to you.

As we go forward, we run a major risk of applying the behavioral paradigm of the past – models, assumptions, and behaviors – to the opportunities of the future. If so, as with all those other change initiatives that somehow faltered, stumbled, and submerged, we'll fail. To succeed, we have to change not just our intentions but how we actually work day-in, day-out, with one another inside the organization and out into the marketplace.

* * * * * * * * * *

To make sense of the next part, I need to share with you what I've learned about paradigms and paradigm shifts, and about how behaviors change and don't change.

Chapter Six

PARADIGMS, MASTER MODELS AND PARADIGM SHIFTS

Paradigm shift is one of those phrases like "empowerment," or "right-sizing," whose meaning has been diffused by repetition and sloppy application. I want to reclaim the meaning.

The term *paradigm shift* was first used by Thomas Kuhn in 1962 in a book called *The Structure of Scientific Revolutions.*[1] This is one of the toughest books I've ever read, and one of the most fascinating. Kuhn describes how, for scientific knowledge to be cumulative, scientists of a particular discipline have to agree on how they define the basic nature of reality. They have to school themselves to follow the same laws, models and rules for exploring it.

Kuhn describes scientific paradigms as *models derived from experience and experimentation* that allow for the practice of what he calls "normal science."

The focus of normal science is to solve problems. The accumulation of all this problem-solving is to figure out what reality is and how the world works. For this work to have value, it needs to be capable not just of being replicated but also of being built upon by others. If my work as a scientist is to be useful, my observations need to fit like jigsaw puzzle pieces into the development of larger patterns of understanding, to build on or illuminate what's gone before, and to be capable of being extended by those who come after.

Here is his basic logic:

Kuhn says that he takes paradigms "to be universally recognized scientific achievements that for a time provide model problems and solutions to a community of practitioners."[2]

Notice that, from the very beginning, he describes these universally recognized achievements as providing model problems and solutions *for a time*. Even in something as elemental as basic science, where a lay person's logic would suggest that the definition of reality ought to be constant and agreed upon, it is neither constant, agreed upon, nor permanent.

He describes pre-paradigm, paradigm, and post-paradigm periods in the development of a science. In the pre-paradigm period, a number of schools compete for which school of thought will assume supremacy. During the paradigm period, one model dominates. Under rare circumstances in the post-paradigm period, he says, "two paradigms can coexist peacefully."[3]

Kuhn documents how historians of science have come to understand that science never proceeds smoothly and cumulatively. As different schools of thought gain supremacy, there is a tendency to consider the worldview of prior schools as unscientific, e.g. "What was wrong with those folks that they thought the world was flat?" He says that "the more carefully historians study concepts that once held sway, concepts such as Aristotelian dynamics, phlogistic chemistry, or caloric thermodynamics, the more certain they feel that those once current views of nature were...neither less scientific nor more the product of human idiosyncrasy than those current today."[4]

I find this very comforting. Our current and prior models, no matter how insufficient they may be to the problems we now have to solve, were as thoughtful and accurate as we knew at the time to solve the problems we had to solve then.

He describes the early developmental stages of most sciences as having "been characterized by continual competition between a number of distinct views of nature, each partially derived from, and all roughly compatible with, the dictates of scientific observation and method."[5]

Kuhn further describes how every scientific group needs "some set of received beliefs."[6] Before it can do good work, the scientific community needs firm answers to such questions as: "What are the fundamental entities of which the universe is composed? How do these interact with each other and with the senses? What questions may legitimately be asked about such entities and what techniques employed in seeking solutions?"[7]

He says that "in the mature sciences, answers... to questions like these are firmly embedded in the educational initiation that prepares and licenses the student for professional practice. Because that education is both rigorous and rigid, these answers come to exert a deep hold on the scientific mind." In fact, he says, when scientists then conduct normal research, that research is "a strenuous and devoted attempt to force nature into the conceptual boxes supplied by professional education."[8]

He writes that "normal science, the activity in which most scientists inevitably spend almost all their time, is predicated on the assumption that the scientific community knows what the world is like." Normal science will often suppress "fundamental novelties because they are necessarily subversive to its basic commitments." However, "the very nature of normal research ensures that novelty shall not be suppressed for very long." If "a normal problem, one that ought to be solvable by known rules and procedures, resists the reiterated onslaught of the ablest members of the group within whose competence it falls," and when "the profession can no longer evade anomalies that subvert the existing tradition of scientific practice – then begin the extraordinary investigations that lead the profession at last to a new set of commitments, a new basis for the practice of science."[9]

These "extraordinary episodes in which that shift of professional commitments occur are the ones known...as scientific revolutions." "Each of them necessitates the community's rejection of one time-honored scientific theory in favor of another incompatible with it." And each affects "the scientific imagination in ways that we shall ultimately need to describe as a transformation of the world within which scientific work was done."[10]

This shifting is never a smooth transformation. Institutions, careers, reputations, and lives are built on each paradigm. For those who reigned supreme in the prior paradigm, seeing a different one take ascendancy also means that their stars are descending and their life's work will be discarded as a model for the future. The value of their prior work is likely to be devalued as well.

I think this is what is happening now.

* * * * * * * * * *

There are important parallels between the practice of normal science and the practice of normal business.

The focus of normal business is to solve problems, realize opportunities, and keep work flowing. The accumulation of all this problem-solving is to produce a product or service, provide employment, gain and keep customers, exchange value, create wealth, and keep the business alive and growing.

For our individual work to have value, it also needs to be cumulative and to fit together with other parts of the organization and out in our ecosystem, to build on what's gone before, to self-correct, and to prepare the organization to be effective and viable in the environment that is to come.

We, too, derive insight from the success stories of our industry hero-leaders. The model problems they've solved, and the business models they built to solve those problems, become the basis for our own models.

We, too, in our history, had competing worldviews jockeying for supremacy. We are not far removed from the time that Juan Tripp was island-hopping in the Pacific to identify places where flying boat bases could be built to allow for worldwide expansion of this dream of commercial aviation.

Thomas Petzinger, Jr., does a beautiful job in *Hard Landing*[11] in describing the battle of the titans of aviation, similar to the battle of the Big Four of the railroads. But there were alternative views of the marketplace – some that died, some that are succeeding: People Express among them, and Southwest.

My mind goes to Battles Royal over whether it's hub-and-spoke or point-to-point. Is it "competitive anger" and "labor *against* management" or is it "serve the customer" and "labor *with* management?" Do we best succeed by being flesh-eating raptors competing with each other in Jurassic Park or by being decent and resilient Hobbits with our roots in the Shire?

We, too, go through rigorous and rigid educational sequences that prepare and license *us* for professional practice. It can be in our MBA programs; it can be as we study to be professional engineers or A&P mechanics. We are also taught by the keepers of the keys that "this is the way the world is." The formal and informal educational indoctrination we receive about how to make the world work comes to exert a deep hold on *our* minds as well.

* * * * * * * * * *

Willis Harman, in a wonderful book called *An Incomplete Guide to the Future,*[12] took Kuhn's definition of a scientific or technical paradigm and applied it to the social sciences. A social paradigm, he said, "refers to basic ways of perceiving, thinking, valuing, and doing associated with a particular view of reality held by a community."

These basic ways of perceiving, thinking, valuing and doing form a Master Model that we use to shape how we approach, and seek to solve, our problems. It's like having a big Sectional map for life. You use the Sectional to get from Point A to Point B, but you have to remember it's a map; it's not the terrain. I'm not sure we ever really see the terrain.

Sometimes we find our map isn't adequate to describe the terrain. For example, quantum physicists have conducted experiments in which the only logical conclusion is that one particle can be in two places at the same time. Well, either you throw out the experiment, which has been replicated again and again, or you decide your current map for reality at the sub-molecular level isn't sufficient.

Some of us in aviation come from parts of the world where folks consult with psychics who foresee the future. Many of us in the West don't believe that anyone can see the future. But that's based on our problem-solving model for time, our paradigm, which says that time is linear and unfolding and the future hasn't happened yet.

The point is, our paradigms are models or maps. Sometimes they're useful; they help us navigate the terrain. Sometimes they aren't; we crash into mountains that our map says aren't there.

And sometimes the terrain changes. When that happens, it's important to change the map.

Chapter Seven

HOW MANAGERIAL MODELS EMBED AND PERSIST

To understand why managerial paradigms tend to persist beyond their useful lives, I had to trace back to how each of us as human beings set out to figure out how to make the world work. I then needed to relate that to how we moved into organizations as problem-solvers, managers, winners, leaders, and creators of organizational culture.

I'm addressing this segment especially to those of you who are in upper management. If you decide you need to take your organizations down this path, you will be pointing them toward a future that you will probably never fully enter, a future in which you'll never fully feel at home, and you'll need to build in special mechanisms to keep yourself from derailing the very efforts you initiate.

In *The Prophet*, Kahlil Gibran writes of parents and children.[1] He likens the role of parent to that of the bow, with our children being the living arrows.

He talks of the bow shooting the arrows into a future which we can't visit, not even in our dreams.

This is a similar situation.

Those of us who have risen to the top in our organizations have done so because our current paradigm for organizational problem-solving and decision-making worked wonderfully well for us. It is deeply embedded in all our instincts, and deeply related to who we are.

Paradigm shifts don't typically start in executive offices. The Swiss watch business leaders didn't even want to hear about electronic watches. They held onto belief in their design superiority and onto the assumption that people aspire to exquisite quality, and Swatch blew them away. It's unusual for people who earn millions of dollars a year to decide that the model on which they based their success will sabotage the future.

A couple of concepts from the Bible helped me start to comprehend how deeply committed we are to the paradigms that worked for us. One is the quote, "It is easier for a camel to go through the Eye of a Needle than for a rich man to enter into the Kingdom of Heaven." The Kingdom of Heaven is about paradigm shifts – really hard to do when the current mindset has served you personally so well.

I struggled with the story of Moses leading the Children of Egypt into the desert. They wandered around in the desert for many years. With the exception of a few advanced scouts, no one who left Egypt with Moses entered the Promised Land, though many died within sight of it, on the threshold. This had to be so. If they had entered, they would have established the same culture they had left, only this time they each would have been a Pharaoh or a member of the ruling class. It took the kids born in the desert to create a different model for how we live in society with one another.

The fact that you've read thus far puts you in a special class. But you need to know that if you approach the future with your old mindset, you'll mess it up. It takes a special vision to turn an organization toward a promised land that you yourself may never fully enter. But it will let your organization go forward.

So here is some background on why our paradigms for human interaction are as deeply embedded as they are, and why we need to build in mechanisms to offset our own instincts.

* * * * * * * * * *

One of the wonders of human beings is that inside each of us are several separate selves. Eric Berne, creator of the theory of *Transactional Analysis*, refers to these selves as ego states.[2] It's quite literally as if three distinct selves (and little encapsulated subsets of these selves) co-exist within your skin as parent, adult, and child ego states. At various times, each ego state is in command of the organism that is you. There are ideal situations in which each one should be in command, and there are less ideal situations.

You might think of the *adult* ego state as a dispassionate, data-processing, devoid-of-feeling, near-computer. Your adult ego state should be in the driver's seat when logical, analytical, unemotional, data-processing and probability-estimating need to take place.

We internalized the *parent* ego state in its entirety from our perceptions and experiences of our

135

own parents or caregivers when we were very young. The parent ego state should be in charge when the environment calls for parental activities – authoritarian, standard- and expectation-setting, as well as nurturing. Gerhard Neumann was in his authoritarian parent ego state up there on top of Building 45 with his binoculars in the early morning hours.

And the *child* ego state should be in command when the situation calls for play, creativity, feeling, being right here right now, in touch with the emotional richness of life. Those of you who took a course in Transactional Analysis may remember that the child ego state consists of the Natural Child in all its sweetness, enthusiasm, magical thinking and fears, and the Rebellious Child, which is a kind of permanent teenager at odds with authority figures, an "elf with attitude."

So, there is inside each of us our own small child. Sometimes our child ego state is let out to play; sometimes it just takes over. What's important to remember is this child is alive and present in each of us.

The actual child in real life, and the child ego state in all of us, not only is the natural province of play, creativity, and energy, it is also the starting point for scientific exploration. Transactional Analysis calls this part of our child ego state The Little Professor. This is where we start our own map making for how to survive and succeed in our world.

Those of you who have children of your own see this every day. Kids are, by nature, little scientists. Each one of them has to, as each of us had to, figure out how to make the entire world work. We started out from birth to do this.

Freud's Definition of Mental Health

When I was in graduate school, a colleague asked if I knew Freud's definition of mental health. I imagined some dense multi-syllabic statement.

"Five words," he said. "To work and to love."

William Glasser and Reality Therapy

Years later, I read a book called *Reality Therapy* by William Glasser,[3] whom I like because he's not only a psychiatrist, he is also a mechanical engineer. He says that each of us as a human being has to figure out for ourselves a patterned way to do two things: *to meet our needs and to gain and keep the approval of others.* It's identical to Freud's definition. This is our psychological, lifelong journey.

In our various environments, each of us has to first *find* and then *refine* patterned and habitual ways to do meaningful work that meets our needs, and each of us has to be in relationships of friendship, acceptance, inclusion, "attaboys," and love. The better the solutions we find, the healthier we are mentally. By so doing, we satisfy the needs that Maslow described. We exist in networks of work and relationship.

So each of us repeats in microcosm the experience of the human race, seeking our own answers to profound questions: Where am I? What is the nature of reality? What is this place I find myself in? To what extent is it friendly? To what extent is it hostile? Who am I? Who are you? What is the nature of our relationship? How do I meet my needs? How do we meet our needs? What's it all about?

We replicate the search of our ancestors for survival, health, and meaningful existence.

This is an enormous task. You took on this task when you were a little kid, and you figured out the basics. And those of you who have kids or grandkids probably sit and marvel at your little guys as they set out to figure out how to make the world work, just as you did.

We not only had to figure everything out for ourselves, we had to find ways to share that common knowledge with those around us, because from the beginning human beings have had to work together to make things happen. And we have to pass it on to those who come after, so the tribe, the organization, can survive beyond us.

We are hardwired to seek to do these things, so much so that our very balance, happiness, and sense of self-worth depend on it.

And all we had, as little kids starting out, were just three things: the natural tendencies we were born with, what we did, and what happened as a result of what we did (reactions of our parents, injunctions about the appropriateness of our behavior in the culture we're members of, and so forth). This last item might be thought of as environmental feedback.

What we do depends in part on the natural tendencies and capabilities we're born with. And we're born with different natural tendencies, probably more so than we used to think. Longitudinal studies of twins separated at birth, and now the human genome mapping studies, have produced some fascinating insights into the inborn differences – tendencies to shyness or boldness, tendencies to prefer the color red, even tendencies to marry women named Mary.

From the time we were born, we experimented. We did something to get what we wanted. And one of two things happened. It worked, or it didn't work. And another of two things happened. The people around us, on whom we depended for our very existence and our connectedness, either approved of it (and therefore of us) or disapproved.

If it worked, maybe Mom called Dad and said, "Come see what the baby just did!" You were a smart little kid; guess what you did? You did it again. And again. Your little mind was laying in observations, conclusions, and recommendations: "This works; they like it; they like me! This is how you make the world work! I think I'll do this again."

If it didn't work, you didn't do *that* again; you did something else. And if you ran into disapproval, you not only didn't do it again, you concluded that whoever did that was suspect because that obviously *wasn't* the way to make the world work. And if you ran into someone who did that regularly, you concluded that they were out of touch with reality. You didn't understand them, and you probably came to distrust them.

This experimentation got more complex. Some things worked, but your folks disapproved. There were times in your development when that *in itself* was enough reason to do it again, in part because you needed to differentiate yourself from them. Or because you needed the approval of your peers right then more than you needed the approval of your parents.

The truth is you needed not just the approval of your folks, but also of your classmates, peers, and teachers - of your larger environment. So over time you tended to reinforce those things that worked and were approved of, and you tended to shift away from those things that didn't work and were disapproved of.

Kurt Lewin, organizational theorist out of MIT, proposed this concept.[4]

$$B = f (P, e)$$

Behavior is a function of the person and the environment.

Stuart Atkins,[5] developer with Allan Katcher of a wonderfully versatile behavioral-styles instrument called LIFO, taught me that if you're by nature oriented toward action and quick decisions, and finding out how big you are by how much you can do and how much you can confront, all your life you've done those things and succeeded. You've looked at your successes and concluded, "This is how you make the world work."

If you're oriented towards thinking things through, gathering data, being slow to shift into action, and using your head, you'll tend to succeed at things that require those skills. Your worldview and your definition of how to make the world work will be derived from those experiences.

In these two instances, both of you were perfect little scientists, missing some of the pieces, each coming up with very different definitions of the world and how to succeed in it. So we all project ourselves and our experiences onto the world and call it reality.

Because the word "relativity" was not an important part of our mindsets when we were little, our conclusions were not that "this seems to be a good map for reality in this environment, in this culture, in this small town/big city, 20th century, 21st century, as a man, as a woman, with this set of inborn predispositions and capabilities."

We were concluding that this *is* the way the world works. Period. If I want to win at the game of life, this is how to play it. And because when we are young (and perhaps forever), we ourselves are the centerpoint of the universe; we each extrapolate from our egocentric vantage point that everyone *should* play the game of life this way.

Now as soon as the word "should" enters the equation, we have shifted from observation and analysis to *evaluation*. We have started to build a value set for what the nature of reality is and what people *should* do to make the world work.

As in all science where the experimenter is also an actor and therefore is influencing the event, the data and the analysis, sometimes the conclusions we draw are questionable.

As little kids and in our child ego states, though we're as perfect little scientists as we know how to be, we're missing a lot of data points. We fill in the gaps with magical thinking; we did then and we still do.

There was a time in my life when I was afraid of flying commercially. I didn't know the pilot. And I was entrusting my life to him or her, turning over control. But I needed to fly. My magical solution: I gripped the armrests of my seat and maintained constant vigilance throughout the flight. As long as I did this, I personally could hold the plane up in the sky.

A recent TV commercial captured for me the wonder of magical thinking. In it, a little boy and a little girl are sitting on porch steps in the predawn light. The little boy is sucking on a straw inserted into a small carton of orange juice. As he sucks, you can see the juice rise in the straw. Simultaneously the sun starts to rise in the sky. He stops sucking, the juice falls back from the straw, *and the sun slips back below the horizon.* The little girl's eyes grow wide. The little boy sucks on the straw again, the juice rises in the straw, and the sun rises in the sky.

We augment our developing models by what we learn in school, school being the institution set up to be the transmitter of culture and current paradigms for problem-solving. Most of us learned to fit our emerging worldviews sufficiently into our schools' boxes, and we took pride in being rewarded for learning and applying the "correct" models.

Because of magical thinking, each of us, no matter how grown up we are, is convinced that it is by doing some things and not doing other things that we personally cause the world to work. As long as we behave in these ways, the sun rises in the morning and sets in the evening. Because we behave in these ways, gravity works. When we don't or can't, the world quickly "goes to hell in a hand-basket." We *have* to behave in these ways everyday to keep the world working, to feel personally grounded and in balance.

Another element embeds these assumptions and behaviors even more. I'm told that every time you think and behave in a certain way, electrons flow in a particular pattern in your brain. When you think and behave in these habitual, patterned ways, electrons flow in that same pattern over and over again, building pathways of lowered electrical resistance in your brain.

I can picture this best when I imagine droplets of water falling on a hillside. Initially, they fall to the ground and drain off rather randomly. But then they find a pathway of slightly less resistance, and more of them flow that way. As this continues over time, rivulets appear. Then streamlets. Then a streambed. Then a river. Then a canyon.

So though we have thought in the past, and can still think, different thoughts, come to different conclusions, choose different actions, and build different habits, over time we have developed a model for how to make the world work through experimentation and observation. It is based on our own innate capabilities, reinforced by success, approval and magical thinking, doubly reinforced by a culture that has come to many of the same conclusions and rewards them, and now reinforced by brain structure.

How Corporate Cultures and Paradigms Embed

And then we went to work. Most of us had the luxury of going to work at places of our own choosing. Though we may not have ever recognized it, we probably each chose a place that felt right to us. I walked into a place filled with six thousand people like my Uncle Jay.

The best job in the world is one that requires for success and rewards those things we do as naturally as breathing. The best organization in the world is one that shares and reinforces our own worldview.

You already had your own personal style, formed through predisposition and experimentation in the environments you grew up in. Now you're in another environment. You still need to meet your needs and to gain and keep the approval of others. Now these others are your managers and the folks you need to collaborate with to get work done.

So you used your personal style in your particular business. If it worked, you thought it was because you were extraordinary. Though I take nothing away from your insight and hard work, it's probably as much a matter of the kind of natural selection that occurs in evolution. There happened to be a match between your preferred style of responding and what your environment required for success at that time.

Winston Churchill is a wonderful example of this phenomenon. He was the perfect leader for England during World War II. But who he was, what he did, and how he saw the world was not a fit before or after.

Most observers whose job it is to tell everyone else how to play the game in order to anchor success, transfer it, and make it cumulative in our business culture – business school professors, esteemed writers for business magazines, and the like – tend to look more at the person than at the person/environment mix, and the world suddenly *is* as Bob Crandall defines it, or Stephen Wolf or Frank Borman or Gerhard Neumann.

And so you're quoted or written up in articles in the *Harvard Business Review,* or *Purchasing* magazine, or *Air Transport World.* The Young

Presidents' Association highlights you as *the* person who knows how to make the world work.

So some of us rose toward the top through success - success being defined as, "Thus far, you seem to be winning." Based on our track record, press, and admiration, we each concluded, "I make the sun come up. I've figured the world out. I'm a winner."

As we grew, we needed to hire additional people to work with us to make our business succeed. Who are we going to hire? Out of that group of potential people who can do the job, we tend to hire people we trust. People we trust tend to have personal styles similar to ours. They have come to the same conclusion about how the world works; they speak the same stylistic language.[6,7]

Though people with other worldviews exist in every organization (and this is one of our saving graces), as we rose into major leadership roles, the top jobs in the organizations we influenced tended to skew toward our personal style. Other folks drifted elsewhere.

We then collectively took our paradigms, assumptions, and desired behaviors and used our paraphernalia of culture to embed these personal attributes into our organizations' cultures. Our hiring processes screened for them. Our evaluation processes favored them. Our pay criteria, policies, procedures, and measurements encouraged them.

And as successive waves of newer folks got hired into organizations that already fit their personal styles, they absorbed by osmosis the cultural imperatives. Given that they also were eager to win, guess how they learned to define and play the game? It never dawned on them that these imperatives were projections of their collective assumptions.

* * * * * * * * * *

This is how organizational paradigms embed. Southwest is as different from American as Herb Kelleher is from Bob Crandall. And those of us in leadership roles both at the top and scattered through the organization are immensely invested in our paradigms, our problem-solving models for how to make the world work. These paradigms are in every fiber of our beings. The behaviors that derive from them are what we have to do every day to feel balanced, in control, and right with the world.

This is also why paradigm shifts don't tend to start at the top of organizations. It is why, if you decide to move down this path and encourage this different way to make the world work, you will need mechanisms for reminding yourself and your staff that many of your instincts won't work - mechanisms for holding yourselves in check.

* * * * * * * * * *

The good news is that many of our top managers are deeply invested in having their businesses succeed. The best ones very much want to leave their business better than they found them, positioned for growth beyond their tenure.

They are experiencing clear signs that our current models aren't working. They know the environment has radically changed. They know the problems we're seeking to solve are eluding solution. They know we can't seem to get from where we are to where we need to be.

All these symptoms, according to Thomas Kuhn, Joel Barker and others, describe the events that occur in the final stage of an old paradigm that once served us well.

Chapter Eight

ASSESSING OUR CURRENT BEHAVIORS AND OBJECTIVES

If you review the implosion I've sought to sketch out, you'll see that I'm suggesting that a major aspect of our dilemma is a disconnect between our stated strategic objectives – the things we're clear we need to accomplish in order to be effective in this changed and changing environment - and the assumptions and behaviors we've been using to seek to achieve those objectives.

Let's align our objectives with our behaviors and ask ourselves two simple questions: Does this compute? Can we get from here to there doing this?

Here is a sampling of our objectives. They are culled from strategic objective and mission statements of airlines, engine companies, commercial airframers, general aviation airframers, and aftermarket service companies.

In Relation to Our Own Organizations:

We know we need to shift our cultures so as to engage the discretionary energy of all our employees, to create the best working cultures in the industry. One company described it as "engaging everyone's minds, hearts, and creative spirit." Another identified that they needed to attract, keep, and empower the best people, encouraging creativity, lifelong learning, growth and leadership. One identified the need to build a culture of autonomy and accountability, of having fun and taking responsibility. One wrote of building enterprise-wide professionalism across the function. Others wrote of building and maintaining operational excellence and a strong management team, of increasing productivity and cost competitiveness to achieve superior financial results, while strengthening our infrastructure and investing in the development of our people.

In Relation to Our Business Networks:

We know we need to work seamlessly along the value chain, to streamline operations and infrastructure both inside the organization and throughout our networks. One described the process as caring about and caring for customers, employees, partners, and shareholders – simultaneously. They were clear they were part of an interrelated system and the entire system had to be healthy. The logic was that as they built a high performance culture of accountability, strategic thinking and business acumen, as they acted with integrity and honesty in all their relationships, those shared goals, behaviors, and values would drive world-class results.

In Relation to Our Customers:

A major theme had to do with providing total customer satisfaction, addressing *their* needs and priorities, and being easy to do business with. One company described their objectives as creating "customer delight." One described their responsibility as providing global customer service that would *exceed* customer expectations.

In Relation to Our Suppliers:

Whether defined as supply management and procurement, supply chain management, purchasing, materials, materiel, or sourcing, these organizations identified how their work, interfacing between the outer world of sources and their own internal operations, could contribute to the company's short-term and long-term success. They knew they needed to enlist the suppliers to work with them to create and maintain a more seamless flow of material, to streamline operations and infrastructure, to contain and reduce the cost of materials over time, to be in long-term, mutually advantageous relationships. Many identified the need to link suppliers with customers in profitable alliances.

In Relation to a Changing Marketplace:

We are seeking to think less as organizational silos. The engine services businesses see the opportunity to use superior engine services to influence future engine sales. Maintenance and engineering organizations see the opportunity to take an internally focused resource and turn it into a profit center, to leverage their capabilities to improve profitability. Airframers are redefining their corporate charter from designing, manufacturing, and selling aircraft to providing the greater ease of one-stop shopping for the customer, or selling "capability" instead of hardware and services.

In Relation to Crafting a Common Corporate Entity:

Many, if not most, of us have been involved in absorbing multiple businesses. We're identifying the need to craft a common culture from multiple businesses, streamline operations, and build a common infrastructure with greater ability to communicate with each other. We're clear we need to take the benefits and strengths from each of our heritage companies and our diverse cultures.

In Relation to Operating in Ways That Are Congruent With Our Core Values:

More than one organization understood the importance of clarifying what it stood for, its corporate values, and for pursuing its goals in ways that were consistent with its values. The values had to do with speed, simplicity, honesty, integrity, being responsible and responsive.

* * * * * * * * *

When you look at the common themes in these strategic objective statements, the current environment in aviation seems to include these elements:

151

- the marketplace is more competitive;
- everything is interrelated;
- we need our people, customers, suppliers and partners;
- we need a seamless flow of material and decisions;
- we're in long-term relationships;
- we need strong cultures, values, organizations, infrastructure, and people;
- we need employees' discretionary energy and creativity;
- we need to do things differently;
- and we need to do more with less.

Now, it's possible that our stated strategic objectives are false, and our behaviors are actually rather well aligned with our true intentions.

Maybe we never intended to partner with our employee groups, or to form truly functional international alliances in the marketplace. Maybe we never intended to create "customer delight." Maybe our talk about suppliers being key corporate partners was just an elaborate ruse to soften them up so we could take advantage of them in negotiation. Maybe the management presentations about needing our people to be dedicated members of our team were myth and public relations.

The funny thing is, I don't think so. For the most part, I believe these strategic objectives do define our *intentions.*

* * * * * * * * * *

152

So here we are. The environment has changed and is changing dramatically. We are charting different courses to be effective in the emerging environment. We need far better solutions. So where will these better solutions come from?

In what is basically a mature business I am convinced they will come from managing the human side of change, the behavioral side of enterprise.

Years ago, I heard Tom Peters talk about productivity improvement. He was convinced, he said, that the opportunity existed not for 5% to 10% improvement, but for hundreds of percent.

When I first heard that, I was in the trenches at GE, working to slog out 2%, maybe 3%, productivity improvements, and I remember thinking, "Yeah, right." But what if he is right? What if there are 100%, 200% productivity improvements just lying there waiting for us to pick them up?

The longer I've worked in industry, the more convinced I am that he is right. I'll seek to make this case for you; it's at the crux of everything.

Content/Process Model

Rich Hodapp, the man who taught me to focus on satisfying the customer instead of competing against the competition, introduced me to this concept.[1] Rich suggested that a mature business can gauge its effectiveness in terms of two things – its *content* excellence and its *process* excellence.

Content is *what the business does.* It includes things like the excellence of your research, designs, products and services, your manufacturing, assembly, test and repair capabilities and facilities, information systems technology, yield management technologies, distribution systems, the know-how in the heads of your technical folks, marketing folks, capacity and pricing folks, and so forth.

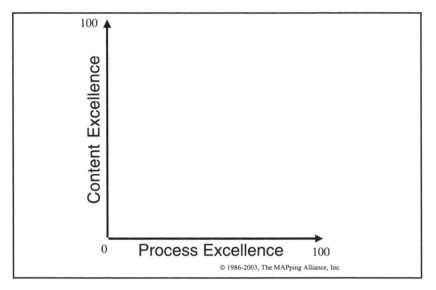

© 1986-2003, The MAPping Alliance, Inc.

I want you to think about your own organization and to rank it on a percentile basis on your *content* excellence, with 100 percentile being perfect. Imagine an "x" somewhere on the "content excellence" axis.

Then imagine, as fully as possible, what it would take - in terms of money, resources, people, time, and effort - to grow that another five percentile points.

Process excellence has to do with *how* you do what you do with one another – inside your own organization, with your employee groups, across organizational silos, as well as out into the marketplace with customers, suppliers, partners, and regulators. These would include people management skills, problem-solving skills, communication skills (sending and receiving, written and verbal, up and down and sideways), personal interaction skills, customer satisfaction skills, coordinating skills, account strategy skills, group decision-making skills...

If you blow away stuff like this, you call it soft skills. If you're slightly more open, you might call it *behavioral* skills.

Again, if you were to rank your own organization on a percentile basis on your *process* excellence, where would you put yourself on this scale? Imagine an "x" somewhere on that "process excellence" axis.

And what would it take in terms of resources to grow *that* five percentile points? Ten percentile points?

I have asked this question many times – to individuals, at conferences, to management associations, to top officers in aviation and aerospace companies of all sizes. Invariably, they tend to mark their content excellence between the 75th and the 90th percentile. (Engineers mark it highest.) When asked what it would take to grow that another five percentile points, the answer is always, "A lot!" And they're right. The closer you get to 100, the resources required for incremental improvement increase at an exponential rate.

When asked about the current state of their process excellence, almost every person asked put it much lower – from the 35th to the 50th percentile. When asked what it would take to grow their process excellence by five or even ten percentile points, the answer was almost always, "A lot less."

I agree with that, too. First, there is so much room for improvement. And, more importantly, it doesn't take huge investments in systems, technologies, bricks and mortar, or equipment.

Rich Hodapp says that, in mature businesses, these two together roughly define your business effectiveness and your marketshare.

In developing businesses – such as, until recently, the technology market – there is a period of time in which you can be boorishly interpersonally *incompetent* and get away with it, so long as you keep coming out with quantum-leap product improvements three to six months ahead of your competition. There comes a time, though, when content excellence - technological excellence - is not sufficient.

Now, we *have* to keep our content excellence high – it's our ticket to the ballgame. And we'll continue to pour resources into it, just to maintain parity. Yet this chart suggests that massive leaps in effectiveness are available to us by growing our process excellence.

I think this is at the base of what Tom Peters was saying. And, compared to the resources required to grow content excellence, we can get a lot of bang for the buck by doing so.

I'd like to suggest that the thread that ties all these process skills, these behavioral skills, together – management, communication, problem-solving, decision-making, agreement-shaping – is this game of life, is negotiation. Our student was right: It's not about "Sharpen your pencil" and "You've got to do better than that." It's about everything we do with one another, every day.

What's wonderful about our current situation is that should we decide to get serious about growing our process excellence, given where most of us are now, so much improvement is possible!

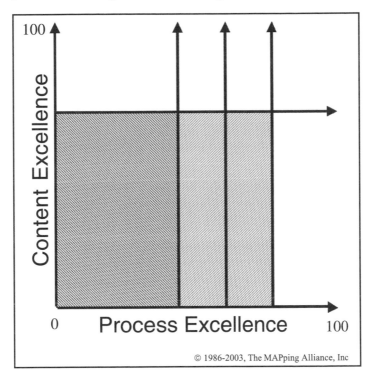

© 1986-2003, The MAPping Alliance, Inc

So let's talk some more about behaviors.

The First Premise: The purpose of our behaviors is to achieve our objectives in a particular environment.

To the extent that our behaviors are rational (and much of the time they're more rational than not) we do things to get what we want and need for ourselves and for the folks we represent - for our constituents. Hopefully, to get the very best solution possible within the time frame and other constraints we have to work with.

This gets complicated because as a species we get taught much of how to behave and what to do by the communities we find ourselves in. When we go to work in a particular business, we learn the operant ground rules of our culture by sitting next to folks who have been there longer than we have. They transmit to us the rules of the tribe. "Do this." "Don't do that." "That's the way we've always done it."

Rarely do the instructions come with environmental perspectives or explanations. We get the short version.

So a lot of what we do in organizations we learned from others, who learned from still others, about *how to be effective in an environment that presumably existed when the behaviors were first codified.* And at the time, they probably were the best thing folks could come up with for how to be effective in that particular environment.

But what happens when our environment changes? Are the behaviors still effective? Sometimes the environment changes so much that the behaviors that were the foundation of our success in our old world are now making it more difficult, or downright impossible, to achieve our objectives in the emerging one.

I think that now is such a time.

Let's add the second premise.

The Second Premise: Negotiation underlies the behaviors we use to achieve our objectives.

Negotiation is one of a series of problem-solving methodologies that human beings developed over the years when they didn't know how much their self-interests might overlap, and when they had varying degrees of interest in building and maintaining a long-term relationship with each other.

Negotiation involves those things that we do in order to solve problems, shape solutions, and reach agreements with others over whom we don't have direct control, in what is called a "mixed-motive environment."

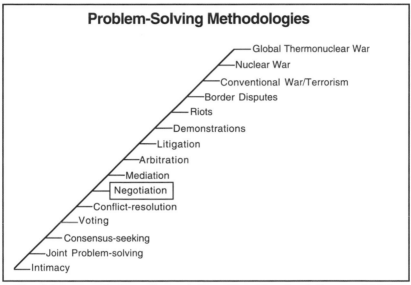

Problem-Solving Methodologies

- Global Thermonuclear War
- Nuclear War
- Conventional War/Terrorism
- Border Disputes
- Riots
- Demonstrations
- Litigation
- Arbitration
- Mediation
- Negotiation
- Conflict-resolution
- Voting
- Consensus-seeking
- Joint Problem-solving
- Intimacy

Used by permission. Copyright ©The Mattford Group, 1988.

A mixed-motive environment is a situation where some of our interests overlap with those of the other person (or we won't be negotiating very long), and some don't and may be in direct conflict with those of the other person.

So if we're too open too soon, or with the wrong folks at the wrong time, we can do great damage to ourselves and to our organizations. But if we don't find a way to share what actually matters to us and to our constituents, and to learn what matters to them and theirs, it's almost impossible to craft near-optimal agreements.

Under these circumstances, the behaviors we use for coming to agreement - that's negotiation. It can take place in the marketplace, cross-functionally, with your boss, subordinates, peers, employees, regulators, internal customers, suppliers, external customers, partners, husbands, wives, sixteen-year-old kids - no limits. The game of life.

If the purpose of our behaviors is to achieve our objectives in a particular environment, and if we've identified our objectives, then what are our current behaviors? What is our current model for negotiation?

* * * * * * * * * *

An amazing project, the Program on Negotiation, was put together in Cambridge, Massachusetts, in the early 1980s.[2] It involved a consortium of New England colleges and universities – Harvard, MIT, Simmons, Tufts, etc. This group, in collaboration with the Harvard Negotiation Project under the leadership of Roger Fisher, Williston Professor of Law at Harvard Law School, set up a massive study to answer some simple questions: "What is the best way for people to deal with their differences? How can you best come to agreement without giving in?"

The approach needed to be applicable to crafting agreements with family, colleagues, bosses, counterparts - up to and including nations.[3] They were looking for a practical method for negotiating doable, durable, near-optimal agreements. Doable, in that you could implement them, durable, in that they'd last, and near-optimal, in that people would support them because they felt their needs were being met.

As part of the study, they identified our current model for negotiation. Roger Fisher and his colleagues call our current model "Positional Negotiation." In one variant of this model – *Hard Positional Negotiation*[4] - the premise is that the pie is fixed, negotiation is about claiming value, and my job is to get more than you.

Here are the key elements they identified as to how the game is played:

- Participants are adversaries.
- The goal is winning.
- Demand concessions to continue the relationship.
- Be hard on the people and the problem.
- Distrust others.
- Dig in to our position.
- Make threats.
- Mislead as to our bottom line.
- Demand one-sided gains.
- Search for the single answer - the one we can accept.
- Insist on our position.
- Apply pressure.

If we operate in the marketplace, we're reasonably comfortable with negotiation being a game whose purpose is winning. Sometimes beating the competition, sometimes winning a battle of wits with suppliers or government regulators, and so forth.

When we operate internally, maybe we use other words. But no matter how subtle the language, each of us learned that our job is to get *our* job done, meet *our* measurements, get *our* head count, or get *our* employees (or children or spouses) to do what we want, and so forth. And since we honestly believe that our position is the right one, our job became getting others to fall in step with us, liking it (hopefully) or not. Gentler words, same underlying assumptions.

Sometimes we're not good at this hard positional game, or we're uncomfortable with it, or we want to establish better relationships and think we can do so by being "nice." So some of us play another version of the game, whose purpose is *agreement.* Roger Fisher and friends call it *Soft Positional Negotiation.*[5]

Here are the major behaviors they identified for this version:

- Behave as if we're friends.
- Make concessions to improve the friendship.
- Be soft on both the people and the problem.
- Trust others, believing that reciprocity will cause them to be trustworthy.
- Change position easily.
- Make offers.
- Disclose our bottom line.
- Accept one-sided losses.
- Seek the single answer - the one they'll accept.
- Readily yield to pressure.

Positional Negotiation

Soft Positional	Hard Positional
♦ Participants are friends.	♦ Participants are adversaries.
♦ The goal is agreement.	♦ The goal is winning.
♦ Make concessions to cultivate the relationship.	♦ Demand concessions to maintain the relationship.
♦ Be soft on the people & the problem.	♦ Be hard on the people & the problem.
♦ Trust others.	♦ Distrust others.
♦ Change your position easily.	♦ Dig in to your position.
♦ Make offers.	♦ Make threats.
♦ Disclose your bottom line.	♦ Mislead as to your bottom line.
♦ Accept one-sided losses.	♦ Demand one-sided gains.
♦ Search for a single answer - theirs.	♦ Search for a single answer - yours.
♦ Insist on agreement.	♦ Insist on your position.
♦ Yield to pressure.	♦ Apply pressure.

Adapted from Fisher and Ury's Getting to Yes, page 13.

You can see it's the flip side of the same game.

So that's the pattern Roger Fisher and his colleagues identified: *Positional Negotiation.* I take a position more extreme than I'm willing to settle for. You do the same. Then through a series of tactics and ploys, measures and countermeasures, we ratchet in toward the middle, finding out through a variety of means where there seems to be room for movement and what seems to be unyielding. It typically is time consuming. It frequently worsens the relationship.

We in aviation didn't invent it; it's been a pattern for how people have negotiated for thousands of years. But we're really good at it.

* * * * * * * * * *

Now, let's get back to the original premise. The purpose of our behaviors is to achieve our objectives in a particular environment, and negotiation is the medium for doing this. Some of us include an additional element: The purpose of our behaviors is to achieve our objectives in a particular environment *in ways that are consistent with our values.*

So let's add the objectives and see.

Here's where I need to ask for your involvement. I'd like you to jot down your organization's strategic objectives on the next chart. Ideally, these objectives would encompass elements having to do with your own organization and people, your business networks, your customers and suppliers, and the changing marketplace. If your organization has been absorbing other companies, they would address this as well.

My Organization's Strategic Objectives

Behaviors	Objectives
◆ Participants are adversaries.	◆ _____
◆ The goal is winning.	◆ _____
◆ Demand concessions to maintain	◆ _____
the relationship.	◆ _____
◆ Be hard on the people & the problem.	◆ _____
◆ Distrust others.	◆ _____
◆ Dig in to your position.	◆ _____
◆ Make threats.	◆ _____
◆ Mislead as to your bottom line.	◆ _____
◆ Demand one-sided gains.	◆ _____
◆ Search for a single answer - yours.	◆ _____
◆ Insist on your position.	◆ _____
◆ Apply pressure.	◆ _____

Now, take a look at what you're seeking to do. Then ask yourself the operational questions:

1) Does this compute?
2) Can we get from here to there using these behaviors?

On the following pages I've charted some of our organizations' strategic objectives side-by-side with our current behaviors.

In relation to our own organization:

Does this compute?

Behaviors	Objectives
♦ Participants are adversaries.	♦ Attract, keep, and empower the best people, encouraging creativity, lifelong learning, growth and leadership.
♦ The goal is winning.	
♦ Demand concessions to maintain the relationship.	
♦ Be hard on the people & the problem.	♦ Engage the discretionary energy of all our employees, creating the best working culture in the industry.
♦ Distrust others.	
♦ Dig in to your position.	
♦ Make threats.	♦ Engage everyone's minds, hearts, and creative spirit.
♦ Mislead as to your bottom line.	
♦ Demand one-sided gains.	
♦ Search for a single answer - yours.	
♦ Insist on *your* position.	
♦ Apply pressure.	

In relation to our business networks:

Does this compute?

Behaviors	Objectives
♦ Participants are adversaries.	♦ Work more seamlessly together along the value chain, streamlining operations and infrastructure both inside the organization and out to our networks.
♦ The goal is winning.	
♦ Demand concessions to maintain the relationship.	
♦ Be hard on the people & the problem.	♦ Care about and care for customers, employees, partners, and shareholders.
♦ Distrust others.	
♦ Dig in to your position.	♦ Build a high performance culture of accountability, strategic thinking, and business acumen, acting with integrity and honesty in all our relationships.
♦ Make threats.	
♦ Mislead as to your bottom line.	
♦ Demand one-sided gains.	
♦ Search for a single answer - yours.	
♦ Insist on *your* position.	
♦ Apply pressure.	

In relation to our customers:

Does this compute?

Behaviors	**Objectives**
◆ Participants are adversaries.	◆ Provide total customer satisfaction, addressing their needs and priorities, and being easy to do business with.
◆ The goal is winning.	
◆ Demand concessions to maintain the relationship.	
◆ Be hard on the people & the problem.	◆ Create customer delight.
◆ Distrust others.	◆ Provide global customer service that will exceed customer expectations.
◆ Dig in to your position.	
◆ Make threats.	
◆ Mislead as to your bottom line.	
◆ Demand one-sided gains.	
◆ Search for a single answer - yours.	
◆ Insist on *your* position.	
◆ Apply pressure.	

In relation to our suppliers:

Does this compute?

Behaviors	**Objectives**
◆ Participants are adversaries.	◆ Enlist our suppliers to work with us to create and maintain a more seamless flow of material.
◆ The goal is winning.	
◆ Demand concessions to maintain the relationship.	
◆ Be hard on the people & the problem.	◆ Streamline operations and infrastructure to contain the cost of materials over time.
◆ Distrust others.	
◆ Dig in to your position.	
◆ Make threats.	◆ Establish and maintain long term, mutually advantageous relationships.
◆ Mislead as to your bottom line.	
◆ Demand one-sided gains.	◆ Link suppliers with customers in profitable alliances.
◆ Search for a single answer - yours.	
◆ Insist on *your* position.	
◆ Apply pressure.	

In relation to a changing marketplace:

Does this compute?

Behaviors	Objectives
◆ Participants are adversaries.	◆ Use excellence in our services business to influence future engine sales.
◆ The goal is winning.	
◆ Demand concessions to maintain the relationship.	
◆ Be hard on the people & the problem.	◆ Leverage our internal services and capabilities to improve profitability for the company.
◆ Distrust others.	
◆ Dig in to your position.	◆ Provide the greater ease of one-stop shopping for the customer.
◆ Make threats.	
◆ Mislead as to your bottom line.	
◆ Demand one-sided gains.	
◆ Search for a single answer - yours.	
◆ Insist on *your* position.	
◆ Apply pressure.	

In relation to crafting a common corporate entity:

Does this compute?

Behaviors	Objectives
◆ Participants are adversaries.	◆ Craft a common culture from multiple businesses.
◆ The goal is winning.	
◆ Demand concessions to maintain the relationship.	◆ Recognize and incorporate the benefits and strengths from each of our heritage companies.
◆ Be hard on the people & the problem.	
◆ Distrust others.	
◆ Dig in to your position.	◆ Build a common infrastructure with the ability to communicate with each other.
◆ Make threats.	
◆ Mislead as to your bottom line.	◆ Streamline operations so we can work in concert with each other.
◆ Demand one-sided gains.	
◆ Search for a single answer - yours.	
◆ Insist on *your* position.	
◆ Apply pressure.	

In relation to our current environment:

Does this compute?

Behaviors	Environment
◆ Participants are adversaries.	◆ Marketplace more competitive.
◆ The goal is winning.	◆ Everything is interconnected.
◆ Demand concessions to maintain the relationship.	◆ Need our customers.
	◆ Need our suppliers and partners.
◆ Be hard on the people & the problem.	◆ Need seamless flow of material.
◆ Distrust others.	◆ In long-term relationships.
◆ Dig in to your position.	◆ Need employees' discretionary energy and creativity.
◆ Make threats.	
◆ Mislead as to your bottom line.	◆ Need to do more with less.
◆ Demand one-sided gains.	
◆ Search for a single answer - yours.	
◆ Insist on *your* position.	
◆ Apply pressure.	

When we ask, "Can we achieve these objectives using these behaviors?" I think the honest answer is, "For a while longer." Managers and employees regularly do incredibly difficult things. But the rest of the answer is, "With exponentially increasing difficulty." It's like trying to run a four-minute mile while folks are throwing airplane tires and engine cores in your path. Or trying to get from San Francisco to Seattle by way of Cape Horn.

Even now, we can't do it in ways that are consistent with our corporate values, unless those values are along the line of "slash and burn."

Now, we're not dumb. We've known we need to change how we work with one another. The problem is, we've been trying to change behaviors through strategic visions, edicts, and sheer effort.

For example, a few years back, as part of its culture change efforts, American Airlines brought in very able consultants to report on their assessment of American's management style. The consultants reported that their management style was too *red*, that it needed to be more *green*.[6]

Red as a management style is authoritarian, hierarchical, "my way or the highway." Green is more democratic, inclusive, interactive, and organic.

I agree. Given what American was working hard to do inside its own organization, with alliance partners, and in the marketplace, they did need to be more green in their management style.

Then the request went out. Managers were to be more green. They were to walk the shops more, listen to people, ask about their children, ask how people were doing. These are all behaviors that green managers regularly employ.

So they did. Many of them also concluded that they'd been told to bend over backward and be "nice" to people, so they shifted from hard positional negotiation to soft positional negotiation, even if they didn't identify it as such. They knew it wouldn't work, and they'd get frustrated and slip up, but they tried hard, shaking their heads all the while.

For months afterwards, when the maintenance and engineering managers walked into the Tulsa shops each morning, their people would look up, tilt their heads, smile somewhat crooked smiles, and ask, "Hey, Joe, you green yet? Hey, Gilly, you green yet?"

This is one of my all-time favorite wall charts:

SINCERITY

IS THE MOST IMPORTANT THING...

ONCE YOU CAN FAKE THAT,

YOU'VE GOT IT MADE.[7]

When we think about it for more than a nanosecond, we all know you can't *be* more green by *acting* more green. You act more green because you *are* more green.

For American's managers to be more green, you'll have to fire over half of them and hire naturally green folks, buying into Southwest's mantra of "Hire for attitude; train for skills."[8]

Or, and this is more likely, a critical mass of American's managers and management will have to be involved in a mind-changing, life-changing experience that causes them to see the world differently and to act differently.

Upper management will also need to go through this mind-changing, life-changing experience so that they, too, choose to change and stay the course. Then they will need to change much of the paraphernalia that holds their cultural paradigm in place so that people can be more green and have it constitute individual as well as organizational success.

We have worked with enough of them to know that they, too, know the system is broken and want very much to change it. And that they, too, have a wondrous capacity to see the world anew and to work out of that new perspective. The desire to change is there; the ability to change is there.

And then several thousand more folks will need the opportunity to go through similar experiences so they, too, *choose* to change. The good news is that it doesn't take open-heart surgery. It does take about a week.

Chapter Nine

CHANGING BEHAVIORS

Historically, when we've decided we need to change our behavior, we've done two things.

First, we have *intended* to change and *tried* to change.

In dealing with my teenage daughter, I realized the contests of will weren't working, the ones that escalated into screaming matches culminating in brilliant pronouncements like, "As long as you live under my roof, you'll abide by my rules!" I made a decision to change: "I'll never yell at Mindy again." It was well-intended. It didn't work. It couldn't work.

And then we've sent people to behavioral training, sometimes thousands of people. American once sent thousands of people to a wonderful three-day workshop called *Commitment to Leadership*. Your organizations may well have had their equivalent experiences. Everyone found the program valuable. Not much changed. Since training and development has been my profession for many years, I've struggled with this. I knew we needed to change our behaviors to do what we wanted to do. I knew that most managers were reluctant to send their people to what they saw as a waste of time. There seemed to be a missing piece.

I recently came across a quote attributed to Einstein that helped me understand this better. He says that *you can't solve the problem at the level of the problem.*

In relation to this situation, you can't change behaviors by seeking to change behaviors. That's not where our behaviors come from.

Our behaviors flow out of largely unexamined assumptions, which flow out of our paradigms for how to make the world work. These paradigms are deeply embedded. They're now keeping us stuck in old assumptions and behaviors that are working at cross-purposes with our own objectives. To be effective now, we have to get beneath the visible behaviors to the invisible models and assumptions that drive them.

On the next page is a model for behavior change a colleague introduced me to years ago.

This change model starts with our paradigm for how to make the world work. It says that our master model drives our *assumptions,* which include our vocabulary and our metaphors - the images we use to define reality. I believe this is what Bill Moyers means when he says that when we get our metaphors right, we tend to do the right things.

Our assumptions drive our *behavior.* Our behavior tends to (not always, but tends to) elicit *reciprocal behaviors.* And these behaviors have certain *consequences.*

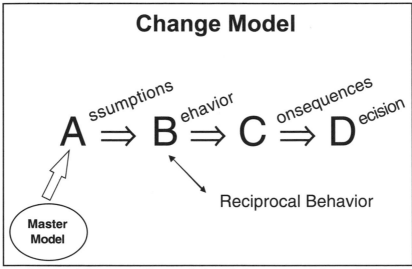

Adapted from a colleague's hand-drawn model, ca. 1978.

The model says that if we don't like the consequences, if they don't serve us well, we can make a *decision* to change.

Usually, when we decide to change, we try to change our *behavior.* It doesn't work. You can't change your behavior by trying to change your behavior. You have to go all the way back and change your master model, which drives different assumptions, results in different behavior, tends to elicit different reciprocal behaviors, and results in different consequences.

The hopeful part is that when you do change what Willis Harman calls your "basic ways of perceiving, thinking, valuing, and doing," your assumptions change and your behaviors change, and you can do things with relative ease and simplicity that felt like pulling teeth before.

* * * * * * * * * *

To give you an example of the difference a simple mind change can make, I want to take you through this model twice in relation to negotiation. All I'll change is a couple of words.

Suppose, based on your current paradigm, the words you use to describe the other guy in a negotiation are "my opponent," or "my adversary."

If you're sitting down to negotiate against your *opponent* or your *adversary*, what *assumptions* are you likely to make about your *purpose* in the negotiation?

A. To solve problems, shape agreements, get things done
B. To not lose the negotiation, to defend and protect myself
C. To win the negotiation, to beat them

Form follows function. If your purpose is to win - to beat them - what might your *behavior* be like?

A. Open, trustworthy, collaborative
B. Defensive, suspicious, distrustful
C. Adversarial, aggressive, abusive

Note that your behavior clarifies your actual objectives. If your behavior is defensive, distrustful, covert, and protective, your primary objective is probably to avoid losing.

So if you behave adversarially, abusively, and aggressively, what *behaviors* are you likely to elicit from them?

A. Open, trustworthy, collaborative
B. Defensive, suspicious, distrustful
C. Adversarial, aggressive, abusive

Sure, you tend to get either the same behaviors or their reciprocal.

And what might the *consequences* be? More precisely, what's the likelihood that you and your opponents are going to come up with creative, near-optimal solutions and look forward to working together again?

Somewhere approaching zero? You got it.

Let's take that quiz again. But this time, the words we use aren't "my opponent" or "my adversary." This time, let's describe the other guy as "my counterpart." Kind of like me, works too hard, doesn't get home enough. Has a job to do, kind of like me. My counterpart.

If you're sitting down to negotiate with your *counterpart*, what *assumptions* might you make about your purpose in the negotiation? Here are your choices:

A. To win the negotiation, beat them
B. To make sure I don't lose, defend and protect myself
C. To solve problems, shape agreements, get things done

Form follows function. If your purpose is to solve problems, shape agreements, get things done, what might your *behaviors* be like?

A. Adversarial, aggressive, abusive
B. Defensive, suspicious, distrustful
C. More open, trustworthy, collaborative

So if *you* operate in trustworthy ways, are willing to collaborate, are open to things that are better for you and them, what *behaviors* are you likely to elicit from *them*?

A. Adversarial, aggressive, abusive

B. Defensive, suspicious, distrustful

C. More open, trustworthy, collaborative

There may be a lag time, but most people tend to shift...

And what might the *Consequences* be?

A. Near optimal, mutually beneficial

B. Time efficient, amicable

C. Likely to strengthen the relationship

D. Potentially, all of the above

We once worked with a purchasing group that hadn't realized it had internal customers. Now, when Requests for Material would cross their desks, instead of just processing them like data entry clerks, they started going down to the maintenance and engineering shop to find the requestor to understand what really mattered to that person. Initially the M&E guys gave them a hard time. They said, "Never saw you here before. You sure you're feeling all right?" And they had reason to be suspicious. Was this just a fleeting flavor of the month, or were the purchasing guys serious about wanting to know what mattered to them?

* * * * * * * * * *

I won't pretend that everyone will shift their behaviors toward yours. There are real cretins in the world. Some folks like beating up on other people. Some organizations have measurements on their people that drive them to strangely aberrant behaviors. Some people, based on past experience, won't believe we've changed until they see a sustained difference over a long period of time. And some of the folks we negotiate with just have agendas that keep them from coming to agreement with us.

Roger Fisher and Scott Brown, in their book *Getting Together*, suggest that you don't behave these ways in *expectation* of reciprocal behavior; you decide to "do only those things that are good for you and good for the relationship, whether or not they reciprocate."[2] This is the logic behind their phrase, "Be hard on the problem, unconditionally constructive with the people."

In a nutshell, this is what we're talking about. I just took you through a simple change in an assumption that has the ability to create subtle changes in our behaviors and massive changes in our results. But it's our master models, our invisible paradigms, that drive our assumptions. How do we get to our paradigms?

Chapter Ten

GETTING TO OUR MASTER MODEL

Sherry Crane, a colleague in human resources at Cessna, told me she learned in Psychology 101 that it takes a cathartic event for us to change our behavior.[1]

This probably relates back to Jean Piaget's theories of learning,[2] which suggest that intellectual growth takes a disequilibrium sufficient to call into question your old models. You then have some choices. You can reject the new data. You can alter your perceptions so that, though they may now be false, they can still fit within your old models. Or you can go through the discomfort and unease of creating better models to make sense out of the new data. If you choose to face your own discomfort, in the subsequent process you learn, adapt, grow, and regain your equilibrium.

I think it takes three things:

- a cathartic event,
- our personal identification with the event, so much so that we reconsider our own assumptions about life and work, and

- a readily available alternative model that may work better - ideally, a model already pre-tested in our system.

A Cathartic Event:

A cathartic event is a precondition for true behavior change because your worldview has to be shaken enough for you to rethink the nature of reality.

A graduate of ours who grew through United, Reno Air, Hawaiian Air, and America West, is a member of the "Zipper Club." This elite group has survived open-heart surgery. He described how open-heart surgery dramatically and permanently changed his perspective on what matters and what doesn't. *Who you are doesn't change, but your model, assumptions, and behaviors do.* This is also at the base of 12-Step programs. They know you have to hit bottom before you will choose to change and have a chance to stay the course.

I don't think we have to hit bottom, but something massive enough has to occur for us to come to understand that our worldview is precisely that – a view, a model of reality, not the world itself. This lets us consider the possibility that there may be different models and views that can get us through these times better.

We've had more than enough cathartic events of late, depending on how you count. The dot-com crash. September 11th. Enron. Tyco. ImClone. WorldCom. An endless stream of homicide bombers. The implosion of the stock market. USAirways, Air Canada and United in bankruptcy; Swiss Air and Sabena fail. The Iraqi war and its aftermath. Add your favorite.

Personal Identification With the Cathartic Event:

The second necessary element - personally connecting with these events, seeing their reflections in you such that you rethink the assumptions on which your own work and life are based – has some built-in difficulties.

Peters and Waterman introduced me to *Attribution Theory.*[3] Attribution Theory says that if something positive happens, it's because of what I did. I take credit for it. If something negative happens, it's not me, it's the system, and I render myself innocent of its implications. This makes it harder to see my own reflection in the cathartic event. It's not me that needs changing, it's the other guy or it's the system.

A few years ago, at American Airlines' annual fall management conference, each seat in the auditorium had been outfitted with a real-time response device. A set of questions was posted on the screen about whether people saw the need for substantial system and culture change. As each person pushed buttons in response to the questions, the results were instantly tallied and projected.

"*My management* needs to change how it works with people."   90+% yes.

"*My colleagues* need to change how they work with people."   90+% yes.

"*My subordinates* need to change how they work with people."   90+% yes.

"*I* need to change how I work with people."
                                    90+% no.[4]

181

I once saw an interview with Tony DiCicco, the coach of the U.S. women's soccer team that won the gold medal at the 1996 Atlanta Summer Olympics.[5] He described the difference between coaching a team of men and a team of women. He described how, when you tell a men's team, "You guys are dogging it; you need to dedicate yourselves and get into shape," every guy on the team thinks to himself, "Those guys are dogging it; they need to get into shape. I'm the only one who's fit." With a women's team, he said, every woman on the team thinks to herself, "I'm dogging it; I need to get into shape."

In terms of changing our behavioral paradigm, this second prerequisite – personal identification – has four aspects:

1) You need to be experienced enough to know that what we've been doing in the marketplace, cross-functionally in our own organizations, and between management and employee or union groups, is sub-optimal.

2) You need to have thought to yourself with passion and frustration, "There's got to be a better way."

3) It works even better if you're open to the possibility that, no matter how honorable your intentions or justifiable your actions, the pattern of your *own* behavior over the past months or years may just have contributed to the current situation.

4) And here's the most important one of all. If you really can get far better solutions and results for yourself and your constituents,

now and over time, than you're getting now, it needs to be OK with you for your counterparts to do better, too. I'm not sure this is a prerequisite; it may be OK to grow into it. I do know that it's the core paradigm-shift issue, and it's harder than it appears on the surface. We are deeply conditioned to believe that "winning" means "beating." It needs to be OK with you for the other guy to do better, too.

A Readily Available, Pre-Tested Alternative Model:

And then you need an alternative model that seems to be more able to help us solve the problems we need to solve now. It doesn't need to be fully shaped and proven. We regularly take steps in faith if not leaps in faith, but there needs to be enough evidence that it can work better and be substantially more helpful to us than what we're using now.

* * * * * * * * * *

So is there a better way that's readily available to us, one that's been pre-tested in our industry and that shows remarkable promise?

Let me take you back to the folks at the Harvard Negotiation Project and the Program on Negotiation.[6] As they sought to identify the best way to come to agreement and resolve differences, their basic conclusion was that negotiation isn't about dominance or beating.

Rather, it's about solving problems and shaping solutions to satisfy your constituents' and counterparts' interests and needs better than any alternative reasonably available to you or them, and doing so in such a way that you and your counterparts look forward to creating value[7] and solving problems together again.

They concluded that a good method of negotiation should satisfy three criteria:

- It should produce a wise agreement, if agreement is possible.

- It should be efficient.

- And it should improve or at least not damage the relationship between the parties.[8]

Their researchers laid out the old options against these criteria. Soft positional or hard positional negotiation - which game should you play?

Which Game Should You Play?	
Soft Positional	**Hard Positional**
♦ Participants are friends.	♦ Participants are adversaries.
♦ The goal is agreement.	♦ The goal is winning.
♦ Make concessions to cultivate the relationship.	♦ Demand concessions to maintain the relationship.
♦ Be soft on the people & the problem.	♦ Be hard on the people & the problem.
♦ Trust others.	♦ Distrust others.
♦ Change your position easily.	♦ Dig in to your position.
♦ Make offers.	♦ Make threats.
♦ Disclose your bottom line.	♦ Mislead as to your bottom line.
♦ Accept one-sided losses.	♦ Demand one-sided gains.
♦ Search for a single answer - theirs.	♦ Search for a single answer - yours.
♦ Insist on agreement.	♦ Insist on *your* position.
♦ Yield to pressure.	♦ Apply pressure.

Adapted from Getting to Yes, by Roger Fisher and William Ury, with Bruce Patton, second edition, pg. 13.

You may have seen the movie *War Games*, in which a war simulation computer plays endless sessions of Tic Tac Toe and nuclear war scenarios. Finally it learns: In both cases, the only way to win is not to play.

Which game should you play? Neither, they said. Change the game. Negotiate on the merits.

In interest-based negotiation,[9] they said:

- You are neither adversary nor friend; your role is that of problem-solver.

- The goal is neither victory nor agreement for the sake of agreement. The goal is a wise outcome reached efficiently and amicably.

- You neither demand substantive concessions as a condition of relationship, nor do you make them to cultivate the relationship. You don't link substance with relationship. You separate the people issues from the substantive issues and you're hard on the problem, *unconditionally constructive* with the people.

- You neither trust nor distrust. You learn the incredible power of being wholly trustworthy, not necessarily wholly trusting. Absent good reason, you deal independently of trust, though at times some upfront trust may be a very good investment.

- You neither dig into your position nor change it easily. You get below positions to the interests that motivate them, since beneath conflicting positions you often find shared or complementary or simply different interests - most if not all of which can be satisfied. You identify the interests and needs of the negotiators themselves, of the constituents they directly represent, and of third parties whose interests need to be satisfied sufficiently so that the agreement doesn't come unraveled as you move into implementation.

- You don't mislead as to your bottom line, nor do you disclose it. In fact, you don't have a bottom line. Instead, you clarify ahead of time what you'll do if you don't come to an agreement, so you'll never again agree to something that's worse than your other alternatives, nor will you ever again take an unrealistic stance.

- You don't search for the single answer, the one they or you will accept. You don't accept or demand one-sided losses or gains as the price for agreement. Instead, you invent options for mutual gain. And you develop multiple options to choose from, separating inventing from deciding.

- When elements conflict, you neither insist on your position nor cave for the sake of agreement, nor do you engage in a contest of will, influence, or power. Instead, you apply objective criteria that both sides agree to, criteria that are independent of the will of either party.

- You neither yield to pressure nor apply pressure. You reason and remain open to reason and you yield to principle, never to pressure.

Let's take a look at some of our objectives in relation to these behaviors.

In relation to our own organization:

How about this instead?

Behaviors	Objectives
◆ Participants are problem solvers.	
◆ The goal is a wise outcome amicably reached.	◆ Attract, keep, and empower the best people, encouraging creativity, lifelong learning, growth and leadership.
◆ Separate the people from the problem.	
◆ Be hard on the problem, positive with the people.	◆ Engage the discretionary energy of all our employees, creating the best working culture in the industry.
◆ Be wholly trustworthy.	
◆ Get below positions to the motivating interests.	◆ Engage everyone's minds, hearts, and creative spirit.
◆ Avoid having a bottom line.	
◆ Multiply options for mutual gain.	◆ Build a culture of autonomy and accountability, of having fun and taking responsibility.
◆ Multiply options first; decide later.	
◆ Insist on objective criteria.	
◆ Reason and be open to reason.	
◆ Yield to principle, not to pressure.	

In relation to our business networks:

How about this instead?

Behaviors	Objectives
◆ Participants are problem solvers.	
◆ The goal is a wise outcome amicably reached.	◆ Work more seamlessly together along the value chain, streamlining operations and infrastructure both inside the organization and out to our networks.
◆ Separate the people from the problem.	
◆ Be hard on the problem, positive with the people.	◆ Care about and care for customers, employees, partners, and shareholders.
◆ Be wholly trustworthy.	
◆ Get below positions to the motivating interests.	◆ Build a high performance culture of accountability, strategic thinking, and business acumen, acting with integrity and honesty in all our relationships.
◆ Avoid having a bottom line.	
◆ Multiply options for mutual gain.	
◆ Multiply options first; decide later.	
◆ Insist on objective criteria.	
◆ Reason and be open to reason.	
◆ Yield to principle, not to pressure.	

In relation to our customers:

How about this instead?

Behaviors	Objectives
◆ Participants are problem solvers.	
◆ The goal is a wise outcome amicably reached.	◆ Provide total customer satisfaction, addressing their needs and priorities, and being easy to do business with.
◆ Separate the people from the problem.	
◆ Be hard on the problem, positive with the people.	◆ Create customer delight.
◆ Be wholly trustworthy.	◆ Provide global customer service that will exceed customer expectations.
◆ Get below positions to the motivating interests.	
◆ Avoid having a bottom line.	
◆ Multiply options for mutual gain.	
◆ Multiply options first; decide later.	
◆ Insist on objective criteria.	
◆ Reason and be open to reason.	
◆ Yield to principle, not to pressure.	

In relation to our suppliers:

How about this instead?

Behaviors	Objectives
◆ Participants are problem solvers.	◆ Enlist our suppliers to work with us to create and maintain a more seamless flow of material.
◆ The goal is a wise outcome amicably reached.	
◆ Separate the people from the problem.	◆ Streamline operations and infrastructure to contain the cost of materials over time.
◆ Be hard on the problem, positive with the people.	
◆ Be wholly trustworthy.	◆ Establish and maintain long term, mutually advantageous relationships.
◆ Get below positions to the motivating interests.	
◆ Avoid having a bottom line.	◆ Link suppliers with customers in profitable alliances.
◆ Multiply options for mutual gain.	
◆ Multiply options first; decide later.	
◆ Insist on objective criteria.	
◆ Reason and be open to reason.	
◆ Yield to principle, not to pressure.	

In relation to a changing marketplace:

How about this instead?

Behaviors

- Participants are problem solvers.
- The goal is a wise outcome amicably reached.
- Separate the people from the problem.
- Be hard on the problem, positive with the people.
- Be wholly trustworthy.
- Get below positions to the motivating interests.
- Avoid having a bottom line.
- Multiply options for mutual gain.
- Multiply options first; decide later.
- Insist on objective criteria.
- Reason and be open to reason.
- Yield to principle, not to pressure.

Objectives

- Use excellence in our services business to influence future engine sales.
- Leverage our internal services and capabilities to improve profitability for the company.
- Provide the greater ease of one-stop shopping for the customer.

In relation to crafting a common corporate entity:

How about this instead?

Behaviors

- Participants are problem solvers.
- The goal is a wise outcome amicably reached.
- Separate the people from the problem.
- Be hard on the problem, positive with the people.
- Be wholly trustworthy.
- Get below positions to the motivating interests.
- Avoid having a bottom line.
- Multiply options for mutual gain.
- Multiply options first; decide later.
- Insist on objective criteria.
- Reason and be open to reason.
- Yield to principle, not to pressure.

Objectives

- Craft a common culture from multiple businesses.
- Recognize and incorporate the benefits and strengths from each of our heritage companies.
- Build a common infrastructure with the ability to communicate with each other.
- Streamline operations so we can work in concert with each other.

In relation to our current environment:

How about this instead?	
Behaviors	**Environment**
◆ Participants are problem solvers.	◆ Marketplace more competitive.
◆ The goal is a wise outcome amicably reached.	◆ Everything is interconnected.
◆ Separate the people from the problem.	◆ Need our customers.
◆ Be hard on the problem, positive with the people.	◆ Need our suppliers and partners.
◆ Be wholly trustworthy.	◆ Need seamless flow of material.
◆ Get below positions to the motivating interests.	◆ In long-term relationships.
◆ Avoid having a bottom line.	◆ Need employees' discretionary energy and creativity.
◆ Multiply options for mutual gain.	◆ Need to do more with less.
◆ Multiply options first; decide later.	
◆ Insist on objective criteria.	
◆ Reason and be open to reason.	
◆ Yield to principle, not to pressure.	

Four key concepts form the core elements of interest-based negotiation: separating the people from the problem (dealing with them both, but dealing with them separately); getting below positions to the interests and needs that motivate them; inventing a variety of options for mutual gain; and using agreed-upon objective criteria, standards and procedures.

Behind these behaviors lie very different paradigm-driven assumptions.

- The old one says life is a zero-sum game. The new one says, no, it's not. We can both lose big time.

- The old one says the pie is fixed. The new one says it's variable and can readily be made larger and richer for us both.

- The old one says negotiation is about claiming value. Out of this fixed pie, how much for you, how much for me? The new one says negotiation is about two things: first, it's about creating value, making the pie bigger and better for us both, and then it's about claiming value in a way that your counterpart will choose to create value with you again.

- The old one says that integrity is irrelevant. At most, we need to stay on the slippery side of legal and adhere to the company line. The new one says that personal integrity is core. In this small community, your integrity, or lack thereof, will eventually bless you or curse you...and your organization.

- The old one says that relationship is irrelevant. Why should I care about what satisfaction means to you? The new one says understanding what satisfaction means to your counterpart is critical. Your job isn't to beat them; it's to help them, not because it's nice, but because it's the only way that you can truly, maximally, help yourself.

- The old one says negotiation is about winning, which means beating. The new one says yep, negotiation is about winning, but not about beating. It means crafting solutions that are as good as possible for my constituents, and if doing that means the solution is better for you, too, that's OK.

And that leads to the paradigm-shift question I mentioned earlier that each of us needs to wrestle with. For many of us, it's tougher than it appears on the surface. Here it is:

If you truly can get significantly better decisions and results, now and over time, using interest-based negotiation than you can get any other way, is it OK with you if your counterpart does better, too?

* * * * * * * * *

So let's assume you buy off on this conceptually. Many of the examples from *Getting to Yes* have to do with students at university or with international political negotiations such as the Law of the Sea Conference. Neither describes our reality.

How do we implement these ideas in an industrial environment in which getting ever better results remains paramount?

Chapter Eleven

IMPLEMENTING THIS IN OUR ENVIRONMENT

As I reflected on how positional negotiation has been our model for negotiation and on why it might be time to change the game, I thought about Chester Karrass, who began his formal study of negotiation in the late 1960s and early 1970s. He published *The Negotiating Game* in 1970 and *Give and Take* in 1974.

My colleagues at GE and I discovered his books and tapes in 1977. This encompassed the timeframe when Gerhard Neumann was seeking to grow the commercial side of GE's Aircraft Engines business and Bob Crandall at American Airlines was figuring out how to survive and thrive in what was about to be a deregulated environment.

I thought back to how Karrass started his own journey. He had grown up in the purchasing organization of one of Howard Hughes' aerospace companies in Southern California. His personal experience in our industry traces back to the 1950s.

He was sent to USC by his company in the 1960s to get a doctorate in business. He chose negotiation as the topic of his dissertation. He sought to put patterns on how people have negotiated for thousands of years.

He reported on how the Russians negotiated. They were the powerhouse we had to contend with at the time. They had circled the earth with Sputnik before our space program was off the ground. They were the competition to beat at their own game. So how did they negotiate? They started low, they conceded slowly, they were patient, they focused on what mattered to them, they always asked for something in return when they made a concession, they became emotional, and they used limited authority.[1]

Chester Karrass did a wonderful job of cataloguing tactics, measures and countermeasures for what he described as the five elements that exist in every negotiation: both win, one win, personal, attitudinal, and organizational.[2]

Many (though not all) of the tactics he catalogued were for one-shot, never-see-the-other-guy-again negotiations. Many of the issues were in conflict. And even though he talked about the power of integrity, the power of hard work, and the power of good will, the preponderance of the measures and countermeasures he taught were hard positional tactics. Certainly, this is what people who took his seminars and read his books took away. What are the tactics I can use to beat the other guy? And what are the countermeasures I can use to protect myself if the other guy uses those tactics against me?

Hundreds of thousands of people have since - with great glee - applied his authority, power, and bottom line tactics. Karrass defined hard positional negotiation at a time when it was a fit for the world we projected and created. He sketched out for us behaviors we could use that were consistent with our assumptions of "competitive anger" and "Beat Pratt."

He didn't envision the driving need to "move at the speed of business." How could he? This was the era of telexes, mimeograph machines, and multiple carbon copies. Many of our telephones still had dials on them. Faxes were relatively newfangled inventions. Much of long distance still involved operators. Word processors, much less personal computers, hadn't yet been introduced.

There was a time when you could take your time to play the negotiating game in the souks of Egypt, or the conference rooms and shop floors across multiple continents. You could sit and sip tea in the souk, enjoying the give and take of the game, all the while taking measure of each other's skill, each knowing the game would end finally with a price each could live with, and each enhanced by participating once again in a game well played. Satisfaction was in graceful execution of the game, not in efficiency. And if sometimes it eroded the relationship, we could live with that.

We in aviation competed suppliers annually on the basis of price. We inspected for quality at the receiving dock. Our purchasing organizations grew to hundreds or thousands of people moving paper in manila envelopes with tie strings and routing slips.

Karrass did not identify the different environments in which these negotiations took place. Might there be a difference between a purely transactional one-shot negotiation for a serape in Mexico and a negotiation with Skip Kundahl of Mal Tool, a company that had in the past and would again fill critical needs for your business?

That was never his purpose. He was cataloguing tactics, measures, and countermeasures, and advising how to use them and how not to. He was not advising *when* to use them and when not to.

But this matters. When you were buying a serape in Mexico, or selling a horse to a stranger in the Far West, or shipping ice from New England to China to trade for tea, dealing with someone you probably would never see again, "Let the buyer beware" was a reasonable assumption to shape your behaviors. Whether you personally operated that way or not, you needed to be open to the possibility that the folks you were negotiating with might be working that way. You needed to protect yourself. We are part of the Great Ape family; we are not descended from dolphins.

* * * * * * * * *

At some point, all of this shifted. Time sped up. The world got smaller and it got very, very interconnected.

We needed our remaining suppliers as much as we needed our shops. We needed repeat customers. We needed to be in functional worldwide alliances. We needed an educated, involved, committed workforce. For our wiser organizations, it was to our interest as management that our employees' interests in meaningful, well-paid work and job security not be overwhelmed by the company's need to provide profit to its shareholders. We needed them to care about the continued success of the enterprise.

Suddenly, everything was interconnected and needed to flow together smoothly.

Neither hard nor soft positional negotiation could get us from here to there. Interest-based negotiation might.

So how do we apply interest-based negotiation concepts in our very interrelated world of business, profits, and bottom-line results? Are there ways to take all this good information and put it into patterns so we can organize it for application, action, and results?

* * * * * * * * * *

Over the years, we have built several basic tenets around these concepts, extending some, adding some others. The tenets and tools seem to help folks think about and find those better solutions in the marketplace with customers, suppliers, and partners, as well as inside their own organizations.

The most important one may be this first realization:

Negotiation is Problem-Solving and Decision-Making in a Mixed-Motive Environment

There comes a time in our lives and careers when it dawns on us that the kind of negotiation we're involved in, *where we usually have to deal with the other guy again and again,* really isn't about beating opponents with artfully employed thrusts and parries, tactics, measures, and countermeasures.

It's about solving complex problems together, keeping work flowing, and realizing opportunities.

It's about getting to the point where you can do good problem-solving with your counterparts in a mixed-motive environment.

So how can you usefully assess and influence the environment? How can you and your counterparts do good problem-solving together, understanding that some of your interests and needs will overlap and some won't?

Identifying the Environment

I mentioned earlier that because some of your interests and needs may be in direct conflict with theirs, if you're too open, too soon, you can do great damage to your organization. Yet if you and they don't find ways to share what matters to you and to them, you'll never be able to craft those more elegant solutions.

They are Neither Opponents Nor Friends; They're Your Counterparts

First, you recognize that the people you're dealing with, as Roger Fisher pointed out, are neither your adversaries nor your friends. They're your counterparts. It is, at its core, a commercial relationship.

Like you, they're seeking to solve problems and realize opportunities while keeping work and business flowing. Like you, they're seeking to satisfy their *own* driving interests and needs. Should they conclude that you (and your business, capabilities, products, and services) are part of their solution now or in the foreseeable future, they will want to include you. Should it seem to them that you are *not* part of their solution now or in the future, they won't. Notice that this is a matter of perception.

This, obviously, is equally true from your point of view. No matter how warm and wonderful as human beings your counterparts may be, if what they have to offer in terms of product, access, opportunity, or service is not useful to you, you are unlikely to do business with them this time. And, no matter how difficult they may be, up to a point, if what they have to offer is critical to your interests and needs, you will.

Other aspects of the environment come into play.

Past, Present, and Future

Most business decisions don't start from scratch. Most of our decisions derive from prior decisions, many of which are still being implemented. Whether or not we participated in past events, our organizations have histories together, some of which greatly influence where we are now. So we need to understand what may have happened in the past that is still exerting an influence on the present. What ghosts, skeletons, or black holes might there be? To what extent will they need to be addressed before you can go forward together? What is your level of risk in going forward?

Interests and Needs

You need to assess to what extent your interests and theirs might overlap in this particular situation or over time. You need to identify how collaborative you can be and how careful or competitive you must be. To what extent can you trust them and the people and organization behind them? To what extent can they trust you and the people and organization behind you? How open is it safe to be?

The more we can quantify and put a pattern on the environment, the better our decision-making can be, and the better actions we can take to navigate it well. Clearly, a variety of parameters can and sometimes should be used to define and quantify our negotiating environments.

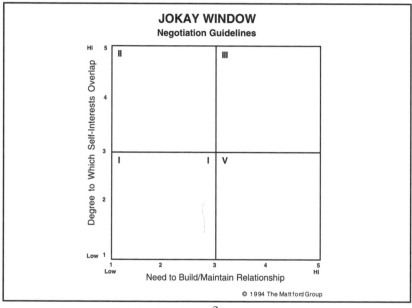

JOKAY WINDOW
Negotiation Guidelines

Degree to Which Self-Interests Overlap

Need to Build/Maintain Relationship

© 1994 The Mattford Group

The JOKAY Window[3] invites you to consider these two key parameters:

1) to what extent might my interests and those of my counterparts overlap in this particular situation? And,

2) to what extent do I, and might they, have an interest in building and maintaining a long-term relationship?

In every negotiation, there will be some ways in which your self-interests and theirs overlap, or you'd have no reason to negotiate. This could be as simple as you want to buy and they want to sell. It could be that both of you have a vested interest in keeping your organizations alive. This is why the bottom coordinates of the JOKAY Window are 1/1, not 0/0.

And, in every negotiation, there will always be some ways in which your self-interests and theirs don't overlap, or you won't be negotiating either, you'll be farther down on the Problem-Solving Methodologies scale.

Negotiating the Environment

The JOKAY Window suggests that the more people *perceive* (that's a key word – perceive) that their interests overlap, the more collaborative their behavior will tend to be. The less overlap they perceive, the more competitive their behavior is likely to be. So if you can help your counterparts conclude that their interests overlap with yours more than they might originally have thought, their behavior will tend to shift toward the collaborative. It takes collaborative behavior to come to maximally beneficial solutions.

Similarly, if they see no future in the joint relationship, the less inclined they will be to work for joint and mutual advantage over time. When they decide that they do need to build and maintain an ongoing relationship with you, unless they're really dumb, their behavior will tend to shift toward the collaborative. (There are some really dumb people out there.)

Modes of Interest-Based Negotiation

So if you're in what truly is a Quadrant I environment, where neither of you cares if you ever see the other guy again, you and they can still get at least as good and probably better results using interest-based negotiation than what you're doing now.

But, bearing in mind that we are not descended from dolphins, you'll approach it differently. You'll listen for what's not said. You'll negotiate the level of authority of the person you're dealing with before you begin. You'll triangulate on information. You'll ask the same question two or three different ways, listening for consistency. You'll be very careful with the wording of your questions, and you'll listen carefully for the wording of the answers. (I believe that most people in industry today don't lie, but they may be selective with the truth.) You'll get it in writing and signed. And you'll make sure that all elements of the contract are concluded in present time so that you're not captive to a future the other party has no investment in.

In Quadrant II, though there may be many overlapping interests in this particular situation that can lead to a satisfying solution for you both, neither side sees the need for a long-term relationship. Again, you'll make sure that implementation is not captive to decisions that need to be made in future time, and you'll assure that this agreement, in and of itself, is sufficiently satisfactory to you.

In Quadrant III, where you have a lot of overlapping interests and a strong need to be in a continuing relationship, it would make sense to be supportive, to put things in a long-term context, to be more open to sharing and less concerned about looking for where they might be out to get you. You'll probably continue to clarify with each other that this is, in fact, a Quadrant III negotiation.

And in Quadrant IV, though there may not be a fit this time, you will be aware of the long-term potential in the relationship. You will tend to make sure that what you do now and how you treat each other sets up a time in the future when working together or doing business together can proceed smoothly.

You might fill out the JOKAY Window both in relation to how you see the negotiating environment, and in relation to how you think your counterparts see it. It's important, obviously, to avoid wishful thinking and projection. School yourself and your colleagues to ask, "What data do we have that suggests this is how they see it?"

Sometimes you need to fill out a JOKAY Window on several participants in your counterparts' decision process, as well as on the organization itself. For example, a manager who wants to get a quick success and use it to move to another job may have very different motives and perceptions than the head of the project who will be dealing with the long-term implications of the agreement reached.

Time can frequently affect how your counterparts see the JOKAY Window. You may have been in a Quadrant III relationship with them for years, but something has now changed in the environment, and they no longer perceive a need for a long-term relationship. So you need to continue to consider how you perceive it and how they perceive it, not just the one person you may have a great relationship with, but their function, organization, and management.

Be aware that behaviors that may be appropriate for a Quadrant I situation, used in a Quadrant III environment, will tend to pull your counterparts into Quadrant I behaviors and will keep all of you from finding those near-optimal solutions. This too often describes the current state of union/management relations.

So it's important to look *behind* the behaviors to the situation. Regardless of what they're currently doing, might a long-term relationship be important to you? To your constituents? To them? To their constituents? Might there be more overlapping interests than you originally thought?

And, just as you negotiate "Can I trust you?" so you can negotiate a process for shifting from where you currently are in the JOKAY Window to where it would better serve both of you to be.

Problem-Solving and Decision-Making

For years we've taught our students that negotiation is about shaping joint solutions in a mixed-motive environment in order to solve problems and realize opportunities. If this is true, our already existing models for problem-solving can help us see the pattern for the whole, which in turn would let us put a logic and sequence to our planning activities and to the course of our negotiations.

The four-stage problem-solving model on the next page is adapted from one Roger Fisher and his colleagues introduced in *Getting to Yes.*[4] They call their model the Circle Chart. They use it to demonstrate how to multiply options for mutual gain.

Notice the four stages for solving problems:

1. You first identify the problem or opportunity,

2. then you analyze the situation,

3. you identify possible alternatives, and

4. you choose the best among them to take forward into the implied fifth stage - implementation.

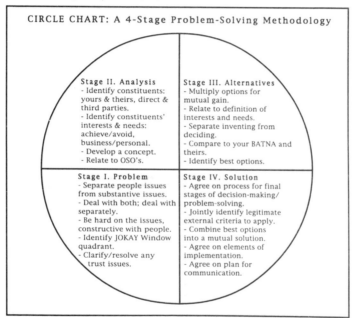

CIRCLE CHART: A 4-Stage Problem-Solving Methodology

Stage II. Analysis
- Identify constituents: yours & theirs, direct & third parties.
- Identify constituents' interests & needs: achieve/avoid, business/personal.
- Develop a concept.
- Relate to OSO's.

Stage III. Alternatives
- Multiply options for mutual gain.
- Relate to definition of interests and needs.
- Separate inventing from deciding.
- Compare to your BATNA and theirs.
- Identify best options.

Stage I. Problem
- Separate people issues from substantive issues.
- Deal with both; deal with separately.
- Be hard on the issues, constructive with people.
- Identify JOKAY Window quadrant.
- Clarify/resolve any trust issues.

Stage IV. Solution
- Agree on process for final stages of decision-making/ problem-solving.
- Jointly identify legitimate external criteria to apply.
- Combine best options into a mutual solution.
- Agree on elements of implementation.
- Agree on plan for communication.

Adapted from Fisher and Ury, Getting to Yes, pg. 68.

Roger Fisher and his colleagues, in their lectures, make the point that, in the real world, we tend to shuttle from Stage I to Stage IV: Problem→Solution. We're bright, we've done things like this before, we like action, and we need quick results. The dilemma is that many times we haven't identified the true problem or opportunity, and the solution therefore doesn't solve things.

In Academia, they say, people can make entire careers cycling back and forth between Stage II, Analysis, and Stage III, Alternatives, with little need to ground their analysis in real world problems, and little obligation to put all those alternatives into action.

Their suggestion: Move through all four stages.

I like the Circle Chart because it makes it easy to see that your decision-process or problem-solving process can flow forward from one stage to another, clockwise around the chart, but it can also flow backward. For example, suppose your solution isn't adequate. You can move back a stage to ask yourselves, "What were the other alternatives we considered?" You can move even further back, to review your analysis: "Was it complete?" "What was missing?" Or even further back: "How did we identify the problem or opportunity?"

In positional negotiation, the equivalent to our tendency to leap directly from Problem to Solution is our tendency to leap directly from Problem to Position. On the surface, it seems this would be more time-efficient and effective. It is neither. Frequently you conduct a good definition of the problem or opportunity, but only your half of it. You don't consult with your counterparts; you just present to them a position that is acceptable to you.

Skipping Stages II and III completely, you never identify all your constituents or the range of their interests, much less those of your counterparts. You never experience the richness of the alternatives that emerge when you and your counterparts do good Stage II Analysis together. And though you zip through the first three stages by skipping two of them, you bog down in Stage IV.

More to the point, you end up with sub-optimal solutions, and you typically worsen the working relationship. This sets up a contentious and time-consuming Implementation stage. You find you have made it harder to do good business together next time and the time after that.

The Flow of a Well-Made Decision

The Circle Chart becomes a graphic way to display the four elements Roger Fisher and his colleagues identified as core to the process of interest-based negotiation:

1. Separate the people from the problem.
2. Focus on interests, not positions.
3. Multiply options for mutual gain.
4. Use objective criteria.

Stage 1. Problem

In the problem (or opportunity) identification stage, you recognize that there are "people problems" and "problem problems." So you identify the perceptual, emotional, and communications issues, and you also identify the substantive issues. Both must be dealt with, but separately.

People problems can range from mis-perceptions to miscommunication to emotions. Sometimes they simply don't know you. Sometimes they don't trust you. If someone key to the decision doesn't know you or trust you, this needs to be addressed. You can't get someone to trust you by cutting your price. Sales people seek to do this all the time. Price is a "problem" issue; trust is a "people" issue. Deal with them separately.

And there are substantive issues that will need to be resolved. So identify, analyze, and prioritize both sets of issues.

Be hard on the problem, the data, and all aspects of the substantive issues. And be unconditionally constructive with the people[5] - doing only those things that are good for you and good for the relationship.

Clearly, much analysis can and should be done by you and your colleagues prior to meeting with your counterparts. Some of it is best done together with your counterparts. Think of interest-based negotiation as sitting on the same side of the table, scoping out the environment and the issues together, in order to come to a joint conclusion that both of you can honor and support.

Overarching Strategic Objectives (OSOs)

Another element of problem definition differs widely depending on the particular problem you're seeking to solve, or the opportunity you're seeking to realize. Most of us work in large organizations. More often than not, everything we do in our businesses is a piece of a larger picture or larger pattern of problems, opportunities, and objectives. Too often, individual decisions are made without regard to the larger patterns they are part of or the impact they may have on other parts of the organization. Not infrequently, individual decisions made in isolation make it far harder to accomplish the organization's strategic objectives.

The clearer we are about the larger whole of which what we're doing is a part, the better we can align our efforts in the interest of those overarching organizational strategic objectives.

For example, if, as a design engineer, you make an improvement to the product that will reduce its manufacturing cost, without considering the impact this change might have on supporting the product in the field, it is very easy to increase the total cost to the business, or to make the product less user-friendly, or both.

Or, if you understand that selling this product to a particular customer can directly link to upcoming decisions by a series of organizations that historically have followed this customer's lead (even if those customers are not part of your territory), how you work with this customer should be influenced.

Before you plan your approach to internal or external problem-solving and decision-making, school yourselves to ask, "What's our OSO of which this decision is a part?" Spend at least as much time identifying what your counterparts' OSO might be.

It's been suggested that OSO is pronounced "Ohhh....sooo," because as soon as you identify it, many things become clear.

One good way to find your counterparts' OSOs is to follow Deming's advice and ask "why?" five times. Why do they want to buy this product or make this deal? What will it be used for? What problem might it solve? What opportunity might it let them realize? Why might they want to do that? Why might they want to do *that*?

Sometimes you find some surprising answers, which reinforce the next concept - that people act to satisfy their underlying needs and interests, both business and personal. We once concluded that the main reason a customer from the Far East wanted to come to Cincinnati for a plant visit had nothing to do with the superiority of our products or how they fit into the customer's current fleet plans. When we asked "why?" five times, we learned that his daughter had just started college at Ohio State University in Columbus, just two hours' drive away.

This, too, was helpful. Rather than structuring his visit to try to sell him something right now, we could design the visit so that he could talk with us about the future plans for his airline, and we could leave him with some ideas about possible future joint activities. And we could also suggest that he meet with us on a Friday.

Stage 11. Analysis

In this stage, you identify the interests and needs of those involved in, or affected by, the decision. Your purpose is to derive a working concept from the pattern of those interests and needs. This, in turn, should address the problems you and your counterparts need to solve or the opportunities you wish to realize.

So, you identify everyone with a stake in the outcome – big stakeholders and little ones, yourselves included. You identify your direct constituents. You spend at least as much time identifying the constituents your counterparts represent. Sometimes you know; sometimes you ask. Sometimes you guess and then seek to confirm in later conversations. You also identify third parties who will be affected by any decision you jointly make.

Once you've identified your constituents, their constituents, and affected third parties, you identify their interests and needs. You identify your counterparts' direct and indirect constituents, and you clarify their interests and needs. As you do so, options for mutual gain start suggesting themselves. You and your counterparts will need to resist moving prematurely to Stage III, Alternatives. You stay focused on working to jointly agree on a common concept. Ideally, together you will draw up a conceptual statement of purpose that will shape the movement into Stage III.

My father was a doctor. He said that the most important part of medical practice is physical diagnosis. If you listen carefully, he said, the patient will tell you what's wrong with him. Prescription then follows naturally. The same is true here. Stay in Stage II long enough to fully identify all your constituents, and to scope out their interests and needs in order to find the overlapping pattern of those needs and to derive a conceptual statement that will solve them. This lets Stages III and IV go quickly and well.

Needs and Interests

Keep in mind that, in every negotiation, people have problems they need to solve and opportunities they wish to realize. A position is simply one solution acceptable to them. Behind every position, no matter how ridiculous it may look, are interests and needs. Find those, and creative options for mutual gain start to fall out of the woodwork.

Very frequently we don't ask, we just assume.

THE SIX STAGES OF PROJECT MANAGEMENT

1. Great enthusiasm
2. Chaos
3. Search for the guilty
4. Punishment of the innocent
5. Promotion of non-participants
6. Establishment of objectives

6

Adapted from unknown source, ca. 1975

The VP of our commercial engine business once asked his new marketing communications director to write a thirty-minute speech about a particular topic. The marketing communications director wrote a beautiful speech. The VP rejected it. The marketing communications director wrote another speech. That one was rejected, too. Finally, the marketing communications director sat down with the vice president and said, "Jim, what are you trying to accomplish here? What matters to you?"

Perhaps the lasting brilliance of the work of Roger Fisher and his colleagues lies in how they help us get away from positions to the needs and interests that lie beneath them.

The clearer we are about our own needs and interests and those of our constituents, the better we'll be at deciding what is a good agreement and what isn't. The more we understand our counterparts' needs and interests, the more creative we can be at coming up with ways to help them find satisfaction.

Shape of Satisfaction

Chester Karrass first taught me that negotiation really isn't about dollars, goods or services. It's about satisfaction. People buy satisfaction.

Shape of Satisfaction: Needs & Interests

We want to achieve	We want to avoid
Business Personal	Business Personal
They want to achieve	They want to avoid
Business Personal	Business Personal

The Shape of Satisfaction chart lets us scope out the needs and interests not just of the negotiators, but also of the constituents they directly represent and of third parties whose interests need to be satisfied enough that they won't derail the agreement down the road. Someone's Shape of Satisfaction includes things they're trying to achieve and things they're trying to avoid, on a personal level as well as on a business or role level.

Fisher says that one definition of a good outcome is that our interests are satisfied as fully as possible, our counterparts' sufficiently, and third parties' tolerably.[7]

Positions are almost always in conflict. We can develop far more satisfactory solutions when we work with interests precisely because so many of our interests are *not* in conflict.

As the next chart suggests, some of our interests are held in common (I want to be treated with respect and so do you. We both want the enterprise to succeed. We both want to feel we got a good deal). Some are complementary (I want a product more than I want money, and you want money more than you want the product). Some are just different (I like vanilla, you like Rocky Road... Look, here's Baskin Robbins!). And only some may be in conflict.

Interests & Needs	
Common	Complementary
Conflicting	Different

Frequently, as people first work to fill out the Shape of Satisfaction chart, they ask, "How do I know what their interests are?" To some extent, you can guess. The truth is, the best way to find out is to ask.

We have gone into negotiations with folks from companies widely known for being hard positional negotiators. We regularly start by saying, "We want to put together our proposal to address your interests and needs as well as possible. We'd like to review with you what we think those are so we can use them as the basis for our proposal. If you like, we're happy to share with you what we're trying to accomplish." And we receive their permission to go ahead. We then lay out our best sense of their interests and needs, even when some of them are in conflict with each other. We then ask, "Which are correct? Which aren't? Which have we missed completely? Which matter most to you?"

I've been amazed at how willing most people are to help you make their list better, either in preparation for a meeting or at the meeting itself. I've come to believe that most people negotiate positionally because it's what they've been taught. Most (though not all) are surprisingly open to working in this different way.

This approach also differentiates you from almost everyone else they're working with. In order to come up with your best sense of their interests and needs, you have to spend time thinking about what matters to them as seen by them.

As we work together to identify the common, complimentary, and just different interests, almost all of which can be satisfied, we craft solutions far better for both. Here's where we create value together. As we do so, those interests-in-conflict become a smaller piece of the whole. Having created value together, we are highly motivated to find ways to resolve the remaining issues.

Stage III. Alternatives

As I mentioned, if you and your counterparts have done a good job of identifying constituents, interests, and needs, you've had to resist moving prematurely into identifying alternatives and options for mutual gain. A good way to resist is to use the Parking Lot concept. Jot those ideas on a flipchart page taped to the wall. They won't get lost.

Some of us, as we approach the end of Stage II, suddenly flash on an intuitive grasp of a picture of the whole. The separate interests and needs coalesce into a big picture, a conceptual "Wow!" We find ourselves saying, "If we can do this and this and this, it will satisfy this and this and this." We find ourselves at a whiteboard or a flipchart, drawing an interrelated whole.

For others, the analytical pieces start to coalesce into logical sequences. We can create charts that make visible those interests that are shared by multiple constituents and those that are random. We identify which interests need to be fully satisfied, and which don't.

Whether your natural pattern is intuitive or analytical, this data becomes the base from which you jointly derive options for mutual gain.

This is a point where brainstorming can be a powerful tool, used by yourself and your colleagues prior to meeting with your counterparts, and, far more than you might initially think, used jointly with your counterparts. When you brainstorm possible concepts, nothing is agreed upon until you've put together the agreement as a whole. Just as people discover that sharing interests and needs is not risky (it's sharing bottom line positions that causes problems), so they quickly discover that brainstorming with their counterparts can be incredibly valuable.

As with all brainstorming, you get all the ideas and possibilities out first, writing them down verbatim, and not judging them. You do divergent thinking, separating inventing from deciding.

Only later do you identify which ideas can be grouped, which tweaked a little bit, which discarded, and which kept. And then you compare them to your joint conceptual statement, and to the interests and needs that motivated that statement. If we were able to dovetail these items, would it satisfy the concept? To what extent would it satisfy the interests and needs? To what extent would it let us solve the problem or realize the opportunity? What's missing? What could be even better?

This is also where you can make wonderful use of the original Circle Chart from *Getting to Yes* to do what Roger Fisher and his colleagues call "shuttling between the specific and the general."[8]

Whatever the problem, whatever the interests and needs, a variety of options can satisfy them. The end product of Stage III, after you have considered several of those possible options, is to identify what seems to be the best option, and to spend time together making it just as good as possible.

It will need to pass several tests:

- Is it consistent with, and does it advance, our OSOs?
- Does it satisfy our interests as fully as possible, their interests sufficiently, and third parties' tolerably?
- Is it feasible?
- Can it be implemented within the time frame and the other constraints we're working with?
- Will it cause problems down the road?

Stage IV. Solution

At this point, you've agreed conceptually on how to proceed, and you've sketched out key elements. Sometimes your managements have publicly announced their intentions to proceed into implementation.

Whether they have or not, you need to draft a joint agreement that turns the decision from concept to contract. As you do so, you often discover that your perfectly clear understanding of what was meant differs remarkably from their perfectly clear understanding. Partisan perceptions are alive and well, and the discussion runs the danger of deteriorating into intractable positions, or of disintegrating. And you're coming face to face with the distributive elements of negotiation, with those elements where, if it's a dollar more for you, it's a dollar less for them.

Yet together you've done a good job of creating value. You've identified the common, complementary, and different interests, and you've incorporated ways to satisfy them into the agreement. Now you need resources for managing the conflicting elements of the negotiation; for coming to a successful conclusion; and for setting a base to move successfully into the longest stage of all – implementation of the decision, which requires a good working relationship over time, one that can indeed deal well with differences.

Several concepts may be of help here:

- Partisan perceptions and tit-for-tat
- Negotiating fair standards and procedures
- Pareto's concept of an Elegant Solution
- Settlement ranges
- Alternative currencies

Partisan Perceptions and Tit-For-Tat

Because human beings are indeed members of the Great Ape family, we need to make allowances for some of our less lovely tendencies, including our tendencies to view the world through our own partisan-colored glasses, to desire more than is fair, and to feel justified in those desires.

This first resource may help rebalance our perceptions and reduce our misperceptions.

Roger Fisher and his colleagues once conducted a study of litigators.[9] A series of questions had to do with, "How do you determine your pretrial behavior? Your courtroom behavior?" More than half said, "I take my cue from the other side. If they're reasonable, I'll be reasonable. If they're going to be hard-nosed, I'll be hard-nosed."

On the surface, this tit-for-tat behavior – I'll do to them as they do to me – sounds like a modified version of the Golden Rule. I've been in all too many meetings when we determined how to work with our customers, suppliers, or other counterparts on the basis of how we perceived them to be dealing with us. It seems reasonable at the time, like peeing higher on the post. Because of partisan perceptions, this is a *lousy* way to set your behavior.

The concept of Partisan Perceptions, according to Fisher and his colleagues,[10] says that it is built into our wiring to see our own behavior as somewhat more justifiable, righteous, and understandable than it really is, and to see the other person's behavior as somewhat less righteous, understandable, and justifiable than it actually is. This is true even with people we love.

The two together make up a witch's brew for disaster.

Let us assume that you've initiated relations with your counterparts. They decide to deal with you as you've dealt with them. But they see your behavior as less honorable and reasonable than it really is.

So they seek to come in at that discounted level. But since they see their own behavior as more righteous, reasonable, and honorable than it really is, they undershoot still more. You decide to use tit-for-tat as your strategy as well. But you've seen their behavior as less righteous than it is and your own as more righteous, so you double undershoot as well. And they do the same. And so do you. This is the definition of a flat spin - really hard to get out of, easy to crash and burn.

Fisher says that we need to school ourselves to understand that partisan perceptions cloud everyone's thinking, ours included, and then we build in corrections. We look for the flaw in *our* logic, as seen by them, and for the value in *theirs*. We learn to articulate their viewpoint, maybe even better than they do. I strongly believe that until we can see the world as our counterparts see it, whether or not we agree with it, we aren't in a position to seek those better solutions. We can then set a flexible strategy and avoid letting tit-for-tat become our strategy.

Negotiating Fair Standards

When you get down to the details of an agreement, you will need to overcome a natural tendency to propose elements that favor *you*, and to use criteria that justify *your* position, even though you wouldn't find them legitimate were the situation reversed.

Keep in mind that you're crafting an agreement both of you must honor, and that you're establishing a base for next time and the time after that. It is perhaps wiser to frame the decision with what Fisher calls "a joint search for legitimate external criteria independent of the will of either party."[11]

It also may be wise to set aside your focus on content for awhile and spend time agreeing on the procedures or the protocol you'll use to come to agreement. These agreed-upon procedures may be as simple as "I cut; you choose."

I've heard of union contracts that include a clause that only one person (not one side...one person!) can get angry at a time. I love this idea. It recognizes that people get angry. It further recognizes that anger isn't the danger; the danger is anger escalating. So you get angry. You blow off steam. Everyone else listens. After awhile, someone asks, "Are you through yet?" And you say, "No, not yet!" and you blow off some more steam. Awhile later, you say, "I'm through." Now the other people in the room can get angry if they want to, but they don't feel the need to. Discussions can resume.

One of my favorite procedures for avoiding deadlock is to agree ahead of time that if we don't come to agreement, we have to escalate the decision to our bosses. We'd never do that since both of us know that they'd really screw it up.

I didn't fully understand the importance of negotiating fair standards until I watched the American presidential election of 2000 and what happened in Florida in terms of "What is a vote?" The issue was not just the definition of a standard, but how to implement it. The standard was identified as "the will of the voter." The harder question was, "How do we operationalize 'the will of the voter?'" So we all learned about dimpled chads and pregnant chads and hanging chads.

Pareto's Elegant Solution

Too often in negotiation, we take the situation as if it's fixed and maneuver over how to divide things up. Or we accept the first offer that satisfies our interests enough. Yet if we take the time to search and use a model that can get us there, we will almost always discover solutions that are better for me without being worse for you, or better for you without being worse for me, or both. In the process, we reaffirm the collaborative nature of the negotiation, and we build a base for working together in the future.

Roger Fisher introduced me to the Italian economist Pareto's concept of a more elegant solution.[12]

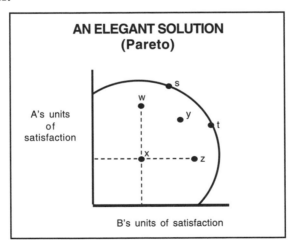

Source: Redrawn from class notes,
Harvard Negotiating Workshop, 1990.

This Pareto diagram looks at a variety of potential agreements in terms of each party's units of satisfaction. Let's assume that we've come to Point X.

A is reasonably satisfied and so is B. We're willing to formalize an agreement at this point. Pareto suggests that A can then say to B, "What is everything I can do for you that makes this agreement better for you without being worse for me?"

This is a radical concept. It goes against the grain. "Wait a minute, if it's going to be better for you, it has to be better for me, too."

But stay with it a minute. We were willing to shake hands and conclude the agreement at Point X. Let's play with it. So we overcome old sibling rivalry patterns and play with ideas. As we come up with ideas, the solution can move toward Point Z. No worse for A, better for B.

Or B could say to A, "What is everything I can do for you that makes this agreement better for you without being worse for me?" As they come up with ideas, the solution moves towards Point W. And if they do this simultaneously, the solution will move toward Point Y.

As we jointly explore, the outcome becomes better and better, and each side's level of satisfaction grows. At some point, Pareto says, there is nothing that can make the solution better for one side without being worse for the other, but we hardly ever find that Pareto Frontier.

Searching for it together builds the relationship, improves the existing agreement, and causes both of us to look forward to working together again.

One of our students, in charge of revenue management for a major airline, suggested that there is great value in looking for things that are significantly better for one side and only a little worse for the other. This greatly increases the opportunity field. This one does require paying more attention to reciprocity.

Settlement Ranges

No matter how good we are at building value together, there comes a time in every negotiation when issues and interests conflict, where a favorable element for one will be less favorable for the other.

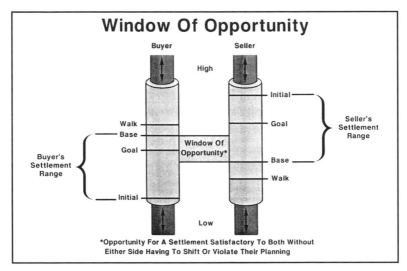

Settlement Ranges says that, *even for the distributive elements of negotiation,* there is usually a range within which both sides can walk away satisfied. The Window of Opportunity chart invites you to think of the numerical aspects of negotiation as being located on moveable sleeves.

In a buy-sell situation, that range is defined as being anywhere from the buyer's initial offer to their base. Similarly, such a range exists between the seller's initial offer and their base. And because our planning is part data, part guess, and part hope – if you, as the buyer, can introduce data or perspective to help me, as the seller, decide that marketplace reality today is not what I thought it was, I may shift my sleeve, and my range will shift accordingly. The same is true if I, as the seller, can help you, as the buyer, change your mind about the nature of the marketplace today.

I think it is the buyer's responsibility to seek to get sellers to shift their sleeves downward, and then to come to an agreement as close to the seller's base as possible. And it's the seller's responsibility to do the reverse.

You need to think long and hard before you *force* your counterparts to break through their base. If you introduce information that causes them to rethink their planning, given time to work decisions backward into their own organization, they will frequently shift their sleeves. But if you force them to break their planning, and if their self-esteem is involved, one way or another, they'll get even. You need to consider carefully what your actions may end up costing you.

Alternative Currencies

Alternative Currencies become one way to make Settlement Ranges less of an issue. There are always items that have more value to your counterpart than cost to you, and more value to you than cost to them. As you work to identify those alternative currencies, you both have more room to negotiate and create value together.

For example, in the 1980s, when Middle East Airlines was making an aircraft/engine decision, they would identify a list of dollar objectives and non-dollar objectives. They privately put a dollar value on the non-dollar objectives. One of these was that the Tech Rep be an old Middle Eastern hand. Their reason was pragmatic. They needed someone to translate from their high-context culture to our low-context culture.

Back in the 1980s, they put a $5 million value on this item. This was a time when GE moved its Tech Reps every two years. Pratt & Whitney left them in place for decades. GE said, "We'll decide when to move our Tech Rep." Pratt & Whitney got a $5 million credit.

When American Airlines and the Association of Professional Flight Attendants were negotiating their contract in 1998-99, the three issues for the flight attendants were Raises, Retirement, and Respect. How do you quantify respect?

When you work with Alternative Currencies, absent good reason, claim the value your counterpart places on them rather than the cost to you.

And finally, a simple statement:

What Goes Around Comes Around

This is a very small industry. Small things you did ten or twenty years ago have the most amazing ways of coming back to bless you or curse you today or next week or next year. If you school yourself to honor and treat with respect everyone you deal with, you'll be so far ahead of the game.

This gets complicated. Honoring everyone, treating everyone with respect, extends out into the environment. It includes your employees, your suppliers, your shareholders. It includes yourself. It includes your customers, those you currently have and those you might have. It includes your partners, those you currently have and those you might have. I think it even includes your competitors. It probably includes your enemies. There is never a time when it works to your long-term benefit to ascribe motive to others or to demonize those you will ever need to work with.

There is a profound element to this. Everything we do is increasingly interrelated. Abraham Maslow explores this at length in *Eupsychian Management*. He describes how your particular enterprise "is embedded in the larger community ... which in turn is embedded in the whole darned human species and the whole darn world."[13] He makes the point that your company's ability to do business rests "on a whole network of assumed relationships and services" that lets you be effective - things as simple as water and electricity, schools and garbage service, and as complex as a standing army, transportation system, and assumed levels of safety, security, and a future that extends logically and sequentially from the present.[14]

He points out that everything you do in your own role and organization has an effect on your immediate town, a lesser effect on your state, your country, and the world. He doesn't pull his punches. He describes how "the unnecessarily bad and insulting treatment of the Japanese in California, partly determined by a stupid system which permitted William Randolph Hearst to have a huge and unlimited power to express his own unnecessary contempt for the Japanese, strengthened the war party in Japan in their internal struggles with peace-loving Japanese and finally led to Pearl Harbor." In the long run, he said, "through these chains of causes and effects, William Randolph Hearst is responsible for the death of many American people including some undoubtedly that he loved."[15]

Individual choices made to cheat on accounting practices inside diverse businesses yielded a $3 trillion loss in the stock market by July of 2002, making it infinitely harder for all those businesses to survive.

> "We cannot live only for ourselves.
> A thousand fibers connect us with our fellow men;
> and among these fibers, as sympathetic threads,
> our actions run as causes,
> and they come back to us as effects."
>
> – Herman Melville

And it applies at our level, too. Years ago, Delta struggled to maintain its marketshare and profitability when ValuJet invaded its backyard as a low-cost carrier. Delta dropped its prices and raised the frequency of its flights to fend off the incursion. These defensive actions, plus the devastating crash in the Everglades of a ValuJet DC-9, removed ValuJet as a challenger in the system.

And then Delta and American gave the resuscitated ValuJet, now flying under the name of AirTran, the market opening it needed. Decisions by the majors to engage in predatory pricing in Wichita set up an opportunity that brought AirTran to town with a far smarter strategy. They knew the majors had deeper pockets; they couldn't compete in a straight fare war. They also knew the community leaders understood that if there were a fare war, ticket prices would rise once the new entrant was defeated. So they negotiated commitments from the government and from area businesses. Joe Leonard, head of AirTran, established what he called "public-private partnerships." Martha Brannigan[16] of the *Wall Street*

Journal describes how "the 'public' part taps municipal coffers mainly for revenue guarantees that protect AirTran against losses during the initial phase of operations; the private builds 'travel banks,' in which businesses pledge to spend a specified amount on tickets. Both elements help to build a loyal following and a cushion against the early losses of expanding into a new city and the invariable backlash from bigger competitors who respond by slashing their own fares and expanding service."[17]

Wichita Mid-Continent Airport reported that prior to May 2002, a full-fare round trip ticket on Delta from Wichita to Atlanta was $1284.24. After AirTran entered the market, it was $376.50.[18]

A failure to honor their customers, present and potential, in the interest of short-term gains, had set up an opportunity not only in Wichita but in dozens of other cities also ill-served by the majors.

I watched Pratt & Whitney's arrogance in the 1970s create an opportunity for GE Aircraft Engines to enter the market. Boeing's arrogance in the 1980s created an opportunity for Airbus.

Might I actually get better profits and a more vibrant business over time if I treat my customers with respect, and if I work to honor their reasonable needs and interests?

Every action has side effects. Roger Fisher says that if you develop a reputation as *untrustworthy*, the cost to you may be expensive. He also says that a reputation for fair dealing can be an extraordinary asset.[19] The longer you're in business, the more true you know this to be.

When American Airlines was seeking to rebuild trust with its employee groups, and at the same time was doing everything on the narrow edge of legal to keep Legend from acquiring landing slots at Love Field in Dallas, guess what lesson many of American's employees took away? Of course, they're not dumb. The question was: "If management will do these kinds of things to Legend when it suits their purpose, what will they do to us when it suits their purpose?"

In the final analysis, this game of life has more to do with character, with establishing a reputation for reliability and trustworthiness based on who you are and what you consistently do, than it has to do with shifting situational ethics.

Here's a strange truism:

- You can't treat your shareholders better than you treat your partners.
- You can't treat your partners better than you treat your customers.
- You can't treat your customers better than you treat your employees.
- You can't treat your employees better than you treat your suppliers.
- You think you can, but you can't.

It's all one fabric.

Initially we gag over this idea; our minds want to reject it. We look for examples to prove it isn't so. I invite you instead to consider the idea and to look for ways that it *is* so.

I suspect that you can't treat your suppliers, customers, employees, partners, or shareholders better than you treat your *competitors.* Once we stop thinking we're competing against competitors, and focus instead on helping our customers decide that our alternative suits them better than any alternative reasonably available to them, then the other alternatives (our competitors) keep us from getting arrogant or complacent. And they may become our customers, our suppliers, or our partners.

What goes around comes around. It's all very interesting.

* * * * * * * * * *

So that's a quick picture of the whole. Before we look more deeply at whether interest-based negotiation may be a better way, I need to address a question that may be in some of your minds – that being whether what I'm proposing is what some people refer to as "win-win" negotiation.

Chapter Twelve

ISN'T THIS THE SAME AS "WIN-WIN" NEGOTIATION?

For years, our students have asked whether interest-based negotiation is the same as "win-win" negotiation. I always responded that I never understood what the term meant. "Win-win" sounds like, "Was it as good for you, dear, as it was for me?" I would remind them of one element of Fisher's definition of a good outcome that I'd mentioned earlier: it satisfies our interests as fully as possible, our counterparts' sufficiently, and third parties' tolerably. This is hardly the same as seeking to make everyone happy.

But it has become important to make a more clear distinction. Recently, a mean-spirited book called *Start with No*[1] was published. Business books come and go, and it probably would have been just a temporary blip on the bookshelves but for the fact that the July 2002 "Forethought" in the *Harvard Business Review*[2] gave more credence to the book than it ever deserved.

In his "Books in Brief" review, John T. Landry wrote,

> "The introduction of the win-win approach to negotiations changed the way companies make deals, turning what had been an adversarial duel into something approaching collaboration. But any good idea can be taken too far, and this executive coach exposes the dangers of adhering too enthusiastically to the win-win ethic. [He] explains how the focus on making everyone happy can expose a corporate negotiator to the manipulations of a wily opponent. He counsels negotiators to always remain skeptical and self-interested; rather than striving to get to yes from the outset, start with no."

The author of the book, through the oppositional title he chose, clearly ascribes "win-win" negotiation to the concepts identified by the Harvard Negotiation Project and described in *Getting to Yes* and *Getting Together*. On the book's dust jacket, he states, "Think win-win is the best way to make the deal? Think again. It's the worst possible way to get the best deal. This is the dirty little secret of corporate America."[3] He could not be more off-base in his attribution.

The *Harvard Business Review* is one of our major conveyors of business culture and effective problem-solving paradigms. The fact that one of its editors gives credence to such an attribution deserves a closer look. Why is it that so many corporate negotiators, seeking to implement the concepts of principled negotiation, fall into the trap of bending over backward to make everyone happy and walk away feeling they've been taken advantage of? Why is it that for all their troubles they also end up with lousy solutions?

This issue is particularly important because negotiation truly is the game of life. It underlies how we work with one another to implement critically important change initiatives. It shapes what union leaders and employee relations people do every day as they seek to find ways to work together. And it defines what those in the marketplace do with customers, suppliers, partners, and regulators.

The purpose of our negotiating behaviors is to achieve our objectives in particular environments. In aviation (as in many of our industries), the environments we must succeed in and our own strategic objectives have changed so much that our old behaviors aren't working.

The concepts, assumptions, and behaviors of interest-based negotiation provide a model far more suited to today's environments and objectives. They have the ability to get us out of many of the managerial and behavioral messes we're currently in, and to get us the superior results we need.

But there has been a tendency in our industry and businesses to believe we were applying the concepts from *Getting to Yes* when we were in fact doing something far different instead. An analogy may be useful.

When mid-level managers at GE Aircraft Engines in the 1970s reluctantly faced into hiring women and members of minority groups in order to meet the quotas that had been placed on them, many of them honestly believed that these folks couldn't cut it in the organization. They also concluded that as managers they were being asked to bend over backwards, that they were not to hold their new employees to the performance standards to which they held the white guys who reported to them.

The mindset that had up to that point in time kept women and minorities out of our organizations persisted, even as they were being brought inside. These managers didn't change their paradigm-driven assumptions, they just bowed to the inevitable and hired "those" people. In many cases, they didn't look for educated and talented "those" people, they just looked for women or for African-Americans. They met the quotas. Then they let their new employees perform at lower levels. They didn't give them the feedback, training, or support they needed, and they justified their own deeply embedded belief system when some of the new hires failed to achieve at "white guy levels." It was a self-fulfilling prophecy: integration doesn't work.

It wasn't until managerial mindsets started to shift, allowing for the possibility that educated, talented, competent, achievement-oriented women, African-Americans, Hispanics and Asians existed, and could bring unique perspectives and skills that actually enriched the organization, that diversity had a chance to work.

The same is true with interest-based negotiation. Most organizations that have intended to shift toward interest-based negotiation haven't provided training for their people. They've set a new tactical direction, notified everyone that they would now behave with each other in win-win ways, or that they would be more "green," and assumed that would be sufficient. If they provided training, it was one to three days of training at the skill level, not at the paradigm-shift level and not reinforced by culture, management, measurements, or reward systems.

So we dutifully set out to "try" to function in this new way. We sought to change our *behaviors*. We tried to be nice to our opponents, to all the folks who were driving us nuts or taking advantage of us. We concluded that management wanted us to come to agreements with these people, whether the agreements were good agreements or not.

Operating inside our old mindsets, *seeking to change our behaviors rather than our paradigms*, all we did was switch from the hard side of the positional negotiation game to the soft side of the same game, calling it "win-win" negotiation. And the folks who were dealing with us were still playing the hard positional game. These folks were indeed taking advantage of us. Frustration was growing. Relationships were worsening. We experienced "win-win" as "win-lose," and we were right. Unfortunately, we ascribed it to interest-based negotiation. Right conclusion, wrong attribution.

Fisher and Ury address this issue in the first few pages of *Getting to Yes*. Here's what they say:

> "Being nice is no answer. Many people recognize the high costs of hard positional bargaining, particularly on the parties and their relationship. They hope to avoid them by following a more gentle style of negotiating. Instead of seeing the other side as adversaries, they prefer to see them as friends. Rather than emphasizing a goal of victory, they emphasize the necessity of reaching agreement. In a soft

negotiating game, the standard moves are to make offers and concessions, to trust the other side, to be friendly, and to yield as necessary to avoid confrontation."[4]

They go on:

"...pursuing a soft and friendly form of positional bargaining makes you vulnerable to someone who plays a hard game. In positional bargaining, a hard game dominates a soft one. If your response to sustained, hard positional bargaining is soft positional bargaining, you will probably lose your shirt."[5]

"Win-win" negotiation is a buzz-word for changing sides within the same game - from hard positional to soft positional negotiation - used by people who have never had the chance, or taken the chance, to change their paradigm instead.

Perhaps more than anything else the admitted failure of both hard positional negotiation and of "win-win" soft positional negotiation to achieve our own strategic objectives in today's environment points to why we need to commit to widespread training at the paradigm-shift level, in order to change the game we've been playing so that we can get the results we so badly need.

I would hate for the incredible benefits – hard on the problem, unconditionally constructive with the people – of the model proposed in *Getting to Yes* and *Getting Together* to be tarnished by a label that refers to behaviors that are the very antithesis of what Fisher and his colleagues are proposing.

* * * * * * * * *

Now, suppose we have concluded that though we may be uneasy about some of the implications of this different path, there truly is a growing disconnect between our objectives and the behaviors we're currently using to achieve them. Suppose we conclude that neither hard positional negotiation nor "win-win" soft positional negotiation can get us there and that we truly have to find a better way.

Suppose, too, that we know it will take a consistent, persistent effort to change our current paradigm and anchor a different one in our culture. And that if we as top management choose to go this way, we will never be wholly comfortable with what we've created.

What evidence do we have that this interest-based approach might indeed be a better way, one worth both the effort and the risks? And what are some of the pitfalls we need to avoid?

Chapter Thirteen

SOME LESSONS LEARNED

Joel Barker described the role of "paradigm pioneers."[1] These are the people who take a step in faith to apply the new paradigm before there is overwhelming evidence that supports it and before their organizations embrace it. They do so because it seems to work better.

Thomas Kuhn sketches out the development of a new paradigm. He says that the person "who embraces a new paradigm at an early stage must often do so in defiance of the evidence provided by problem-solving. He must, that is, have faith that the new paradigm will succeed with the many large problems that confront it, knowing only that the older paradigm has failed with a few. "A decision of that kind," he states, "can only be made on faith."

Kuhn goes on: "That is one of the reasons why prior crisis proves so important." He describes how crises help folks still committed to the old paradigm become more open to taking a look at what otherwise might be regarded as a flight of fancy, a "will-o'-the-wisp."

"But," he says, "crisis alone is not enough. There must also be a basis...for faith in the particular [course] chosen. Something must make at least a few [people] feel that the new proposal is on the right track, and sometimes it is only personal and inarticulate aesthetic considerations that can do that." In our terms, it just feels right.

He says that "if a paradigm is ever to triumph it must gain some first supporters" who can develop it "to the point where hardheaded arguments can be produced and multiplied." Not everyone will be persuaded, he says. "Rather than a single group conversion, what occurs is an increasing shift in the distribution of professional allegiances. At the start a new candidate for paradigm may have few supporters." However, if the paradigm pioneers are competent, "they will improve it, explore its possibilities, and show what it would be like to belong to the community guided by it." More people will be converted, and exploration of its problem-solving capabilities will continue. "Gradually the number of experiments, instruments, articles, and books based upon the paradigm will multiply." More and more people convinced of its usefulness "will adopt the new mode."[2]

The good news is that just through our program a couple of thousand paradigm pioneers have been at work throughout our industry. They've been applying interest-based negotiation on a personal scale and on some broader scales. They have stories to tell.

Here are some good news stories, and some things we've learned the hard way. Some paradigm pioneers have sacrificed their careers on the altar of this better way; they deserve to be identified and honored, not forgotten. Most are thriving based on its benefits.

Our graduates go back into organizations that are still deeply embedded in hard positional negotiation. Many of these folks are finding they can get far better solutions for themselves and their organizations in a world that hasn't yet changed much. Here are some of their stories.

"I think maybe we're listening differently."

I recall a no-nonsense, 30-year veteran of American's Tulsa Base. He and a colleague were on the management team that met with union representatives on first step grievances. About a month after he attended the workshop, he called me, puzzled, to say, "I'm not sure what's going on, but something's changed." Instead of sending 90% or more of the grievances up to Headquarters, almost all were being settled or withdrawn at the first step meetings. I asked why he thought that was happening. "I don't know," he said. "I think maybe we're listening differently."

"I call them Defining Moments."

A managing director of line maintenance for American Airlines – not a workshop graduate – described what he calls Defining Moments. He says, "It can be as simple as having an accident on an airplane while it's in Maintenance. You can say, 'Is the airplane damaged?' Or you can say, 'Is everyone OK?'" The field HR manager reinforced his comments. She said, "That means everything. Employees talk with one another. They say, 'He didn't even ask how I was. He asked, 'How's the company's property?'"

"When they understand you are trying to work with them, they are more likely to offer suggestions to help satisfy both parties."

A young graduate from Chem-tronics wrote to tell us about his successes. He described how, as he explored the customer's true interests and needs, the customer told him that he could extend his turnaround time, which allowed him to lower his price. He said, "We had not known that customer didn't require a fast turnaround time." In another situation, an airline customer lent him tooling they weren't using, allowing him to reduce his prices to them without affecting his margins. Another customer, once they trusted that he was exploring for mutual advantage, suggested that he stop sending engineering data they had requested on each part that was sent. By cutting out this requirement, he was able to cut his costs by $30,000.

"We concentrated on alternative currencies that would mutually benefit both parties."

An Air Medical Market Manager for Bell Helicopter wrote us to say, "After almost two years of work, the customer, an air ambulance company, decided to purchase two twelve-year-old aircraft made by a competitor at a purchase price of $3 million each. We were proposing new aircraft at $4.6 million each. During the last two negotiating sessions, which were not readily agreed to by the customer because 'they had already made their minds up,' we concentrated on alternative currencies that would mutually benefit both parties – a proposed long-term relationship, our superior support as evidenced by the 1992 and 1996 customer surveys, reduced direct operating costs of our aircraft, and our superior training. We also addressed the humanitarian interests of the prime negotiator in terms of the increased likelihood of insured continuation of a public interest emergency medical service program as weighted against the potential failure or increased down-time of the twelve-year-old aircraft. I personally feel that this approach was substantially responsible for helping us reopen this contract."

"This is very different than beating on the vendor to reduce price."

A senior commodity manager for American wrote, "With the constant upgrades and changes to our computer systems, we spend about $1M every six months or so to recertify our computers. In talking with the vendor, I learned they recertify before shipping. Our testing was redundant. The customer made it clear to me they didn't trust the vendor, and therefore preferred to test redundantly. Before, I would have dropped it. Now I saw the issue as one of negotiating trust. I got the customer and the vendor together to identify how the vendor could do the recertification so that the customer would trust the process, quality, and results. This is very different than beating on the vendor to reduce price."

"Our new VP said we needed to add value for the customer."

A young customer service manager for Interturbine wrote to tell us, "As a repair facility, it is slow suicide to compete against other repair stations as low price producer. Our new VP said we needed to add value for the customer. I agreed with this, but didn't exactly know how to do it. The concept of alternative currencies helped put this into focus, as did focusing on the customer's driving interests and needs. I recently worked with a major customer, showing them how we could reduce turn time from the industry standard of thirty days to ten days, which would help their internal cycle time. By meeting this turn time, along with buying a set of hardware as a fail-safe mechanism, we could reduce the level of inventory they carried by several hundred thousand dollars. Their total added value in doing business with us allowed us to provide the repair at a good profit."

"We asked about their underlying interests and needs."

A senior purchasing agent for American learned the power of asking what mattered to his internal customers. He wrote to us: "Engineering and Maintenance wanted to bring some outsourced repair work in-house. When we asked about their underlying interests – which we didn't use to do – they were concerned about turn time and reliability. They also needed to reduce their cost of inventory. We came to a 'power by the hour' agreement with the supplier, which will drive the supplier to make their work reliable, because they don't want to see the stuff coming back. The supplier also agreed to set up a local satellite shop to reduce time in transit, and therefore further reduce turn time. And they loaned us a tester so our shop can screen and do internal testing, as well as keep work hours in-house."

"Maintaining the customer's confidence is key to an on-going business relationship."

The Director of Middle East Operations for Pratt & Whitney's Military Engines organization wrote to say that, in his career in the region, "I find it very easy to work with the customer when you are honest and discuss freely and openly any issue of mutual interest..." He said the customer will accept information, *even if it is costly to them*, provided it is accurate and your company is not taking advantage of them. A key element of his job therefore became scrutinizing communications from his company and its representatives to make sure the relationship was not jeopardized by anything other than credible information.

"By sharing dissatisfactions, we were able to find common interests and reach an agreement."

A supply manager for Westinghouse wrote to say: "Two years ago, we forced our second and third largest suppliers of skilled technicians to work as subtiers to our primary supplier. This was done to reduce our administrative efforts and prevent wage creep caused by employees jumping between companies. The process and forced marriage created dissatisfaction for all four parties. The two subtiers filed termination notices. Two of us worked with our staffing manager to develop a 'lessons learned' meeting, which was the negotiation of a *process*. At the end of the meeting, the three suppliers joined forces and recommitted to make it work. By sharing dissatisfactions, positives, goals, and stakes in the ground, we were able to find common interests and reach an agreement."

"Taking the time to understand resulted in much good business and many positive referrals."

A sales director for a general aviation company described how, for one of his customers, "the back-and-forth-ness of the deal has been much less important than the validation of personal, non-financial objectives." He explained that this gentleman was deeply involved in health and educational charities.

He said, "While striking a fair deal for the purchase of the airplane, we realized that an informal commitment to participate in an annual charity ball and charity golf tournament had great value. It has resulted in millions of dollars of repeat business, and in many positive referrals."

Taking the time to understand your counterpart's shape of satisfaction – what they're trying to achieve and to avoid on a personal as well as a role level - gives you more room to craft an agreement better for both.

"Now I can put a face on the safety, reliability, and performance we aspire to."

The same general aviation sales director wrote: "Sometimes the interest-based approach is more about communications than a specific negotiation. In many manufacturing organizations, a high wall is built between customers and shop floor workers. Over the past several years we have facilitated meetings between customers and workers. Standing in front of the people who built his airplane, one customer said, 'When I place my baby and wife in your airplane, I want to know that I'm flying in the safest product there is.' After examining the finished airplane with that customer, one of our employees said, 'Now when I make a decision that will affect an aircraft, I'll think of how my decision would affect your satisfaction. Now I can put a face on the safety, reliability, and performance we aspire to.'"

"We have a problem; let's solve it together."

A sales manager for a US airframer's airline logistics support organization briefed me on a negotiation his company concluded with a Japanese airline for spares and aftermarket support for the airline's fleet of wide-body aircraft – all supplied by his company. I mentioned to him that it's not unknown for an American management team to size up such a situation and say, "Hey, they *have* to deal with us. Screw 'em!" He said that his company wanted to keep the airline as a loyal customer, and the airline was interested in being the launch customer for his organization's worldwide inventory management program. In today's business model, he explained, an airline buys their inventory, puts it on a shelf, and issues it to the mechanic when needed. Under this new concept, the airframer owns the inventory up to the point when it's issued to the mechanic; they control the actual consumption. He said. "You can imagine the regulatory and procedural issues surrounding such a conceptual shift that needed to be worked out."

He worked with his counterparts at the airline for nearly two years to sign the agreement – two years and thirty-five trips to Japan. "The entire negotiating experience was collaborative," he said.

The Japanese had proposed using a concept called "Wa" to underlie the negotiation. "Wa" is a traditional Japanese concept; it has to do with maintaining a totally round sense of group harmony.

"That is typical of them," he said. "They swept us into it. There were very few points at which it lapsed into, 'We need this and we're not moving off of it.' Everything was stated as, 'We have a problem; let us solve it together.' Without that collaborative approach, this agreement never would have happened. It resulted in a groundbreaking solution that was extremely good for both companies."

He made a point to post the symbol for "Wa" prominently on the whiteboard behind the table where the contract was signed. Everyone brought digital cameras to the signing ceremony.

"Same principles, different situation."

The Manager of Engine Management Systems for Pratt & Whitney Engine Systems wrote to say: "Although I do plenty of negotiating with our internal customers, I think I apply the principles most often in managing my own team. When a project went poorly, I used to try to isolate the person or thing that had caused it and hold them responsible. I've found it a lot more effective since [the workshop] to call a group meeting and say, 'Let's list all the things that went wrong in this project and see if we can come up with some processes to avoid them next time.' Working together with the common interest in improving runs a lot more smoothly than working against each other to make sure the blame falls on someone else. It's not really a win-lose game. Same principles, different situation."

"New entrants are striving to create a Southwest-type culture..."

An attorney specializing in aviation employment law wrote to say, "I've heard it said among labor relations professionals that interest-based bargaining is simply what good negotiators have always done." He recognizes there is some truth in the statement, but says that "it grossly understates the differences in approach and mindset" that accompany a real paradigm shift. He believes "it is no coincidence that the new entrants like jetBlue are striving mightily to create a Southwest-style culture where the employees identify with the Company and feel that the Company cares about them and listens to them." He warned that as companies such as Southwest grow substantially, maintaining their culture will be a major challenge. I suspect that part of the challenge is figuring out what it is that makes you as good as you are. It's really not about being nice, going to parties, and drinking Wild Turkey.

"Walk away with mutual respect so the relationship can continue..."

Quadrant IV in the JOKAY Window defines those situations where your interests and needs and theirs may not overlap sufficiently in this instance, but where there may be an interest in establishing a relationship over time. Too often, we sabotage future possibilities through how we handle the frustrations of the current impasse.

An Integrated Supply Chain VP for Honeywell wrote to say, "We were in intense negotiations with a supplier for months trying to get significant productivity improvements and concessions from them. We were going nowhere. The frustration level reached the tops of both organizations. The ironic part is that both sides knew there was ample opportunity to work together but had let other issues get in the way. I was asked if there was anything I could do - or wanted to do - to salvage the relationship."

"I met with my counterpart and briefly discussed the frustration level and some issues that were being hotly debated. He asked me, 'What do you want to do?' Reflecting back on interest-based discussions, I asked him, 'What are you looking for? And, given the current environment, why are you interested in doing business with us?' This opened up a two-way dialogue about what we wanted, where we were going, and how we could help each other."

"We did not strike a deal at that time; it simply was not the right structure. But we walked away with professional respect and a relationship that continues today. Sometimes, out of nowhere, one of us will call the other to see if, by some slim chance, there may be some interest in an opportunity. It has also led to a few deals that benefit both companies today. It seems obvious now, but in the heat of negotiations, you tend to forget the simple things and try instead to outsmart the other side."

"I would have never done something like that before."

An inventory controller for Air Canada called us after he attended the program side-by-side with the on-site rep for Pratt & Whitney. He described how Air Canada had experienced a major engine failure. He said, "It was going to cost us a lot of money. My boss negotiated a settlement with Pratt; then it was my job to negotiate a repair cost. I had a client who had purchased an engine which she had intended to put out on the lease market. She had sent it to us for repair. There was so much wrong with it that we suggested she break it down to piece parts and sell it. My engine broke at the same time. We jumped at the opportunity to rob the engine that I was stripping and take the parts we needed, but I couldn't get the percentages to meet my goal. I called her and said, 'I have to buy $1.5 million worth of parts from you. I have to meet a certain percentage. I assume you have to meet a certain percentage. What's your percentage?' She said, 'Why should I tell you?' I said, 'I know people who need parts.' She trusted me and gave me her percentage. I knew that Pratt needed non-cutback stators and that these stators were good. They bought the stators from us. I shipped them to Pratt and added it to my bottom line so my client could meet her minimum goal. I met mine, and Pratt had an extra set of these stators. I would have never done something like that before. I had the integrity I needed from Pratt because the people I was dealing with had taken the course. The only one taking a risk was my client, because she didn't know about the program."

He went on to talk about his relationship with Pratt's on-site rep: "Even today I sent him a set of blades that are useless to everybody because there's no traceability. I said, 'Get your researchers and find certification. Get these serviceable, do what's reasonable, and send me the bill.' I never would have taken that kind of risk before. Now, it's not a risk."

"I asked why he wanted this and why he wanted that."

An engineering section supervisor for Cessna explained to me how they custom-build every aircraft's avionics. A repeat customer had come in to replace his current aircraft. This gentleman flew charter

251

operations; the airplane was his livelihood. He sat down with Marketing to review twenty-two avionics changes he wanted. There's a tendency, our student said, to run and get quotes for every inquiry. "Among other things," he said, "the customer was very insistent that we replace his Cockpit Voice Recorder. Certifying this change would take more time and cost him significantly. Since we sometimes end up absorbing some of the cost of the changes, it might cost us, too. I asked Marketing if I could speak with this customer, since I wanted to make sure we delivered the airplane he wanted and needed. I asked him why he wanted this and why he wanted that. In terms of the Cockpit Voice Recorder, he was concerned about the reliability of our existing product. I got the numbers from our Reliability Department, and he was satisfied. He thought we were using an older tape-driven recorder instead of our current solid-state version. Together we whittled his changes down from twenty-two to six. Taking the time to understand his mission and interests made his purchasing experience more pleasant and both of our end results more satisfactory."

"We started a Wall of Fame."

There's a big difference between structured management attaboys and peer recognition in their community-building impact. And a big difference between trying to be green and just being green.

The VP of aircraft maintenance for America West called to brief me on how the airline is turning itself around. He said, "We're excited here; people are pretty upbeat. In June 2003 we made Number One in on-time performance."

"When I arrived, the attitude was terrible. People walked around without making eye contact. I started saying hello to everyone in the hall; I asked my staff to do it, too. The atmosphere started to change. I told my staff, 'You don't say 'Thank you' enough.'"

"I'm straight with the union guys. I tell them, 'Don't bring me B.S. We're here to solve problems. If we're treating people unfairly, let's stop it. If employees are skipping out on work, let's fix it.'"

"We started a Wall of Fame. To be on it, you have to be nominated by a peer."

"For example," he said, "we had a plane flying out of Phoenix. A Fire Protection warning light had come on in the Number Four galley. They diverted to El Paso. We didn't know if the warning was real or not. One of our guys was on his way out the door on vacation - reservations all made. He flies from Phoenix to El Paso, pulls the report, checks it out, calls Engineering to say nothing's wrong, and goes back to Phoenix. He didn't even mention his vacation; he'd missed his flight."

A colleague nominated him for the Wall of Fame.

"The customer is happier, life for me is easier, and we're getting what we want."

A major concern people have as they start to use interest-based negotiation is: "Do both sides have to be skilled at this for it to work?" And the answer seems to be "No," though it works even better if they are.

Here's what I think:

In interest-based negotiation you learn to be hard on the problem, unconditionally constructive with the people. When you're unconditionally constructive with people, most respond.

You want to understand what satisfaction means to your counterparts. When you want to understand what matters to folks, not so you can manipulate them, but so you can make sure the agreement meets their needs too, it has an effect.

You want to shape an agreement that provides them more satisfaction than any alternative reasonably available to them, so you're open to exploring, to asking open questions and listening. When you actually listen to someone, instead of just waiting until you can leap in with your rebuttal, it makes a difference.

One of our graduates was in charge of business development on a commercial application of a military helicopter. When asked the difference this approach was making, in a situation where his customer hadn't been trained in this, he said, "The customer is happier, life for me is easier, and my organization is getting what it wants." When asked what would need to be put in place to keep him from reverting, he said, "It's very simple. When I forget, the pain returns."

"The value of these mutual benefits is staggering."

Pratt & Whitney Engine Services has had a joint materials management program with Delta for some years. Counterparts in that effort attend the workshop together. A few years into the venture, the P&W program manager said, "We're looking for solutions that provide more value to all parties. The dollar value of these mutual benefits is staggering when compared to the dollar value of the things we 'positionally' worry about on a daily basis." This was part of the effort that led Delta to identify Pratt & Whitney as its most improved supplier.

"A union cannot afford NOT to use an interest-based model when contract negotiation time rolls around."

An international purser for American Airlines wrote: "As a workshop graduate from the labor side of an airline bargaining unit, I have a unique perspective on the importance of an interest-based solution. The political environment is such that a labor union cannot afford NOT to use an interest-based model when contract negotiation time rolls around."

She continued: "The Railway Labor Act has needed overhaul for many years. The National Mediation Board has their hands tied if one party or another stalls, filibusters, or just plain refuses to negotiate. The ability to strike was labor's ultimate strength, but it's no longer an available or desirable option. The Presidential Emergency Board (PEB) is now the most likely outcome of a strike. Arbitration will result. A lengthy bargaining period is never desirable and is very costly to labor and management. It is in the best interests of a labor union to get a negotiated agreement *before* the National Mediation Board is called in."

"We found the workshop an ideal place to build relationships and to begin to practice another way to negotiate in a safe, non-threatening environment before the stakes became too high."

Typically, their reaction is, "Say What? We Own You!"

A commodity manager for Hamilton Sundstrand's Engine and Control Systems reminded me of two teams who attended an open enrollment session in August of 2001. He placed the decision to attend within the context of a larger need at United Technologies. To achieve significant business-wide cost reductions, they had to get cost reductions from "the big spend sole-source suppliers."

"Normally," he said, "a single source supplier does not leave their customer in a very good position to leverage cost. Typically, their reaction is, 'Say what? We own you!'" The Hamilton Sundstrand people asked themselves, "What can we do differently?"

He wrote, "You'll remember that Hamilton Sundstrand and Honeywell teams came together to participate in the workshop. To set the stage for what these two companies meant to each other, they are very much competitors in the very same aerospace marketplace for nearly identical product types. Hamilton Sundstrand's acquisition of the Externals and Controls group from Pratt & Whitney earlier in 2001 now meant that we had complete control over procurement decisions and strategy on engine controls and externals for all of the P&W engine programs. This certainly caused some tension with companies like Honeywell and made for business discussions that were not open to things like cost reductions, value stream mapping events, etc."

I asked him what the management decision process was that led to counterparts attending together. He laughed. "The reaction was that we'd tried everything else, why not? There was nothing to lose."

He continued, "To put the financials in perspective, Honeywell was the largest supplier spend to Hamilton Sundstrand and was a single source supplier on all their products. By having our procurement people and their program management people at the same seminar, key relationships were

256

fostered which helped pave the way to more open communications. We carved out a long-term agreement later in 2001 which proved to be a winning combination for both companies. The methodology and ideals that the Negotiating Solutions workshop brought to bear in that session were key to the agreement's success for both companies. Each side started asking, 'What can we do for you?' That approach paved the way; things started coming open. For example, we agreed to identify them as a preferred supplier. We built in performance *incentives* rather than just penalties, so they benefited if they excelled."

I asked what kind of volume was involved. He described it as a five-year, $200 million deal, regressed 3-5% per year.

"OSHA's not a four letter word at Delta."

The Occupational Safety and Health Administration (OSHA) designed the Voluntary Protection Program (VPP) in 1982. This program, which is open to all U.S. industries, was set up to recognize worksites with outstanding comprehensive safety and health programs. An OSHA area representative says, "The VPP is designed to establish a relationship between employers, employees and OSHA that is based on cooperation and partnership rather than confrontation."[3] This is as much a change for OSHA as it is for the people at the worksite, since most inspectors have long been convinced that the only way you can get people to do things right is to confront them and fine them.

Since 1982, of the more than seven million worksites in the United States, less than a thousand have been recognized with VPP STAR status. Achieving it is a big deal.

The Vice President for Base, Engine, and Component Maintenance for Delta's TechOps organization wrote to say he thinks everyone needs to "understand what will make the difference before you start."

He continued: "This is what happens when you decide there are no quick answers, only opportunities to develop partnerships versus individualism. Delta TechOps was recently recommended for VPP STAR status. This is a first in the aviation industry. What made the difference? There were no mandates. The employees and management worked together to build the program from the bottom up. Communication and education were exercised at each level. We all listened, developed, and succeeded."

TechOps' General Manager of Safety and Security, also a workshop graduate, explained that when he was asked to pick up the effort in 2000, it had slipped below the radar scope for some of the operations managers. Personnel movement had left the original team leaderless and somewhat rudder-less. To succeed, they needed to rebuild the core team with agreed-upon strategic objectives and to get the entire business committed to it and engaged in it again.

They also worked to build relationships with their OSHA counterparts. One element of complexity was that the on-site inspector changed three times.

The people at OSHA were all former enforcement people and didn't cut Delta any slack. They engaged the airline people from a partnership perspective. When they saw things that were wrong, they required comprehensive programs, but it was never punitive. He described OSHA as working to make sure the bar was set high so as not to water down the significance of the achievement.

Overhaul and Maintenance Magazine came in to write an article about the effort.[4] Delta's Senior VP, TechOps, told them, "OSHA's not a four letter word at Delta."

"Do I have evidence for this? Yes, of course."

The chairman of a ceramic coating center in France, a joint venture between Snecma and MTU, wrote to say: "Whenever I am in a cooperative or partnership environment – in business, social, and family - which is most of my time, the only way for me to interact effectively is to apply this new paradigm. Do I have evidence for this? Yes, of course. Whenever I fail to get the required results or the quality of relationship I'm looking for, I can trace it to my falling back into the old paradigm, which hopefully with time is becoming less frequent. One more thing: I don't follow this new paradigm because it works. I follow it because, as you know, it's the right one."

* * * * * * * * * *

And some things learned the hard way.

Short-term gains can really mess up long-term objectives.

A few years before they worked with us, one of our clients brought in a one-day program in interest-based bargaining run by William Ury, the co-author of *Getting to Yes.* Management and union leaders trained together prior to negotiating a contract. One of the management negotiating team members, looking back on it, said that they used interest-based *words* to get what they wanted.

The union members felt they had been sold out. They voted the presidents at the local level out of office. The new presidents of the locals had no ownership of the contract and zero interest in joint training. The message they took away was: Train in interest-based bargaining, get taken, and get voted out of office.

I have since heard of other situations where management proposed using interest-based bargaining and then took advantage of inexperienced union negotiating committees. In each situation, the union members and leaders learned to say not only "No," but "Hell, no!" when invited in the future to train in and negotiate using interest-based bargaining.

For nine years, I taught GE Aircraft Engines people to be really good hard positional negotiators. I spent three years trying to convince myself that interest-based negotiation was just a sophisticated overlay on positional. It's not. It's an entirely different path. You have to let go of subtly manipulating people to do what *you* want and truly be open to crafting a solution together. It's an odd feeling when you've been rewarded all your life for controlling things.

There are major lessons here.

One is that it takes more than one day of training to get to the paradigm-shift level needed to implement interest-based negotiation. Learning the words doesn't matter if they don't flow out of a different master model. In this case, management superimposed interest-based terminology on hard positional negotiating assumptions and behaviors. The labor leaders attempted to use soft positional behaviors. As Fisher and Ury state, a hard positional game dominates a soft game. The labor leaders lost their shirts and subsequently their jobs. The company seriously damaged the chance it truly needed to work with the union in interest-based ways.

The other lesson is that if you as an organization want to shift this way, you have to make sure those leading your teams truly operate with integrity. This includes making decisions not to take advantage of your counterparts, even when you can.

In the second edition of *Getting to Yes*, Fisher and Ury address ten commonly asked questions about interest-based negotiation. One of them is this: "Should I be fair even if I don't have to be?" They write:

> "Sometimes you may have an opportunity to get more than you think would be fair. Should you take it? In our opinion, not without careful thought. More is at stake than just a choice about your moral self-definition."

They ask you to consider several questions:

> "How much is the difference worth to you? Will the unfair result be durable? What damage might the unfair result cause to this or other relationships? Will your conscience bother you?"[5]

Each time I know of that people chose to use the pretext of interest-based negotiation or interest-based bargaining to take advantage of their counterparts or to advance short-term gains, their organizations have paid for it down the road.

Don't it always seem to go, that you don't know what you've got till it's gone. You pave paradise, put up a parking lot."[6]

Even though large organizations skew over time towards a particular personal style and worldview, especially those that for years have had a strong chief executive, there are always some folks who see things differently. Good organizations have enough flex in them that those who succeed in spite of not fitting the mold are allowed to be different and may even be celebrated. Some rise toward the top.

Some of those folks end up with the chance to try new things. This is one of the reasons that Joel Barker says that the emerging paradigm typically begins as experiments, even as the old paradigm is still paramount as a problem-solving model.

Sometimes one part of a largely "red" management style organization happens to contain a cluster of "green" managers. They're getting great results within their boundaries. They're not changing the organization's view of reality, but they're getting results. The organization recognizes and rewards the results. Too often, after a few years, that group of managers gets promoted and moved elsewhere, a more typical management gets brought in and reapplies more traditional behaviors, and the success story falters.

This happened at Pratt & Whitney's Turbine Airfoils' North Haven facility in the mid- to late 1990s. A manager named Ed Northern was brought in to manage an organization so badly in disarray that top management was very close to shutting the place down. He came from GE Aircraft Engines via MRC via Interturbine. He had been part of the GE Aircraft Engines revolution of the 1970s that almost succeeded.

Mort Moriarty, then head of purchasing for Turbine Airfoils, recalls that he and the other twenty-year P&W veterans, who had all been doing yeoman work to hold the organization together, needed this ex-GE guy the way they needed a hole in the head. He described reacting with amazement at Ed Northern's first staff meeting. Eddie had said: "I need you to know three things about me: I believe in God, I believe in family, and I believe in people. Let's get to work."

People were tired. They adopted a wait-and-see attitude. What would this guy do when things got tough? Things did get tough. One of the managers really screwed something up, which shut down an entire line for an extended period of time. They missed production schedule commitments. Everyone hunkered down waiting for the normal response: the people involved would be fired. At the next staff meeting, as Ed went around the table, he got to the offending manager and said, "What did you learn and what do you recommend?" The manager told him. "Great," said Eddie, "Do it. Who's next?" The message spread like wildfire; this guy may be for real.

They started with basic disciplines like housekeeping. They involved everyone with respect and consideration. Ed Northern did not see or believe in hierarchies. They created cellular manufacturing lines. The role of the cell leader was to be a resource to the employees. Any employee could push a button and turn the traffic light at the head of the line from green to red. This started a timer. The cell leader had to respond within sixty seconds. Any employee could shut down a line. The employees started taking ownership for process improvement. The process engineers became resources to the shop guys, who met with machine suppliers to request design changes to the machine fixtures. "If we can use hard rubber on the fixture here instead of metal, I'll scrap far fewer blade mounts." Done. Eddie wandered the shop in a tennis shirt and jeans. Everybody took a minute of his time.

Their goal became going from a three-shift operation with exorbitant overtime to a two-shift operation without overtime. The union reps and members had been consulted and involved. They agreed. There's such a thing as too much overtime; the guys wanted a life outside of work. They needed to close down floor space. The management team consulted with the union reps, reviewed their reasons for having to reduce people, reached agreement, laid people off and shut down space. Productivity went through the roof. They came up with a business plan to create a blade repair facility that repaired not just P&W blades, but also non-P&W blades. The airlines were involved because they needed to get the other original equipment manufacturers to identify Turbine Airfoils as a certified repair station. This became a way to grow employment. Morale grew.

They sent their people to Kaizan training and then ran Kaizan events. They sent them to Stephen Covey's *Seven Habits* training.

It took four months after I heard that Eddie had moved to P&W to overcome the GE Monogram on my soul and write him a congratulatory note. Ten days later, at 7 a.m. on a Saturday morning Pacific time, he called. "We need your program," he said. But he didn't make the decision. He suggested to Mort Moriarty that he might want to look into what we did.

Mort decided to check it out. He brought a team to one of our open enrollment sessions. He personally attended with two of his purchasing managers. They invited three key business unit managers – their internal customers. They invited the regional sales managers for Howmet and PCC, companies that supplied 80% of the cost of their input materials. It so happened that the head of purchasing for Delta, Fred Phillips, was at the same session. The entire value stream from metal sales to purchasing to purchasing's internal customer to Turbine Airfoils' external customer was there.

They ran our workshops starting in 1995 in a way that was radical for the time. We called it "counterpart-matching." If you really want to get those far better solutions, we suggested, invite the people you negotiate with to attend the program with you. They did precisely that, with profound and lasting benefits. When we had proposed this to other organizations at the time, the response had been, "What do you mean – teach our opponents our negotiating ploys and tricks?"

Turbine Airfoils continued to thrive. When someone would make a particularly thoughtful presentation at staff, Ed Northern had a habit of putting both his hands on the sides of the person's face and kissing him on the top of the head. Embarrassing, but somehow you felt good. He believed in "taking a swing." Sometimes you missed. That was OK. What did you learn?

Customers came in for plant tours. The machine operators and cell leaders conducted the tours. George David, head of UTC, visited Turbine Airfoils and declared it the happiest day of his life.

Harvard sent down folks to write a series of case studies about the place. They didn't see the people-revolution that was going on; their rational business practices mindset kept them from seeing it. They wrote nothing about how Turbine Airfoils built community, creating a network of people from the sweeper to the vice president who understood what they were doing, felt like they mattered, and knew that they were making a difference.

They didn't write about how he provided his people, union and management alike, the education and the access to leading industry best practices that let them take the revolution further. Tom Petzinger writes that "tools magnify the user."[7] So does respect.

Resentment started to build elsewhere in Pratt & Whitney. Managers in other module centers, who happened to be working *their* tails off but were getting none of the adulation, were deep into sibling rivalry. "Everyone keeps going on and on about how great Turbine Airfoils is. How about us? How about me?" They started referring to Turbine Airfoils as "Eddie Northern's cult."

And then management suddenly decided to promote Eddie to a much bigger job at United Technologies Automotive in Detroit. The decision was made that he had set Turbine Airfoils up for success, but this "take a swing" philosophy was a bit messy. Let's bring someone in to squeeze out the next modicum of profitability and maybe build in more professional discipline.

The next vice president of Turbine Airfoils was Ed Northern's stylistic opposite – brilliant, analytical, intense, private, drawn to methodologies and procedures. He sequestered himself in his office and analyzed reports. He put a level of management between himself and his people. He didn't talk with the shop stewards and union leaders; his subordinates did. While driving home late at night he dictated endless detailed memos that got typed up and put on his staff's desks the next day for action. The union stewards confronted him: People didn't trust him because he wasn't accessible to them or straight with them.

His staff told him, "You've got to get out into the shop more; you've got to listen to people; you have to manage people as they need to be managed. A benefit is that they'll tell you what we need to do to continue on course and to make things better." Their efforts to get him engaged approached the point where they were endangering their own performance appraisals and careers. So high a level of commitment had been built that some hung in for over two years, because they owed it to the community. Then they gave up and posted out of the organization.

Within a few years, Pratt & Whitney shuttered the North Haven facility.

But the image of potentiality remained. Everyone who worked in that facility remembered in his or her bones what work and work-life could be like. They remembered the community, and they remembered the high performance. And many are still scattered throughout the Pratt & Whitney organization. Some went to AlliedSignal before it merged with Honeywell, some retired. Most are still there, and they would do it again in a heartbeat if given the chance.

What I learned as a 21-year-old, teaching students in that rural North Carolina junior/senior high school, came back. If you don't have the concept, you can't think the thought. Neither George David, as brilliant and successful a leader as has graced our industry, nor the Harvard case writers understood the core of what it was that Ed Northern was doing. Their paradigms didn't let them see it. Not grasping it, there was no way they could embed or extend it.

Peters and Waterman write that "management's prime task is to select, after the fact, from among 'experiments' naturally going on in the organization. Those that succeed and are in accord with management's purposes are labeled after the fact as harbingers of the new strategic direction."[8]

When you don't have the conceptual framework that lets you see paradise, all too often, with the best intentions, you put up a parking lot.

Everyone needs the chance to change their model.

When Thomas Kuhn talks about those who embrace a new paradigm at an early stage, he describes situations in which the first brave souls understand that the older paradigm isn't working. He talks about those who take steps in faith, somehow having a gut feeling, an aesthetic sense, that the new paradigm will help them solve the large and intractable problems they face.

What is evident with the clarity of hindsight is that some paradigm pioneers sacrifice themselves on the vision of that better way. A shop manager at GE in Lynn once likened to the invasion of Normandy the successive waves of management coming in to seek to turn around a failing manufacturing shop. The first wave that comes in, he said, you don't even find their bodies. The second wave goes home in body bags. The third wave is decorated as heroes.

If this paradigm shift in aviation succeeds, some first-wave heroes need to be remembered.

Among them are Denise Hedges and the 1998 negotiating team for the Association of Professional Flight Attendants.

A lesson that has emblazoned itself in my soul is this: Especially in union/management situations, *everyone* needs the chance to change their perceptions.

American Airlines and the Association of Professional Flight Attendants – an in-house union representing more than twenty thousand flight attendants – both trained with us in the summer of 1998 in interest-based bargaining. They exchanged openers in September of that year.

You may remember Thanksgiving of 1993, when Denise Hedges, president of the APFA, led the flight attendants in a strike that would have shut down the airline if Clinton had not intervened on the fifth day.[9] White House-encouraged interest arbitration resulted in an agreement.

The union claimed victory and printed and distributed this bumper sticker:

Vote for Clinton/Gore . . . and their husbands, too.

So here's the union three years later, representing a membership with a history of having victoriously stood down an arrogant management, a membership that clearly saw management as the Evil Empire. Denise Hedges and her team realized that a repeat of 1993 would be a disaster. If they break the airline, that doesn't help the membership – it's an in-house union. Denise called us in April of 1996.

"I want to come to your workshop," she said. I told her that we knew nothing about union/management relations. I had no idea whether what we did would be useful. What she said was apocryphal: "There's got to be a better way." She came to a session that summer with Sherri Cappello, chairperson for their Los Angeles base. A year later, at Denise's request, her counterpart, Sue Oliver, then Managing Director of Employee Relations at American, brought a key colleague with her to check out the program. Both Denise and Sue agreed to train their negotiating teams in interest-based bargaining.

When Denise's team was identified, though she didn't have the training budget, she first took them to the George Meany Center for a week to understand the Railway Labor Act. She brought them out to Lake Tahoe to train with us. We suggested that they attend with their counterparts. "We don't trust them," she said, and she had good reason. "You need to understand how things look through management's eyes," we told her. They gave us permission to invite "surrogate management counterparts" to the session. Three operations managers from Pratt & Whitney Turbine Airfoils attended, as did the top two employee relations managers from Bell Helicopter, the director of human resources from Bristol Aerospace, and a representative from Delta's Flight Attendants' Forum.

She then took her team to Harvard's three-day program on interest-based negotiation. A very interesting thing happened. One of the team members called to say they were passing out our business cards. As we talked, it became clear that by going to Harvard – the equivalent of going to the

Mount – they realized they already knew what they were doing. They were ready. They didn't need to be afraid.

Six weeks later, when Sue Oliver brought her negotiating team out to train with us, nine members of the APFA's Board of Directors joined them at the session.

In less than nine months, instead of the more typical two to four years, American's team and the APFA negotiating team put together an incredible contract – better than the union had seen for over twenty years, and better for American, too. Together, both sides built a better model.

In announcing the tentative agreement, Denise Hedges said:

> "Unlike prior negotiations, American dealt with us as partners in a process designed to ensure that our members' interests were the number one priority, while recognizing that for flight attendants to prosper, the airline must prosper, too."[10]

Here's Sue Oliver, by then Vice President of Employee Relations for the airline:

> "The interest-based process used in these talks created a climate where we could openly share all of our interests and work together to explore creative ways to meet the needs of both parties."[11]

In mid-May of 1999, the lead sentence in the *Wall Street Journal* article announcing the tentative agreement read:

> "AMR Corporation's American Airlines Unit, without rancor, sickout or strike, reached a tentative agreement with its

flight attendants' union on a new six-year contract after nine months of bargaining."[12]

And then the APFA Negotiating Team held membership meetings in the various cities where American has its bases. They stood in front of their members and stated that they had worked with management to ensure that their members' interests and needs were satisfied. It was a true statement.

What do you think the members – perfectly intelligent folks who had not had the opportunity to change *their* paradigms – concluded?

Sure. Our leaders sold out to management.

Many among the twenty thousand members attacked the team. When we asked why, the answer was: "Without rancor, sickout, or strike, our leaders couldn't possibly be representing our best interests." When the ballots were counted, 73% of the members voted down a contract that would have put them significantly ahead of United and Delta – the then industry leaders – in compensation, flexibility, benefits, and retirement.

The day after the Tentative Agreement failed ratification, a very painful APFA Board of Directors meeting was held. It became clear that some members of the negotiating team would be asked to step down while others would be asked to remain on a newly configured team. The members had so much investment in the team they'd formed and the agreement they'd reached that they would not dishonor each other by being separated. Everyone except Denise, who remained in her role as president, resigned. A new negotiating team was set up. Shortly thereafter, national officer elections were held, and a new APFA president emerged. Sue Oliver's employee relations team said they were open to shifting around items inside the framework of the agreement, but the agreement itself was already the best they could do. The final agreement was ratified on September 12, 2001, three years after the start of such a hopeful process. Getting to that final agreement involved a process quite full of rancor, frustration, and discord.

Some corollary learnings:

1) People interpret others' behavior based on their *own* model for reality. If their model hasn't changed, don't be surprised if the behavior is misinterpreted. We're back again to that North Carolina school. If they don't have the concept, they can't receive the thought. Everyone needs the chance to change. Union members do. Chairmen and presidents and boards of directors do. And everyone in between.

2) If you're setting out to change a system, such as labor relations at an airline, it's not enough that your negotiating teams work with each other in interest-based ways. In fact, this may not be the best place to start. You probably first start with top management. If you don't get top management on board at the paradigm-shift level, no matter how long and hard people throughout the organization have been working to effect this change, one misstep can bring it all tumbling down around you.

"What the hell were you thinking?!"

In June of 1995, Hugh Grant, while his beautiful consort Elizabeth Hurley was at home in England, pleaded no contest to lewd conduct after Hollywood police discovered him in his car engaging in oral sex with a prostitute. When he appeared on *The Tonight Show with Jay Leno* in July, Jay's incredulous opening question was, "What the hell were you thinking?"

To his credit, Hugh owned up to his behavior, saying, "I think you know in life what's a good thing to do and what's a bad thing, and I did a bad thing." On *Larry King Live*, he elaborated, stating, "In the end you have to come clean and say, 'I did something dishonorable, shabby and goatish.'"[13]

By mid-April 2003, many among American Airlines' management group had been working hard for several years to change the airline's culture from authoritarian and hierarchical to more inclusive, egalitarian, and thoughtful.

Yet two colossal blunders by their management team and Board of Directors nearly scuttled the airline and forced the retirement of their CEO. Worse perhaps than the decisions was the mindset that let those decisions be made. In combination, the mindset and the decisions demand that Jay Leno's question be put to them as well: *What the hell were you thinking?*

The facts themselves are relatively clear.

In April 2003, to save $1.8 billion in operating expenses in order to stave off bankruptcy, the airline struck somewhat forced and time-pressured deals with the Allied Pilots' Association, the Transportation Workers' Union, and the Association of Professional Flight Attendants for multi-year wage rollbacks of 27%, 16%, and 16%, respectively. The employee groups agreed to cuts in benefits and greater flexibility in work rules. Changes to pay, work rules, and benefits for non-union employees, support staff, and management were also identified.

Don Carty, Chairman and Chief Executive Officer of the airline, stated publicly, "I know I need to lead the way, and I will, with a pay cut of 33%." He said that it was only right that he do so, that the restructuring effort was based on a model of shared sacrifice. "Working together," he said, "we have made hard choices, but they are choices that are ultimately in the best interest of American Airlines and its employees."[14]

The balloting was extremely close. Initially, the APFA members failed by a few hundred votes to ratify the agreement. A twenty-four hour extension was granted from the April 15th deadline. Reballoting resulted in an agreement.

The cost savings were reported as follows:
- Pilots: $660 million
- Flight attendants: $340 million
- TWU represented employees: $620 million
- Agents, representatives and planners: $80 million
- Management and support staff: $100 million.[15]

I find it fascinating that "management and support staff" were lumped into the same category. One wonders about the split.

On Thursday, April 16th, one day after agreeing to the cuts, union leaders learned from reporters that American's 10(K) compulsory annual filing with the Securities and Exchange Commission – a filing that had been granted a two-week extension from the March 31st deadline - contained two items that hadn't been clarified before:

1) In March 2002, the Board of Directors had approved generous retention agreements for

Mr. Carty and six other executives, so generous that they would receive as much as twice their base salaries if they stayed with the airline through 2004.[16] So much for shared sacrifice.

2) In October 2002, the Board of Directors had also partially funded a Supplemental Executive Retirement Program to the tune of $41 million to provide guaranteed retirement benefits to 45 of its officers. The $41 million funded the SERP to the 60% level. Fully funded, it would be $68 million – averaging out to a $1.5 million guaranteed pension fund for each of the 45 officers.

Why was everyone so upset? Why did aviation analysts refer to these sins of commission and omission as the most colossal blunder in union/management relations in the past ten years?

According to Jane Allen, vice president of Flight Service for American Airlines, "The regular pension plans at American hold all funds in a trust, and creditors in the event of bankruptcy cannot touch that money. But in order for there to be enough money in the trust to pay everyone's pension fully when they retire, the company must continue to make cash contributions to each fund every year. ...the bankruptcy judge can terminate the company's requirement to fund those obligations in the future." She went on to explain that, "If a bankruptcy judge relieves a company of the obligation to make future payments...the plan is taken over by the Pension Benefit Guarantee Corporation." The PBGC adds funds to the plan to pay benefits.

However, she says, there is a big caveat. "The PBGC 'caps' the amount of pension any participant is allowed to receive...irrespective of what the plan might have otherwise paid."[17] People could end up getting twenty or thirty percent of the pension they had worked for thirty years to guarantee.

Unlike the regular pension plans, the SERP for officers (and, by the way, a supplemental retirement plan for the pilots called the "B-Fund") is protected from creditors in the event of bankruptcy and cannot be affected by any decisions of the bankruptcy judge or the PBGC.

Bottom line: The officers saw fit to put themselves and the pilots in a different life raft than everyone else. And, somehow, the officers and the Board of Directors saw this as appropriate to do, even as they made public statements about shared sacrifices and pulling together.

If you assume that American's officers and Board members continue to think of themselves as persons of integrity (which I believe they do), then how can you make sense of such actions and explanations? Perhaps the only way this makes sense is if their worldview is still based on privileged assumptions deriving from a multi-tiered class society. In such a world, privileges devolve to the top members of the organization that do not need to be shared or even discussed with those from lower classes.

After the disclosure, airline management ingenuously sought to explain that the SERP program had been in existence since 1985 – nothing new – it had just never been funded.

So what happens when we ask "why?" a few times?

Q: Why had the SERP not been funded until 2002?
A: Because we saw no risk of the company going under.

Q: Why was it being funded now?

A: Because there was now substantial risk the company, and the pension fund, could indeed go under.

Q: Why fund a SERP for officers when the rest of the employees remain at substantial risk of lowered pension benefits, and when these folks probably have fewer financial resources than the top 45 members of the corporation?

A: Because we matter more than they do.

If we're going to go forward together, we may actually have to go forward together. And top management will have to demonstrate they buy this concept with every decision they make, visible or not.

Can you quantify the difference?

The answer is "Yes" and "No."

To get back to Peters' and Waterman's theory that the potential exists for hundreds of percent of productivity improvement, let me suggest some benefits or losses.

It's easiest to quantify union-management failures to agree. The ten-day sick-out in February of 1999 by American's pilots is said to have cost the airline $225 million in lost revenues. The pilots' union was fined $45.5 million by Judge Kendall. Tens of thousands of passengers were alienated. The pilots, who believed they'd been working to defend principles guaranteed by the Scope Clause, felt they'd been made into the fall guys and started refusing overtime. Flights were scrubbed because of incomplete flight crews. This contributed to American's logging in 1999 "the worst on-time performance among the ten major carriers," according to the DOT.[18] And since a lot of American's flight attendants were married to or dating pilots, I suspect the pilots did everything they could to scuttle ratification of the tentative agreement between the airline and the flight attendants.

And the residual distrust carried over to 2003. Even though the pilots ratified the concessions and accepted Don Carty's apology, Steve Blankenship, a spokesman for the APA, said, "Trust has been violated."[19]

I would suggest that the same kind of dynamic potentially exists in all our shops, or at the professional level, for example, between purchasing, suppliers, and engineering. People bring their discretionary energy to work, or they withhold it. They can make things easier for you, or harder. Multiply those individual decisions by five thousand people 20 times a day, and it has a significant impact.

I recall a supervisor of subcontract administration for a helicopter company – very bright, ambitious, and aggressive for success for his company. Halfway through our program, he turned to a colleague across the room and called, "Wow, I just got it! Half our workload is self-induced!" He then described how, in pushing for the best solution for his organization he was creating situations with the supplier that ended in failures to perform, terminations, termination negotiations, recriminations, law suits from both sides, all of these endlessly sucking up time and worsening relationships.

When Delta TechOps' General Manager for Safety and Security set out to quantify the benefits of establishing a workplace that so focused on employee health and safety it could qualify for OSHA's VPP STAR status, he compared Bureau of Labor statistics for the industry with Delta's results. Delta implemented their system in 2000. Just considering medical costs for workers' compensation and medical claims costs, they went from $7 million in 1999 to just over $2 million in 2002. The trendline for everyone else had been going up since 1999; the industry had been experiencing a 10% to 25% increase per year. Delta's trendline has been decreasing by 30% per year.

He wanted to find a way to make the savings more visual, more meaningful. So he took the lost workday cases and other elements and turned the results into jobs saved. He told his senior vice president, "Ray, go upstairs and look off the balcony that overlooks the shop floor. Twenty-eight to 34 people are working every day who wouldn't have been here if we'd stayed on the track we were on. That's one shift for one entire bay."

I think this relates to what the manager of Pratt's MMP program with Delta was referring to when he said that the dollar value of the mutual benefits they were finding was staggering when compared to what they used to haggle about positionally.

* * * * * * * * * *

If this alternative model looks promising, perhaps enough so as to go down the path of being a paradigm pioneer, how do you take yourself and your organization from here to there?

Chapter Fourteen

TAKING OUR ORGANIZATIONS FROM HERE TO THERE

Those of you who are still convinced that winning in business means winning for yourself in the grand tradition of Robert J. Ringer's *Looking Out for Number One*, regardless of its short- or long-term impact on the business, its networks, or its people, will find little value in what I now have to propose. Neither will those of you who are still convinced that your job is to meet your current measurements and position yourself personally to meet your future measurements - no matter how ridiculous the measurements, and no matter what it takes, what it undermines, or whom it hurts.

But if you have concluded – however reluctantly - that perhaps the only way your own business can survive and succeed in the next months, years, and decades is if you all pull together – inside the organization and out into your networks - what I have to say may be of help.

If you suspect we need to move our businesses away from unseemly servitude to Wall Street analysts so we can again focus on a healthy balance of short-term *and* long-term objectives, and so we can again play the value game rather than financial shell games, it should help.

If you believe that though the purpose of business certainly is to make money and generate cash flow, it is also to provide not just jobs but *meaning*, the meaning that comes from working together to make something happen that matters, my next suggestions may help define the path.

And if you have long suspected that the purpose of business should also be to provide as much job security as is possible in an imperfect world, to share benefit (at multiple levels of meaning) fairly with all who help the business succeed, and to secure the future for those who contribute to its success, what I have to say may help you conclude that we can and must reclaim these purposes.

Here are some initial recognitions that underlie what we must do to set up for a present and future in which our businesses and people can survive and succeed. Keeping them in mind as you reshape your managerial and behavioral models will help assure we don't fall back into the assumptions of dying, unsustainable models.

Recognize that our own models, assumptions, and behaviors are part of what's gotten us into this mess.
This one is really important. As soon as you realize that you yourself will also have to change, rather than looking for one more slick way to manipulate or motivate everyone else into changing, change is actually possible.

Recognize that you need people's best efforts, both individually and collectively.

It is not all right to demand more than their very best. When you force people to produce in excess of their best efforts, as we have done in many of our businesses during much of the 1980s and 1990s, you drive them into squirrelly behaviors that undermine the cohesiveness of the organization, the long-term health of the business, and their own integrity. You drive in fear. Too many otherwise excellent people simply turn off at some point. When they do, their motive energy is no longer available to you.

Those who take the challenge to produce more than is possible wreak multi-layered havoc in the name of results. You bear prime responsibility for the devastation that results, whether it manifests itself as Maximum Allowable Gouge, screw the customer, treating employees as cannon fodder, or other desperate paths to "success."

Recognize that you need people who will work as good stewards of the business.

Most people want to. Many are still doing so in spite of the pressures not to. As you set up a different managerial model, build in mechanisms that let them function as good stewards and that recognize and reward those that do.

Some people have no concept of what this means. No matter how brilliant or credentialed they may be, if they do not choose also to function as good stewards of the business in every decision they make, every action they take, decide whether having them around is worth it.

Recognize that you need people who choose to work together in the interests of the overarching organizational goals, even to the point of sharing their own power to do so.

This gets into a multitude of elements, some of which I'll touch on when I talk about measurements. People usually won't work in the interests of the organization's goals unless they have been consulted as to what those goals should be and find them credible.

And recognize that you need people to conclude that working in support of the organization's driving interests and needs, now and over time, is the best way they have to satisfy their own.

You have your interests and needs that you're seeking to satisfy through business and working; so do they, individually and collectively. You have things you're trying to achieve and things you're trying to avoid, not just in your role, but also as a person. So do they. As you and they work to identify and satisfy those overlapping interests and needs - some of which are similar, some complementary, some simply different – you create value together, build trust, create the working relationships that can deal well with differences, and build community that works.

* * * * * * * * * *

These recognitions point towards a different form of management and leadership. It can perhaps best be called interest-based management. It is not a return to paternalism, which was based on an uneven, though primarily benevolent, relationship between a parental management and a dependent employee population. This one involves a relationship that is primarily adult-adult – people on equal footings of interdependence and respect, regardless of their roles. Though it primarily involves adult-adult interactions, it legitimizes people bringing their whole selves to work – to solve problems together, play together, celebrate together, and sometimes cry together.

Now, many of you are already part-way down this culture-changing, paradigm-shifting path. You've defined values, vision, mission, and strategy statements that are consistent with what I've just sketched out.

You're engaged in major initiatives – lean concepts in your shops and also in your services businesses and business processes, supply chain management extending, as one of our clients put it, "from dirt to scrap." You are restructuring your organizations in efforts to reduce the drag between functional silos and fiefdoms. You're creating global alliances and Internet-based one-stop shopping consortia. You're training your folks to be Black Belts. You're learning to provide "capability" rather than product. You're "grappling with your costs, capacity, pricing, and product features in ways you haven't seriously contemplated since the start of deregulation in 1978."[1]

But these changes probably won't embed.

So my invitation to you is simple: At whatever level in the organization you're working, scope out your business change objectives and processes. Consider all eight of John Kotter's stages.[2]

Then Add the Ninth Factor.

In order to change the assumptions that drive your behavior, change your behavioral paradigm –

your own and that of a critical mass of your people - not as an afterthought, but as a key and necessary element of each step of the entire process.

I think I've demonstrated that it takes more than simply making a decision to change. If we could change our behavior by reading a book or intending to change, we'd all play scratch golf and have fantastic sex lives. There's no lack of books, good intentions, or strong motivation relative to either subject.

Einstein is right. We can't solve the problem at the level of the problem. And we tend to confuse the fact that we're decent people who love our families and mean well by our businesses with our negotiating behaviors. Our behaviors, and the assumptions and paradigms that underlie them, are largely invisible to us.

Attribution theory being what it is, most of us, if asked, would tell you that we already *are* interest-based negotiators; it's everybody else who's the problem. At the point that we each discover that "we have met the enemy and he is us," change is possible. Our next shock comes when we realize what lousy solutions we've been getting, compared to what's out there, just lying around in the environment. This possibility of far better solutions becomes the motive energy for change.

I have continued to struggle with elements of this mind-shift. I know that, at very basic levels, people rethink, "What is this game of life and who are these other folks and what are we doing here?" I know that as soon as our minds change, we see everything differently. It's an either-or situation, a flash of understanding, a revelation.

An engine maintenance manager from Delta tied his week with us to segments from a powerful poem by Derek Walcott called "The Sea is History."[3]

He described Monday this way: "First, there was the heaving oil, heavy as chaos..." By Wednesday, he could begin to see for himself, as if from a far distance, "like a light at the end of a tunnel, the lantern of a caravel, and that was Genesis." By Friday, he discovered, "there was a sound, like a rumour without any echo of history, really beginning."

Out of that different vision, that sound of history really beginning, our assumptions are different and so are our behaviors.

Once the mind change occurs, if your business culture even partially allows it, you can't go back.

Clearly, some folks have been going through this mind change on their own, for a variety of reasons. I suspect a "global mind change"[4] is underway. But if we wait for it to happen naturally, it will happen to folks outside of our current organizations. Too many corporate culture mechanisms are in place to hold us where we are.

So if you want to introduce this mind-change in your organization or your part of the organization, you'll probably need a structured, replicable way to provide the three elements necessary for behavior change: a cathartic event, our personal identification with the event, and a readily available alternative model to practice and check out.

And then you'll need mechanisms that anchor those changes in the organization.

Help a Critical Mass of Your People Change Their Paradigm.

This is where experiential education at the paradigm-shift level can be powerfully effective and efficient. It can provide a safe, replicable way for those reasonably open to considering this shift to experience these three elements and then draw their own conclusions.

If you're trying to shift a culture, you probably best start at the top, and then you extend it to those parts of the organization where the management is open to it and where it can make the most difference. Ideally, you provide it for networks of people who need to work together, so the business benefits immediately from their experience. I think this one cascades down, so that as you involve more entry-level people, some shifts in managerial behaviors and measurements will already be in place to allow and reward the changed behavior.

You don't have to train everybody, even though everybody needs the chance to change their minds. There comes a point when you achieve a critical mass, especially once it's built into your measurements and your managers are managing people in these ways. Then, just as I adapted to GE's culture and you adapted to yours, those entering the organization will adapt to the new culture you're shaping. Those being managed differently will start to experience the differences. There'll be a lag time, but things will change.

I know you will struggle with residual memories and knee-jerk habituated responses for a while. These are old habits stuck in our brain architecture and bodies like memory in metal. But because your minds will have shifted, how you see reality will shift, and even though the old tapes will still play, you'll be able to turn the volume down. And you'll be able to override the knee-jerk reactions. It will take a lot of "Aaah, there I go again," apologies and retakes, but your behaviors will shift.

Change Your Measurements.

Most people operate to measurements, and therefore your current metrics and other cultural elements can hold you back. They'll have to be changed to allow the model, assumptions, and behaviors you now want to encourage. As with any change initiative, you'll embed these concepts into your policies, procedures, planning processes, performance and salary screens, rewards and recognition activities, hiring criteria, and your behavioral training sequences.

This is a huge job, one that I would not look forward to, but I know that it has to be done. And you as management will have to be involved, since most people who naturally delight in measurements tend to think in reductionistic, incremental, tactical terms. We'll need some different kinds of measurements that encourage what you're seeking to make happen. Many of our people who devise measurements will misunderstand initially; they'll need managerial help to evaluate impact in contexts unfamiliar to them.

For example, in mid-2000, Don Carty and his team at American Airlines made the radical decision to expand seat pitch in coach by five full inches *without raising prices.* To do this, they removed rows of seats from each plane. The mood of both passengers and cabin crew on American's flights lightened perceptibly as the company gave personal space and reasonable dignity back to their passengers.

This decision struck me as so out of character that I wondered what was going on. Was this the harbinger of a true change of intent?

I then noticed other out-of-character events, such as a change in the behavior of the drivers of the people carriers at DFW Airport. Before, their drivers had hurtled the carriers down the crowded corridors, leaning on their warning horns, scattering walkers before them with their annoying high-pitched blasts. Now, they wended their way quietly and carefully, rarely sounding their horns and, if at all, gently.

Maybe there was a pattern worth looking for.

About the same time that American expanded seat pitch in coach, United introduced Coach Plus – the same five inches of additional knee room per row – in a segment of the plane that coach passengers had to walk past on their way to steerage, and at prices that approached the cost of First Class. I flew United shortly after this policy was implemented. The Coach Plus rows with their plentiful legroom stood empty; coach was stuffed. I seethed as I walked past those empty seats to jam myself into my tight little coach seat. Anger was palpable in the cabin.

Wall Street declared American's decision a terrible idea. Whatever possessed management to reduce the potential total revenue per flight? Treating passengers with consideration without extracting a price – it made no sense at all to minds that long ago had taken the people equation out of business. I thought it surpassed brilliant. But it will take a different kind of measurement to identify the effect and benefit of this kind of business decision.

Peters and Waterman[6] quote a General Instruments sales executive. He reminisced about his first job, saying, "I spent forever getting to know a small handful of customers really well. I came in at 195% of quota, tops in my division. A fellow at corporate said...'You average 1.2 sales calls a day. The company averages 4.5. Just think of what you could sell if you could get your average up to par.'" The fledgling sales executive had responded, "Just think what the rest could sell if they could get their calls *down* to 1.2."

Some of the measurements you devise will be more permissions than restrictions. I am confident that teams of wise practitioners – those being measured, not the measurers – can help define them creatively and appropriately.

For example, how do you measure the *value* that individuals and work groups create for their function, for the organization, for the customer, and in networks? How do you design measurements that follow people from job to job that relate to their long-term stewardship of the business as well as those that relate to their short-term results? How do you quantify alternative currencies and more elegant solutions? How do you give credit for assisting others in the conduct of their jobs, much as basketball statistics record not just points scored but also assists?

We know some things about measurements. They are supposed to let us know how we're doing so we can decide to stay the course or make timely corrections. Most measurements therefore fall into the category of negative and positive feedback. Feedback by nature is neutral. Positive feedback is not praise; it simply means that if this is what you're seeking to do, it's working. Negative feedback is not criticism. It means that if this is what you're seeking to do, you're getting off course. This also defines the heart of motivation. Motivation emerges when we identify the gap between where we are and where we need to be.

Once we conclude that our current approach to measurements may be counter-productive, we can then ask, "What's wrong with it?" This becomes the basis for coming up with better ways. Here are some elements of measurements that don't seem to help. Add your own favorites to make a more complete list.

1. *Measurements laid on individuals and organizations by upper management don't work well.*

    Here, management decides what the metrics should be and requires that they be met. The message is: Produce or else. No one can impose a measurement on someone else and have it truly succeed. Whenever they try to, they're operating in the arena of positive or negative KITA. Both produce results, but neither works well. Frederick Herzberg proved that conclusively. Positive KITA produces results, but they almost always devolve into "beat the measurements" games such as Art Thom played with such relish at GE all those years ago. Negative KITA also produces results because people and other living creatures are motivated to avoid pain, but you never know what direction the pain-avoidance activities will take. It's hardly ever in the direction of your Overarching Strategic Objectives.

2. *Measurements that pit people against each other don't help.*

    Their energies bounce off the "throughput" walls and are largely lost for productive work. The organization becomes highly politicized; silo walls rise and thicken;

straight communication and collaborative, creative, problem-solving dry up.

3. *Measurements that divide people into "reward," "hold," and "dump" piles don't work, nor do those measurements whose purpose is to humiliate or berate.*

I can think of only two reasons for grading on the curve: 1) to decide who you want to promote, and 2) to decide who to get rid of. Grading on the curve is a lousy way to address either of these issues. It's based on a false assumption that management's job is to identify the winners and the losers. Management's better job is to ensure that everyone who wants to, and who works at it, can be a winner.

The other problem with identifying individual winners and losers is that, by definition of the way this game is played, the vast majority of your people won't fall into the winner category. Those notified by their managements that they just don't make the grade, that they aren't winners (by definition, most of us), waste precious energy dealing with the feelings that come from being judged and found lacking: uncertainty, fear, resentment, withdrawal, self-justification, and anger.

The beatings will continue until morale and performance improve.

---

4. *Measurements that frustrate people's efforts to benefit the larger organization don't help.*

    Recently, commodity team members from a general aviation company went out to their suppliers to identify ways to reduce the cost of input materials. Over and over again, the suppliers said, "If you can specify these design changes in the product, it would let us reduce our cost of manufacture by a significant amount, which would let us reduce our price to you. We do not think these changes will interfere with the mission or quality of the part." The commodity people checked back with the factory and determined that, indeed, the requested changes would not affect the parts' quality or ability to perform. So they went to engineering to ask for the design changes. In this particular organization, engineering was divided into Development Engineering, which focused on new products, and Sustaining Engineering, which worked in support of products in production. Sustaining Engineering said, "Yep, we could do that, but all the funds for activities such as that are allocated to Development Engineering. We don't have the budget; therefore, we won't/can't do the work." Development Engineering said the equivalent of, "Not our job." End of story.

5. *Measurements that force people to violate their own integrity don't work for the benefit of the organization.*

    When Jack Welch required managers throughout GE to identify and get rid of the bottom 10% of their people year after year, to their credit, most resisted mightily. According to his own memoir, after the first year or two, even new managers resisted. They offered forth people who had recently resigned or were retiring. In some cases, they identified dead people. They delayed and avoided until they were told that until those names came in, no one in their organization would receive bonuses. They still delayed, until they were told that if they didn't come up with the names, they themselves would end up in the "bottom 10%." Then they gave up. They violated their own integrity. Breaking someone's integrity sets up a slippery slope. Do it once; it's easier to do it again. Business runs on trustworthiness. Once you force people to give up their integrity, what do you have left?

6.   *And, most importantly, measurements and measurement systems that don't allow people to pull in the same direction verge on useless.*

I witnessed a situation early in my career where every section manager met his measurements, yet the department manager they reported to failed and was removed. If your measurements don't produce cumulative benefit for the larger organization, what good are they?

If your sales guys don't know the impact that each element of the proposal they're making will have on the measurements you use to determine the success of the business, how can they work wisely for you? If your shop people don't know the rules of the game they're being asked to play, or the metrics that constitute failure or success, how can they help the business succeed?

One of our graduates is a supervisor in the maintenance and engineering organization at American Airlines. He and a colleague share supervision of one of the largest production shops at the maintenance base. Close to 140 unionized employees work in the shop, which is also the most successful production shop in the facility. Before he arrived, the shop had not met a dock date in memory. Over the past two years, since he arrived, with basically the same personnel, they have met every dock schedule they've ever had, with no overtime. I asked, "What are you guys doing that's making the difference?"

He said, "When I got here, the people were demoralized. They didn't have any information. The philosophy of the supervisor I followed was that people don't need to know when the ship set is due out. The employees' job is to do their job; they should just shut up and do it."

He described the situation as analogous to taking boys out in the middle of a cow pasture, giving them a ball, and telling them to play football. He said, "They might play catch or keep-away for awhile. At the end of the day, though, they'd be turned off. They certainly wouldn't play football or function as a team. How could they? People need to know the rules of engagement. They need to understand how the game is played and where they fit in it."

"Initially," he said, "I began to build an image about, 'We can be the Number One team in the airline.' It was essential to get them to identify with that culture. I held daily shop meetings. Every day I stood in front of them, told them the schedule, told them what came in yesterday, told them if we had had a good or a bad day the day before. I gave them specifics for every day and every week. Just five-minute meetings. Every day they knew if this was a crunch day or not; I maintained credibility by not crying wolf."

He summed up by saying, "These people are motivated to the point that they care more than I do. It's a matter of pride to each of them for something not to be late on their watch. People want to belong. Everybody wants to be a winner. All you have to do is be realistic, and to treat both issues and problems. You need to be a *leader*, not a *cheerleader*. If you're credible and they know you speak the truth, when you have something negative to say, they'll take it to heart and they'll fix it."

* * * * * * * * * *

So do we need measurements?

Absolutely. In business, numbers and measurements help us define the game we're playing and how we're doing.

You ask, "Are there existing models we can look to?" The delightful answer is a resounding "Yes!" It will take translating into the size and scope of some of our businesses, but a documented, pre-tested, alternative model already exists in microcosm.

Jack Stack puts forth a working model for us in his books *The Great Game of Business* (1992) and *A Stake in the Outcome* (2002).[7] He describes how, in the early 1980s, he was an operations manager at a small International Harvester plant in Springfield, Missouri. The Springfield ReManufacturing Company (SRC) remanufactured truck engines - a low-cost producer commodity business if ever there was one. Everyone in the plant, himself included, was working to measurements imposed by Corporate. Then one day, management arrived from Corporate to announce that they were failing, the plant would be closed, and everyone would be out of a job.

The overwhelming feelings were astonishment and betrayal. "Wait a minute," they thought, "If we were meeting our measurements, how come we failed?" They also thought, "If we had known, surely we could have done something about it." That was when they understood the futility of traditional methods of measurement.

Jack and a small group of fellow managers decided to buy the plant. Partly out of desperation, saddled with enormous debt, yet feeling a personal commitment to keep the plant open and maintain the livelihoods of 119 employees and their families, they set out to involve everyone in the plant in playing the Great Game of Business week by week and quarter by quarter.

They worked together with the entire plant population to identify the measurements that actually told each and every person there how they were doing, how their unit was doing, and how the entire business was doing. They taught people to read and understand those measurements, just as most little boys (and a lot of little girls) learn about batting averages and RBI's and all the other statistics of baseball. They gathered and distributed weekly feedback on where each organization stood, and on where the entire organization stood, feedback that was relayed in cascading meetings to every person in the plant. And they provided ways that people working together could win.

Jack writes, "There's a level of mutual trust and respect at SRC that...comes from being honest with people, from telling them about the realities of business, from having principles and sticking by them, from trying to be fair." He goes on, "We've treated people like the capable, intelligent adults we know they are. We haven't protected them like children. We've created a society built around rules we all know and understand – some of which we've developed, but many of which we've gotten from the marketplace. They're the basic rules of business, the things we have to do to survive and prosper in a competitive economy. Out of this has emerged a special kind of corporate culture...a culture of ownership."[8]

At SRC, the role of management is to help people satisfy their driving interests and needs by helping the business do the same. Management's role is to set up the parameters for an ongoing game that people who pull together can win, to provide the help the people say they most need, and then to get out of their way, report the results, and lead the appropriate celebrations.

And what have the results been? In February 1983, a share of SRC stock was worth ten cents a share. By January 2002, it was valued at $81.60 a share. They have grown from 119 employees to more than 900 and from $16 million in sales to ten-fold that number.

Of those who own shares in the business, just five are original shareholders. The other 722 shareholders, all employees, own 64% of the stock, which truly gives them a stake in the outcome. After a first year in which they lost $60,000, the rest have been year after year of unbroken profits.

He makes the point that "business is not an end in itself. It's a tool that allows us to accomplish the things that matter most to us, and those things must transcend business to have real meaning and value."[9]

* * * * * * * * * *

Now, let's assume you're changing your managerial model, you've surfaced and changed your own behavioral paradigm, and you're redesigning your measurements so that people can pull together to win a game whose rules they understand. As you go further down your path, you'll do some other important things:

Walk the Talk.

You yourself have to walk the talk, consistently and persistently, every day. And when you mess up – as you surely will – you will school yourself to apologize and start again. That itself will send a different, encouraging signal!

Celebrate Small Wins.

And you'll celebrate the successes along the way.

As you move down this path, each element of it will teach you more about its implications and connections. You'll keep cycling back to the basics, understanding each more fully.

Assure Your Management Team is On Board.

Eventually, you'll have to make some hard managerial decisions. When Jack Welch started some major culture change initiatives at GE in the early 1980s, he'd meet with younger managers at GE's corporate training center, and they'd all tell him he had to get *their* managers on board.[10] He's a big believer in four-squares – and he drew one.

Jack Welch & Culture Change

	Meets measurements	Doesn't meet measurements
Buys the values	Hero	You get another chance
Doesn't buy the values	?	You're outta here

Adapted from a hand-drawing by Jack Welch
in a Q&A session at Crotonville, ca. 1986.

For those who bought the values and met their measurements, he said, "They're heroes." Those who bought the values but didn't meet their measurements got another chance. For those who didn't buy the values and didn't meet their measurements, he said, "That's simple. They're outta here."

The hard one, he said, was those who met their measurements but didn't buy the values. For awhile, he said, they'll last. Eventually, he said, they're out of here, too, no matter how high up in the company, no matter how illustrious their careers.

And the reason is very simple. If they remain, espousing the old paradigm, their very existence will poison your change initiative.

I know that what I'm proposing to you will take time. Culture change does.

Years ago, a friend of mine, Ph.D. in Chemistry and ten years in the field, decided he was on the wrong career path. What he had wanted back in college, and now found he still wanted, was to be a psychiatrist. He was agonizing over going back to school. It meant four years of medical school, a year of internship, and three years of residency. He asked, "How can I even consider doing this? By the time I'm done, in eight years, I'll be 43 years old." I said, "How old will you be in eight years if you *don't* do it?"

I think it all depends on whether you truly intend to achieve your strategic objectives.

Tom Petzinger placed this quote from Tom Stoppard in the beginning of his book *The New Pioneers*.[11] Perhaps it can also be an invitation to step forward together into quite incredible times, to create anew our wonderful world of aviation as we know it can be and should be, and to revitalize ourselves.

"A door like this has cracked open five or six times
since we got up on our hind legs.
It's the best possible time to be alive,
when almost everything
you thought you knew is wrong."

- Tom Stoppard, *Arcadia*

If not us, who? If not now, when?

Appendix A

SOME RESOURCES

Here are some of the resources I mentioned. Others are referenced in the Footnotes.

Forum Corporation.
One Exchange Place, Boston, MA 02109-2803.
   The Forum Corporation is one of two premier business training organizations in the United States, with offices and/or affiliates in Hong Kong, Singapore, Japan, Canada, Australia, New Zealand, and the United Kingdom. Their *Influence*® program started me on a path to understand how to be effective working with and through others.
Phone: 1-800-FORUM-11 or 617-523-7300.
Web site: www.forum.com.
E-mail: forum@forum.com.

Harvard Negotiation Project.
   The implications of this project are astounding. I highly recommend the books and resources that have

come out of it, including *Getting to Yes, Getting Together,* and *Getting Past No.* The Clearinghouse on Negotiation provides a wealth of material.
Phone: 800-258-4404.
Web site: www.pon.harvard.edu/publications.
E-mail: chouse@law.harvard.edu.

The MAPping Alliance, Inc.
1330 West Avenue, Suite 1702, Miami Beach, FL 33139.

Rich Hodapp's Decision MAPping® process, also called MAP, is a comprehensive strategic account management process. As I mentioned in Chapter 2, it is as much a way of running the business as it is a training program. Account teams identify the decision the customer is seeking to make that they are seeking to influence. MAP provides a way for analytical people and intuitive people to talk together. It gives management a template for reviewing a variety of account opportunities in relation to a consistent model. And it lets you scope out account activity in relation to patterns of the whole so that you can see not just what you do know, but what you don't, and can then set out to fill in the gaps.
Phone: 305-532-4323
Web site: www.decisionmapping.com.
E-mail: mapping@eos.net

Some of our clients have found Miller Heiman's *Strategic Selling®* to be very useful. One major difference is that Decision MAPping® lets you map out complex business-to-business account activity that may take many months or years to bring to fruition (though it can also be used for events as simple as mapping out how to sell yourself for your next promotion) while *Strategic Selling®* seems to work well when a company needs to track multiple smaller account opportunities in various stages of development, each requiring less integration of multiple functions to bring to fruition.

Springfield ReManufacturing Corporation (SRC).
650 North Broadview Place, Springfield, MO 65802.

Jack Stack, with contributions by Bo Burlingame (an editor-at-large of *Inc.*, the magazine for small businesses), wrote *The Great Game of Business* in 1992 and *A Stake in the Outcome* in 2002. An amazon.com reviewer of *The Great Game of Business* writes that this book became "the primer for open-book management, a new method based on the concept of democracy, the spirit of sports, and the reality of numbers." Jack and his colleagues learned the business benefit of creating multiple businesses. One of them teaches you how to play the Great Game. They provide not just training and plant tours. Should you wish, they also provide coaching.
Phone: 417-862-3501, 1-800-FUN-2PLA or 417-831-7706
Web site: www.srcreman.com.
E-mail: info@greatgame.com.
Also
The Great Game of Business.
Web site: www.greatgame.com.

The Mattford Group.
P. O. Box 5454, Incline Village, NV 89450.

The *Negotiating Solutions*® workshop, a week-long residential program that I designed, brings most participants to and through the paradigm-shift level, so they do choose to change their model, assumptions, and behaviors. If you decide you need such a resource, this matters. Without getting through this level, perfectly intelligent people, believing they're changing their behaviors, simply shift from the hard side of the positional game to the soft side of the same game, and they fail.

Should you decide this program meets your needs, we can transfer the technology to you so you can run it for hundreds to thousands of your people at extremely low cost per person.

The design is operational rather than academic. It does not depend on subject matter experts, and it is scripted for ease of transfer. It can be facilitated by experienced functional managers paired with experienced human resources people, so long as this is a path that they themselves are on, however imperfectly, and so long as they have genuine and contactful presence in front of a group and mean well by their students.

Phone: 775-832-5300

E-mail: mattford@gbis.com or mattford@aol.com

Web site: www.negotiatingsolutions.com.

Appendix B

HOW YOU CAN HELP

To the extent you found this book meaningful, please help us extend the conversation throughout aviation.

Send information about the book to those in your networks you think would want to be part of the conversation. Then play with ideas with one another. Ask yourselves, "If we really wanted to implement these concepts, what difference would it make? What would we do? How would we do it?" Then set out to do those things that make sense.

Should you want to buy the book in bulk to share with your employees or members, please visit www.chartingawisercourse.com for details.

Acknowledgements

By now you've noticed most everything I've learned has been a gift from someone else. Some occurred so long ago I don't know who to thank. But in many cases, I do know, and am profoundly grateful.

I thank Bill Lindsay for opening up his entire organization to me, and Bob Curry, Dave Burton, Chuck Phillips and Austin De Groat for including me in the incredible culture change initiatives they enabled in GE-Aircraft Engines in the 1970s and beyond.

Thanks to Bob McMahon, Doug Mallon, Manny Manasian, Ron Brandstetter and the design team members of our original program on negotiation who kept the program useful for their people, organizations and marketplace realities. I thank Chuck Chadwell, Ken Foley, Mick Thackeray, Frank Byrd, Dave McDonald, Joe Mays and the teams of trainers who took it forward, sometimes taking personal vacation time to do so, and Jean Bilien and Olivier Fagard, who brought it into Snecma to build team and a common approach to the marketplace with their GE counterparts.

My thanks to Rich Hodapp and Ann Rice Mullen for tailoring what they did to help my clients and me learn so much about being effective inside our own organizations and out into the marketplace.

I thank Lisa Crockett and Joni Raycroft, who saw the greater value of what we were doing, sometimes before we did; Mort Moriarty and Ed Northern at Pratt & Whitney for the incredible community they built; John Roe and his team at Hamilton Sundstrand; and Denise Hedges of the APFA and Sue Oliver of American Airlines, who knew there had to be a better way and put their careers on the line to find it.

My thanks to those who sought to find ways the Negotiating Solutions workshop could last beyond Joe and me: Eric and Sharon Jensen, Eric and Jean Rossol, Gerrie Linn, Howard Benden, Diane Beamer, Randy Ward, Kirk Joseph, Lynn Gates, Barb Williams, and Scott Whitman. And to those who read early versions of this book and made it better – Olivier Fagard, Bob Gates, Phil King, Jim Smith, Karen Odegard, Denise Hedges, Larry Ames, Leo Profilet, Jim Bailey, Bill Brown, Christine Probett, Joe Cronin, Wayne Huot, Bob Johnson, Ed Sarsfield and Ron Clegg among them.

My deepest appreciation to Bill Freeman and Jay Donoghue of *Air Transport World*, who decided the book could spur and perhaps focus an important dialogue within aviation, and who offered their resources to make it visible to our community.

And foremost and forever, to my husband, Joe Shackford. We set out to see if what we did could make a difference. We think it has and hope it will. We now pass it forward to you.

About the Authors

Joe and Kaye Shackford lived this book. Kaye wrote it down. She learned the aviation business during twelve years with GE-Aircraft Engines in Lynn, Massachusetts, and Evendale, Ohio. Living in New Delhi, India, from 1986-89, while at the same time working for GE International in South Asia and Europe, taught her more about the global nature and wonder of our industry.

Joe Shackford began his professional career with Sikorsky Helicopter as a flight test engineer. After three years, he moved to GE-Aircraft Engines. Twenty-five years' experience as a functional manager in worldwide commercial sales and military aviation operations led in 1986 to his being named the first National Executive - India – for all GE product lines.

In 1988, Joe and Kaye formed the Mattford Group. Since then, they have helped thousands of people throughout the aviation industry (and from other industries working to reinvent themselves) discover the business and personal benefits produced by interest-based negotiation and interest-based management.

Footnotes

Introduction

1. Douglas McGregor. *The Human Side of Enterprise,* McGraw-Hill Book Company, New York, 1960.

2. Excerpts from *The Structure of Scientific Revolutions,* 3rd edition, by Thomas S. Kuhn. The University of Chicago Press. © Copyright 1962, 1970, 1996 by The University of Chicago. Reprinted by permission of the University of Chicago Press. All rights reserved.

3. Harvard Negotiation Project. The Clearinghouse on Negotiation provides a wonderful wealth of material. Visit: www.pon.harvard.edu/publications. For information, contact chouse@law.harvard.edu.
   Phone: 800-258-4406.

4. Joel Barker. *Paradigms: The Business of Discovering the Future,* Harper Business Books, NY, 1992

5. John P. Kotter. *Leading Change,* Harvard Business School Press, Boston, 1996.

Chapter 1. What's Going on Here?

1. Jack Welch, internal GE speeches and presentations, ca. 1982.

2. Jack Welch with Byrne, John A. *Jack: Straight from the Gut,* Warner Books, NY, 2001, Chapter 11, The People Factory. Jack sketched out the "Vitality Curve" as a managerial

method to force differentiation. Each year managers were required to identify the top 20% of their people, the "vital 70," and the bottom 10. He describes the curve as "the dynamic way we sort out As, Bs, and Cs." He goes on to say, "The first time new managers name their weakest players, they do it readily. The second year, it's more difficult. By the third year, it's war." He said, "We constantly faced tough resistance from even the best people in our organization." I say, Good for them. But when Jack withheld bonus or stock option recommendations if people didn't identify the bottom ten, and when he made it clear that "managers who can't differentiate soon find *themselves* in the C category," he won.

3.   Boulwarism. Lemuel R. Boulware (1895-1990) was GE vice president for employee and public relations. He crafted the concept known as Boulwarism. He felt that the company should be responsive to the employees' needs and that therefore no union was necessary to intervene between employees and management. As a bargaining stance, the company studied employees' requests and what the environment would bear. It then presented a completely shaped final response. This "fair but firm" offer was by definition the company's best and final offer. There was no negotiation; union leaders and members saw themselves faced with a de facto "take it or leave it." Boulware would disagree with this. He honestly felt that the company was obliged to try "to do right voluntarily." He claimed that he was receptive to "any old or new information proving changes would be in the balanced best interests of all." Of course, the company decided what doing right consisted of and what were the balanced best interests of all. ("The Truth About Boulwarism." Lemuel R. Boulware. Bureau of National Affairs, 1969.) The NLRB ruled Boulwarism an unfair labor practice in 1964. It was

held to be illegal by the U.S. Second Circuit Court of Appeals in 1969.

4. Roger Fisher and Brown, Scott. *Getting Together*, Penguin Books, NY, 1988, pg. 92.

5. Cartoon. "You wanted it when?" Unknown source, but ubiquitous. (Thanks to Sharon Royer for finding it.)

6. John D. Drake. *Downshifting: How to Work Less and Enjoy Life More*, Berrett-Koehler Publishers, San Francisco, 2000, pg. ix.

7. Frederick Herzberg. "One More Time: How Do You Motivate Employees," Harvard Business Review, September 1, 1987.

8. *The Human Side of Enterprise*, op. cit.

9. Abraham Maslow. *Motivation and Personality*, Addison-Wesley. Boston. Third edition, 1987.

10. Thomas J. Peters and Waterman, Robert H., Jr. *In Search of Excellence*, Harper and Row, New York, 1982.

11. W. Edwards Demming. *Out of the Crisis,* MIT Press, Boston, 2000.

Chapter 2. Lessons From Our Shared History

1. "High Flight." John Gillespie Magee, Jr., 1941. Reprinted with permission.

2. Input-Thruput-Output Model, adapted from a colleague's hand-drawn sketch, ca. 1975.

3. Michael Macoby. *The Gamesman,* Simon & Schuster. 1977.

4. John Newhouse. *The Sporty Game,* Knopf, New York, 1982, pg. 3.

5. Abraham Maslow. *Eupsychian Management*, Richard D. Irwin, Inc. and The Dorsey Press, Homewood, Illinois, 1965.

6. Dr. Sidney B. Simon is Profesor Emeritus at the University of Massachusetts, Amherst. His books include *Values Clarification, A Practical Action-Directed Handbook*, by Sidney Simon, Howard Kirschenbaum, and Leland Howe. Warner Books, 1995. E-mail: DrSimon@SimonWorkshops.com.

7.   The NTL Institute was founded in Bethel, Maine as the National Training Laboratories for Group Development. It pioneered work in methodologies and technologies for exploring group dynamics. Web page: www.ntl.org/about-bethel. Phone: 207-824-2151.

8.   Eric Berne. *Transactional Analysis in Psychotherapy: Systemic Individual and Social Psychiatry,* Grove Press, 1971. Also, *Games People Play: The Psychology of Human Relationship,* Ballantine Books, 1996.

9.   Excerpt from "Anything You Can Do" by Irving Berlin from *Annie Get Your Gun.* © Copyright 1946 by Irving Berlin. © Copyright renewed. International Copyright Secured. All Rights Reserved. Reprinted by Permission.

10.   One of the great sillinesses of class distinction is that we were proud to be "exempt." In reality, the label meant we were exempt from protective labor laws that required that employees who worked overtime be paid for that overtime. We were special.

11.   Excerpt from "Rhinestone Cowboy" by Larry Weiss, © Copyright 1974 (Renewed) WB Music Corp. All Rights Reserved. Used by Permission, Warner Bros. Publications U.S. Inc.

12.   *Give and Take, The Negotiating Game, Effective Negotiating Workbook and Discussion Guide,* and 11 audiocassette negotiating package. From Karrass Negotiating Seminars, 8070 Wilshire Blvd., Beverly Hills, CA 90211. web site: www.karrass.com., E-mail: info@karrass.com, phone: 323-951-7500

13.   Malcolm Shepherd Knowles. *The Modern Practice of Adult Education: From Pedagogy to Andragogy,* Cambridge Book Company, 1988.

14.   Chester L. Karrass. *Give and Take,* HarperCollins, NY. 1974.

15.   Robert L. Miles. "An Evaluation of Negotiation Skills Workshop Training in the Aircraft Engine Business Group for the Years 1978-81," December 1981.

16.   Forum Corporation, *Influence*. One Exchange Place, Boston, MA 02109. 1-800-FORUM-11. www.forum.com.

17.   I was first introduced to this trust model through Forum Corporations's *Influence* program.

18.   MAP (Managing Account Potential), also called Decision MAPping®, by Richard Hodapp of The MAPping Alliance, Inc., 1330 West Avenue, Suite 1702, Miami Beach, FL 33139. www.decisionmapping.com. 305-532-4323.

19.   Ivan Boesky, commencement speech at University of California, Berkeley, quoted in *Tales of the Eighties*, by Kathleen A. Hughes, Wall Street Journal, December 22, 1989, quoted by Thomas Petzinger, Jr. in *The New Pioneers*, pg. 20.

20.   Harvard Negotiation Project. op. cit.

21.   Thomas E. Ricks. *Making the Corps*, Touchstone Books. 1998.

Chapter 3. The End Stages of Once Useful Models

1.   The extraordinary events of April 2003 that put American Airlines on the brink of bankruptcy, resulting in Don Carty's resignation, can perhaps only be explained by the continuation of a class mentality that made it perfectly acceptable to American Airlines' Board of Directors and management team to fund a separate pension life boat for the top 45 managers than for the rest of the employees. For a more complete description, read Chapter 13: "Some Lessons Learned: What the hell were you thinking?"

2.   Amazon.com quotations re: *Jack: Straight from the Gut*. Welch, Jack, and John A. Byrne. Warner Brothers, 2001.

3.   Amazon.com quotations re: *Jack: Straight from the Gut*. Welch, Jack, and John A. Byrne. Warner Brothers, 2001.

4. *Eupsychian Management,* op. cit., pg. 122.
5. Private conversation. June 2000. Dallas, TX.
6. Internal GE memo from the Corporate Purchasing Czar to materials managers, ca. 1985.
7. Conversation with Mike DeFeo, Farmington, CT, ca. 1998.
8. Thomas Petzinger, Jr. *The New Pioneers: The Men and Women Who Are Transforming the Workplace and Marketplace,* Touchstone Books, New York, 1999.
9. Ibid., pp. 14-15.
10. Ibid., pg. 17.
11. Air Transport World, editorial, "After It Fails: GIRO monitors warranty claims for airlines," J.A. Donoghue. May 2002, Vol. 39, Number 5, pg. 60. GIRO, 8909 South Yale, Suite 240, Tulsa, OK 74137, phone: 918-496-0008, E-mail: www.giro.net.

Chapter 4. We Have Met the Enemy and He is Us

1. Walt Kelly. *Pogo: We Have Met the Enemy and He Is Us.* Simon & Schuster, 1987.
2. Stanley Milgram. *Obedience to Authority: An Experimental View.* New York: Harper & Row, 1974, reported in *In Search of Excellence,* pg. 78.
3. Negotiation Workshop, June 1990. Harvard Law School. Program of Instructors for Lawyers. Cambridge, Massachusetts. Roger Fisher lecture notes.
4. Viktor E. Frankl and Allport, Gordon. *Man's Search for Meaning,* Simon & Schuster, 3rd edition, 1984.

Chapter 5. Current Change Efforts

1. *Leading Change,* op. cit.
2. Ibid., pg. 21.

Chapter 6. Paradigms, Master models, and Paradigm Shifts

1. *The Structure of Scientific Revolutions.* op. cit.
2. Ibid., pg. x.
3. Ibid., pg. xi.
4. Ibid., pg. 2.
5. Ibid., pg. 4.
6. Ibid., pg. 4.
7. Ibid., pp. 4-5.
8. Ibid., pg. 5.
9. Ibid., pg. 5.
10. Ibid., pg. 6.
11. Thomas Petzinger, Jr. *Hard Landing,* Times Business, Random House, New York, 1995.
12. Willis W. Harman.*An Incomplete Guide to the Future,* WW Norton & Company, New York, 1979, pg. 24.

Chapter 7. How Managerial Models Embed and Persist

1. Kahlil Gibran *The Prophet,* Alfred A. Knopf, New York, 1923 and 1951, pp. 17-18.
2. Eric Berne. *Transactional Analysis in Psychotherapy* and *Games People Play.*
3. William Glasser. *Reality Therapy*, HarperCollins. Reissue Edition, 1989.
4. Kurt Lewin. *Principles of topologi psychology.* Lewin believed in the field theory. He argued that "for change to take place, the total situation has to be taken into account." The field theory is the proposition that human behavior is a function of both the person and the environment one finds oneself in. Lewin was also one of the major founders of the National Training Laboratories.
5. Stuart Atkins. *The Name of Your Game,* Bcon LIFO International, Ellis & Stewart Publisher, Beverly Hills, CA. 11111 Santa Monica Blvd., Los Angeles, CA 90025. Phone:

805-480-9313. web site: www.stuartatkins.com, E-mail: info@bcon-lifo.com.

6.   Stuart Atkins, op. cit.

7.   Stuart Atkins, op. cit. Stuart teaches that a corollary of this is that we next most trust our stylistic opposites, because they augment our gaps. If we're quick to move, they take time and think things over. If we're analytical; they're intuitive. If we work with logic and making impersonal, data-based things happen, they take their time and build social networks. We tend to marry them, and we tend to have them as our #2 person in the organization.

Chapter 8. Assessing Our Current Behaviors and Objectives

1.   Richard Hodapp of The MAPping Alliance, Inc., op. cit.

2.   The Program on Negotiation and the Harvard Negotiation Project, op. cit.

3.   Roger Fisher and Ury, William. *Getting to Yes: Negotiating Agreement Without Giving In,* Penguin Books. New York, 1981. Second edition 1991. pg. xi.

4.   Ibid., pg. 9.

5.   Ibid., pg. 9.

6.   Reported by attendees at AA's fall management conference, ca. 1999.

7.   Attributed to Oscar Wilde.

8.   Kevin Freiberg and Freiberg, Jackie. *Nuts! Southwest Airlines' Crazy Recipe for Business and Personal Success,* Bard Press, Austin, Texas, 1996, pg. 66.

Chapter 9. Changing Behaviors

1.   Change model. Author unknown. Adapted from a colleague's hand-drawn diagram, ca. 1978.

2.   Roger Fisher and Brown, Scott. *Getting Together: Building Relationships As We Negotiate,* Penguin Books, New York, 1988, pg. 39.

Chapter 10: Getting to Our Master Model

1. Sherry Crane, Cessna Aircraft Company, telephone conversation, early 2002.

2. Jean Piaget. *Origins of Intelligence in Children,* International Universities Press. 1992.

3. Thomas J. Peters and Waterman, Robert H., Jr. *In Search of Excellence,* Harper & Row, New York, 1982, p. 58. Quoting Lee Ross, "The Intuitive Psychologist and His Shortcomings," in Advances in Experimental Social Psychology, vol. 10, ed. Leonard Berkowitz (New York: Academic Press, 1977), pp. 173-220.

4. American Airlines fall management conference. 1999.

5. Matt Lauer interview with Tony DiCicco, coach of the 1996 US Women's Olympic Soccer Team. The Today Show, NBC, July 13, 1999.

6. Program on Negotiation, Harvard Law School, June 1990. Lecture notes.

7. I first ran across the concept that negotiation is about creating value and claiming value in *The Manager as Negotiator,* by David A. Lax and James K. Sebenius, Free Press, New York, 1986, Chapter Two: The Negotiator's Dilemma: Creating and Claiming Value, pp. 29-45.

8. *Getting to Yes,* op cit.. pg. 5

9. *Getting to Yes,* op. cit., pg. 13.

Chapter 11. Implementing This in Our Environment

1. Chester Karrass. *Effective Negotiating Workbook and Discussion Guide,* Karrass Seminars, 1987, pg. 18.

2. Ibid., pg. 30.

3. I was introduced to the JOHARI Window in graduate school. It helps people visualize ways to improve the quality of communication through self-disclosure and feedback. It had a slightly mystical, Eastern philosophical

feel to it. Shortly after we returned from India, I had the honor to be on the staff of a workshop in interpersonal communication designed by Walt Storey and run by his widow Virginia. One of my colleagues in this program was Dr. Joseph Luft, a professor from Berkeley. He turned out to be the Joe of the Joe-and-Harry who crafted the JOHARI Window. The JOKAY Window is our homage to Joe Luft and Harry Ingham.

4. *Getting to Yes*, op. cit., pg. 68.
5. *Getting Together*, op. cit., pg. 37.
6. The Six Stages of Program Development, author unknown.
7. Negotiation Workshop, Program of Instruction for Lawyers, Harvard Law School, June 1990. Lecture notes.
8. *Getting to Yes*, op. cit., pg. 66.
9. Negotiation Workshop, Ibid. Lecture notes.
10. Negotiation Workshop, Ibid. Lecture Notes.
11. *Getting to Yes*, op. cit., pg. 88.
12. Negotiation Workshop, Ibid. Lecture notes.
13. *Eupsychian Management*, op. cit., pg. 109.
14. Ibid., pg. 109.
15. Ibid., pg. 114.
16. Wall Street Journal. Martha Brannigan. "*Discount Carrier Lands Partners in Ill-Served Cities,*" pp. A1 and A10, July 16, 2002.
17. Ibid., pg. A10.
18. Ibid., pg. A10.
19. Negotiation workshop lecture notes. Op. cit.

Chapter 12. Isn't This the Same as "Win-Win" Negotiation?

1. Jim Camp. *Start with No*, Crown Business Books, 2002, front flap.
2. *Harvard Business Review*, July 2002, Forethought, Volume 80, Issue 7, pg. 26.
3. *Start with No*, op. cit., front flap.

4. *Getting To Yes*, op. cit., pp. 7-8.
5. *Getting To Yes*, op. cit., pp. 8-9.

Chapter 13. Some Lessons Learned

1. Joel Barker. *Paradigms: The Business of Discovering the Future,* Harper Business Books, NY, 1992, pg. 41, pp. 71-83.
2. *The Structure of Scientific Revolutions.* op. cit., pp. 158-9.
3. John Stranahan, Pennsylvania OSHA area director. From a GE Erie web site press announcement entitled "GE Transportation Systems Celebrates Nation's Highest Safety Award." www.ge.com.
4. "Savings and Safety From OSHA Program," by Jerome Greer Chandler. Overhaul and Maintenance Magazine, July/August 2003.
5. *Getting to Yes*, op. cit., pp. 155-6.
6. Words from Big Yellow Taxi © 1970 (Renewed), Crazy Crow Music. All Rights Reserved. Joni Mitchell's album *Ladies of the Canyon*. Used by permission Warner Bros. Publications U.S. Inc.
7. *The New Pioneers*, op. cit., pg. 206.
8. *In Search of Excellence*, op. cit., pg. 108.
9. *Hard Landing,* op. cit., pg. 46.
10. Internal AA communications, May 1999.
11. Internal AA communications, May 1999.
12. Wall Street Journal, May 18, 1999. "American Airlines, Flight Attendants Reach an Accord."
13. CNN Showbiz News. Spin cycle: Hugh Grant finds "honesty" best policy. July 11, 1996.
14. AMR Corporation News Release. April 16, 2003.
15. Ibid.
16. Wall Street Journal. Scott McCartney, "Unions Weigh Options at American," April 17th, 2003, pp. A1 and A5.
17. Jane Allen email to AA Flight Service, April 18, 2003.

18. Wall Street Journal report on July 23, 1999, quoting the Department of Transportation.

19. CNN.com. "Flight attendants scrap deal with American." April 19, 2003.

Chapter 14. Taking Our Organizations From Here to There

1. Business Week. Wendy Zellner with Michael Arndt and Lorraine Woellert. "It's Showtime for the Airlines," September 2, 2002, pg. 36.

2. *Leading Change*, op. cit.

3. Excerpts from "The Sea is History." Poem by Derek Walcott, 1992 Nobel Laureate in Literature. In *Collected Poems: 1948-1984*. Noonday Press, 1987. pg. 364. Copyright © 1986 by Derek Walcott. Reprinted by permission of Farrar, Straus & Giroux, LLC. UK permission from Faber & Faber, Ltd.

4. Willis Harman. *Global Mind Change,* Second Edition. Berrett-Koehler Publishers, San Francisco, 1998.

5. *Eupsychian Management.* op. cit., pp. 88-89.

6. *In Search of Excellence,* op. cit., pg. 185.

7. Jack Stack with Bo Burlingame. *The Great Game of Business,* Currency Doubleday, New York, 1992, and *A Stake in the Outcome,* Currency Doubleday, New York, 2002.

8. *A Stake in the Outcome*, Ibid. pp. 3-4.

9. Ibid., pg. 5.

10. Jack Welch, Crotonville Q&A period, GE Management Development Center, Ossining, NY, ca. 1986.

11. *The New Pioneers*, op. cit., frontispiece.